Through the Moral Maze

Through the Moral Maze

Searching for Absolute Values
in a Pluralistic World

Robert Kane

PARAGON HOUSE
New York, New York

First edition, 1994

Published in the United States by

Paragon House Publishers
401 Fifth Avenue
New York, NY 10016

Library of Congress Cataloging-in-Publication Data

Kane, Robert Hilary
    Through the moral maze : searching for absolute values in a
pluralistic world / Robert Hilary Kane. — 1st ed.
        p.   cm.
    Includes bibliographical references and index.
    ISBN 1-55778-601-1
    1. Ethics. 2. Values. 3. Respect for persons. 4. Absolute, The.
5. Pluralism.
BJ1012.K274   1994
170—dc20   92-36927
                                                            CIP

Manufactured in the United States of America

To my wife,
Claudette

Contents

Preface

This book is written for readers of all ages and backgrounds troubled by conflicting points of view on moral and spiritual matters, who may wonder as a consequence about the truth of their own beliefs and ask what values can be believed and passed on to their children in the face of the unprecedented challenges of modern life. The book results from my own struggles with these issues over a period of twenty-five years and from attempts to pass on what I learned to university honors students and, through lectures, to adult audiences in various parts of the country, who were as deeply troubled, it turned out, by the moral malaise of the times as I was. No special background in philosophy or other academic subjects is required to read the book; the background is supplied as we go along. But neither do I talk down to readers. They are challenged to do some careful thinking about important issues and about the bases of their own beliefs. General issues about ethics and values are discussed in chapters 1–4 and then applied in chapters 5–9 to current controversies about social ethics, public policy, private versus public morality, politics, religion, the environment, feminism, multiculturalism, the teaching of values, and other topics.

The book should also be of interest to philosophers and other academics, as well as ordinary readers, since it offers novel approaches to old questions. It could serve as a text along with other works in many college courses in which current controversies about values and ethics arise, not only in ethics courses themselves, but in courses that deal with current debates about the objectivity of values, political rights, standards of excellence (for example, in art or literature), or debates generated by postmodernist writings or by popular works like Bellah and colleagues' *Habits of the Heart*, Bloom's *The Closing of the American Mind*, MacIntyre's *After Virtue*, or Hunter's *Culture Wars*. The book could also be recommended to students in any courses who are troubled about foundational questions of ethics (including the "Why be moral?" question) and unsatisfied by the familiar answers to such questions, whether utilitarian, Kantian, or whatever. In applied ethics courses, it could be used as a background text addressing foundational issues that usually cannot be given enough treatment in applied courses to satisfy many students. The book defends a so-called "respect for persons" morality (akin to Kant's idea of treating all persons as ends and not means), which would fit nicely into many applied ethics courses. What is different here is the way the idea is grounded. While traditional ethical theories have much to teach us, as I try to show (whether they be Kantian, utilitarian, contractarian, natural law, virtue ethicist, or whatever), I do not think they can do the job by themselves.

I have accumulated many debts while writing this book, first, to a host of contemporary philosophers and other scholars who have influenced my thinking—too many of them to mention, though the works of a substantial number are cited in the footnotes. My special thanks for encouragement and input are owed to Frank Richardson, George Graham, John Moskop, David Braybrooke, John Post, Noah Lemos, Robert Audi, Huston Smith, Thomas Seung, Peter Coveney, and the late Edmund Pincoffs; also to my colleagues in philosophy at the University of Texas at Austin and to various audiences around the country, including faculty and students at Vanderbilt University, Fordham University in New York City, and the U.S. Military Academy at West Point; the meeting of the Metaphysical Society of America held at Notre Dame, a National Teacher's Convention held in Anchorage, the Texas Commission for the Twenty-first Century, the University Research Institute, and a generation of students in Plan II, the interdisciplinary honor's program at the University of Texas. I wish to express thanks also to my agent, Lettie Lee of the Ann Elmo Agency, who believed in this project from the start, and to the editorial skills of Nick Street and the staff at Paragon House. Finally, my greatest debt is owed to the woman to whom this book is dedicated, Claudette Drennan Kane, whose wisdom, wide reading, and forceful arguments have left an imprint on every page.

1

The Spirits of the Times

A TOWER OF BABEL

The ancient image of the Tower of Babel has been used by more than a few modern writers to describe the current state of discourse about ethics and values.[1] There is no one "spirit of the times," but many—*too many in fact*—too many competing voices, philosophies, and religions, too many points of view on moral issues, too many interpretations of even our most sacred documents, our Bibles and Constitutions. Only the most unthinking persons can fail to be affected by this pluralism of points of view and not wonder, as a consequence, about the truth of their own beliefs. Such doubts are the subject matter of this book. Its theme is that we must begin to address old questions about ethics and values in new ways if our moral consciousness is to keep pace with the new intellectual landscape.

Among the consequences of the modern Tower of Babel is a pervasive temptation to embrace relativism, the view that there are no objective or "absolute" values that hold for *all* persons and *all* times. Judgments about the good and the right, it is said, can only be correct for some persons or societies or times, but not for all persons, societies, or times. In support of such a view, there are widespread doubts about the very possibility of making absolute or universal judgments that transcend our always limited points of view. New trends in the social sciences and humanities, some of them with popular names like "postmodernism" or "poststructuralism," make much of the fact that all our views about the world are historically and culturally conditioned.[2] We always see things from a particular point of view (a "conceptual framework," or "language game," or "cultural tradition"). How can we therefore show that our point of view, or any other, is the right one and competing views wrong, when we must assume the basic presuppositions of some particular point of view to support our claims? How can we climb out of our historically and culturally limited perspectives to find an Archimedean point, an absolute standpoint above the particular and competing points of view?

This problem haunts the modern intellectual landscape. One sees variations of it everywhere in different fields of study, and everywhere it produces doubts among reflective persons about the possibility of justifying belief in objective intellectual, cultural, and moral standards. Many modern thinkers, to be sure, deplore the resulting drift toward relativism or skepticism, arguing that we need to restore belief in objective truth and value. But it is one thing to say this and another to show how it can be done. For the problem of finding an Archimedean point above the pluralism of competing points of view is a complex one, which thinkers have been wrestling with for centuries.

I no longer believe the older ways of solving this problem will work as they did for past generations, and we will see why in chapter 2. If we are not to drift into relativism, therefore, some new ways of thinking about the problem of value are needed. Alasdair MacIntyre is right, I think, to say that the current state of moral discourse is one of grave disrepair, but I am not entirely satisfied with his or any other contemporary suggestion for repair.[3] Some fundamental possibilities, it seems to me, have been overlooked in all traditional and modern searches for absolute value. These possibilities will be explored in the chapters to follow. I have no illusions about the finality of what I have to say about these topics, but I hope my thoughts will stimulate others who understand that the problems of relativism cannot be wished away by simple nostrums and lamentations, without confronting the deep philosophical problems that lead to them.[4]

These themes are explored in the first four chapters of the book and then applied to current debates about public morality and social ethics (chapter 5); politics and democracy (chapter 6); religion (chapter 7); the environment, feminism, and multiculturalism (chapter 8); and moral education (chapter 9).

MORAL DISINTEGRATION WITHIN

The issues at stake are deeply philosophical, but they have practical implications. Many distinguished figures have raised the question of whether democratic and pluralistic societies can withstand the erosion of common beliefs about right and wrong that have traditionally sustained them. As the old ideological struggle of the Western democracies with communism has wound down, we are warned by noted exiles from the communist world, like Nobel laureates Aleksandr Solzhenitsyn and Czeslaw Milosz, that a new and more difficult struggle looms for the world's advanced societies—a struggle against moral disintegration from within.[5] The West may have won the world, they suggest, while losing its own soul.

Similar themes have been echoed in popular books by American writers of recent years, including the widely read *Habits of the Heart* by sociologist Robert Bellah and his colleagues, and Allan Bloom's *The Closing of the American Mind*.[6] These were surprising best-sellers, suggesting a loss of moral and spiritual direction in today's America. Bloom is one of those who laments the rise of relativism. Widespread rejection of absolute values, he claims, has led to a pervasive indifference to what is really good or right, and not only in moral, religious, and political matters. In matters of higher culture as well—great literature, music, painting— he thinks relativism leads to an indifference that debases and impoverishes culture as well as erodes its moral foundations.

But Bloom is also one of those whose suggested solution goes little beyond simple nostrums and lamentations. He thinks a return to education by way of the Great Books of the Western intellectual tradition is the "only serious solution" to the problems created by relativism, skepticism, and nihilism (p. 344). To see the limits of this suggestion, one does not have to speak against reading the Great Books of Western culture, or for that matter the great works of non-Western cultures. They contain much wisdom that we ignore at our peril and they will play an important role in the chapters to follow. But, as reviewers of Bloom's book, like Martha Nussbaum, have pointed out, reference to the Great Books is a two-edged sword.[7] For they parade before us a series of conflicting philosophical and moral positions as the wisdom of the ages, which can lead to the same relativism and skepticism they are supposed to prevent—*unless* they are accompanied by adequate arguments to relieve contemporary doubts that lead to relativism and skepticism.

In the end, I think Milosz is closer to the truth than Bloom when he notes that if we are to overcome our present confusions about values, new ideas will also be necessary. If the modern Tower of Babel is to be overcome, we need to clothe our moral and spiritual aspirations in images as yet unborn. Without that, the Great Books of the past can seem like the Great Sphinx—a monument to human civilization that keeps its secrets to itself.

THE SPIRITUAL CENTER

The root of present problems about values, as I said, is the existence of a pluralism of points of views about the right way to live, with no evident ways of settling disagreements between them. The ancient Tower of

Babel is a fitting image for this modern condition. But I now want to add three other images that will stay with us throughout the book because they help to describe important consequences of modern pluralism. These images are associated respectively with the ideas of (1) *spiritual center*, (2) *moral innocence*, and (3) an *Axial Period* of human history.

Mircea Eliade, the distinguished historian of religions, has said that what religions provided for their believers through the ages was a spiritual centering.[8] Primitive peoples often identified a sacred mountain or some other place near their home as the center of the universe. The axis of the world went through that point and reached directly to the heavens. It was the spiritual center of their world and the place through which people found access to the divine.

One of the stories of modern civilization is a gradual undermining of this sense of spiritual centering. When Copernicus said that the earth was not at the center of the universe, European civilization was shocked. It was shocked even more when Giordano Bruno suggested that there were perhaps many other worlds or galaxies. So shocked, indeed, that Bruno—a less cautious man than Copernicus—was burned at the stake for bringing such bad news. This reaction was crude, but not unnatural. For the spatial center of the universe and our nearness to it had always been an image of the spiritual center and our nearness to it. The loss of one seemed a loss of the other.

But the physical center of the universe was only an image of the spiritual center for ancient peoples, and perhaps it was too crude an image. It is also possible to believe that, no matter where we are in the physical universe, we can find the spiritual center if we hold the right beliefs, those that are absolutely true, true for all persons at all times. Realizing this, primitive peoples also thought that *their* beliefs were the true beliefs and their gods *the* true gods, just as they thought that their mountain was the physical center of the universe.

But this approach to the spiritual center has also been challenged by modern civilization—in this case, not by scientific discoveries alone, but also by the existence of a Tower of Babel of conflicting beliefs. In a modern world full of diverse and conflicting religions, sects, cults, denominations, and spiritual movements, we can no longer afford to think about a spiritual center as the ancients did without considerable soul searching. Hans Küng points out that the greatest·challenge for Christians in the twentieth century is coming to grips with the diversity of the world's religions and religious points of view whose presence in the global community can no longer be ignored or lightly dismissed.[9] The same challenge exists for all religious believers. It is the threatened loss of a spiritual center—the religious counterpart of the Tower of Babel and the spiritual counterpart of discovering many worlds or galaxies beyond our own. As Huston Smith has put it, using Nietzsche's image, in the modern world we are summoned to become Cosmic Dancers, who may "have our own perspectives, but they can no longer be cast in the hard molds of oblivion to the rest."[10]

LOSS OF MORAL INNOCENCE: *PERELANDRA*

A second important consequence of the encounter with a pluralism of points of view is that it takes away what might be called our *moral innocence*. How this occurs is nicely illustrated by a scene in C. S. Lewis's fantasy novel *Perelandra*.[11] Lewis describes the journey of a man named Ransom to the planet Venus, called "Perelandra" in the novel, an idyllic world of islands floating on water and covered with exotic foliage (a veritable Eden, unlike the real Venus which is the image of hell). Ransom meets only one humanlike creature there, a green-skinned woman who tells him of her God, Maleldil, and his command that she search for a man of her own kind who also inhabits this world. Ransom and the woman talk until he complains that the floating islands are making his stomach queasy and suggests they move over to the fixed land. The woman is shocked by this suggestion and tells him that Maleldil has commanded that no one should set foot on the fixed land. This is the one thing she is forbidden to do. Ransom's response troubles and confuses her, for he says that in his world, on earth, everyone lives on the fixed land and no one believes it is wrong. Is it possible, she wonders, that there are different meanings of right and wrong and that Maleldil commands one group of people to do one thing and others to live differently? In her confusion she is tempted to move to the fixed land: if others can do it, why can't she?

As the conversation proceeds, Ransom suddenly realizes they are reenacting the story of Eve and the serpent in the Garden of Eden, and *he is playing the serpent*, tempting Eve to do the one thing that God has commanded her not to do: eat of the fruit of the tree of "knowledge of good and evil." In the biblical version, Eve eats of that fruit, Adam does so also, and as a consequence of knowing good and evil they are banished from the Garden. According to the traditional interpretation, this coming to "know good and evil" is coming to know sin through succumbing to temptation. But in *Perelandra* Lewis is suggesting another, modern interpretation of knowing good and evil. The new knowledge that tempts us to sin is the realization that there may be more than one right or wrong way of doing things, and that therefore our way may not be the only "right way." It tempts us because it weakens commitment to our own beliefs. In the resulting confusion we say, like the woman, "if others can do it, why can't we?"

Such a realization that other points of view may be right in their own ways brings an end to moral innocence—the secure feeling that the rights and wrongs learned in childhood are the only correct or true ones, unchallengeable and unambiguous. It hurls persons out of moral innocence into moral confusion, out of the Eden of childhood into the real world of conflict and ambiguity, tempting them to think that since rules are not absolutely unchallengeable or unambiguous, including their own, perhaps none is absolutely binding. One form this challenge takes is the realization that traditional moral commandments ("Thou shalt not kill, lie, steal . . .") have exceptions in the real world; their absoluteness is questioned. But once exceptions are admitted (for example, in cases of self-defense or war), it becomes problematic where the line on exceptions is to be drawn (capital punishment? abortion? euthanasia?). Disagreements proliferate and the question asked by the woman of Perelandra returns: if others can do it, why can't I?

Failing to grasp these possibilities is to live in moral innocence. To grasp them is to learn something about the complexities of good and evil, but it is learning that comes with a bitter taste. Having tasted the fruit of the tree of knowledge of good and evil in this conspicuously modern manner, we live, so to speak, "after the modern Fall." Beliefs formerly held may survive, but they can no longer be looked upon with the same certainty and innocence. Some people have not crossed this divide, even in the modern world. But those who have crossed it cannot easily go back, any more than they can go back to believing that the earth is flat or situated at the center of the universe.

THE AXIAL PERIOD

These consequences of modern pluralism have suggested comparisons with past ages when older ideas were being challenged on a grand scale and new ones were born, periods such as the end of the Middle Ages in the West, or the much earlier *Axial Period* in human history—which introduces the third theme I want to discuss. The expression "Axial Period" was used by Karl Jaspers to describe the remarkable era between the years 600 and 300 B.C.E., during which a spiritual awakening took place simultaneously in many of the advanced civilizations of the world,[12] giving rise to religious, philosophical, and scientific ideas that have guided the human race ever since—until now, that is, when it has been suggested that the ideas of the original Axial Period may have run their course.[13] It was the period of Confucius and Lao-Tzu in China, of the writing of the principal Hindu Upanishads, and of the rise of the Buddha and Buddhism in India. Further to the west, the Axial Period produced the Persian prophet Zoroaster or Zarathustra and the great transformative prophets Jeremiah and second Isaiah in Israel. Finally, in Greece, it was the period in which Western philosophy and science simultaneously arose. Thales, who is said to be the first philosopher of the West, lived at the beginning of this period, while Socrates, Plato, Aristotle, and many of the great scientists of antiquity lived at the end of it.

The Axial Period was a response to the vast changes in human history brought about by the Agricultural Revolution which had been occurring for millennia before it, just as the Enlightenment of the eighteenth century in Europe was a response to the Industrial Revolution then changing Western civilization. These two revolutions, agricultural and industrial, represent what Alvin Toffler has termed the first and second waves of human civilization.[14] He thinks a third wave of "post-industrial" society is now upon us that will bring intellectual changes as great as the preceding two. Other writers agree, without necessarily resorting to Toffler's imagery of waves. The ideas of the Enlightenment, an expression of what is sometimes called "modernity," are widely challenged and there is talk about a "postmodern" era of human thought to go along with a postindustrial society. At the same time doubts are expressed about the viability of older religious and philosophical ideas inherited from the Axial Period.

Whether all this suggests the advent of a new Axial Period is, of course, far from clear. Writers like Alasdair MacIntyre and Huston Smith, among many others, think the answer to modern moral and spiritual confusions lies in a recovery of the basic philosophical ideas of ancient Greece or the religious traditions of East and West—China, India, Israel, and so on—that go back to the original Axial Period. That period, like all other eras of intellectual change, did not create everything anew, but brought to fruition ideas that had been brewing for centuries. Yet even those who wish to retrieve the wisdom of the past acknowledge that the extent of modern challenges to traditional religious and moral beliefs is unprecedented; and this suggests that the idea of a new Axial Period is one that has to be taken seriously.

THREE FEATURES OF THE SPIRITUAL CENTER

In his recent essay "The Idolatry of Politics" Leszek Kolakowski distinguishes three aspects of the loss of the spiritual center in the modern world that may be moving us toward such a period.[15] He says that anyone who wants "to address the danger that our civilization may collapse into nihilistic sluggishness and become an easy prey for tyranny" must attend to "three crucial points in which humanist beliefs seem to have reached a suicidal stage" (p. 31). These points are (1) the *modern rejection of absolute values;* (2) the *reduction of the unique core of human personality* to the objective and impersonal forces of heredity, physical environment, and collective social forces; and (3) the *loss of roots,* or a sense of cultural continuity that makes of the past a source of meaning and provides an "historically defined sense of 'belonging.'"

These three points provide a good description of what it means "to lose the spiritual center," and they will play an important role in subsequent chapters of this book. We can scarcely recapture that center any longer in the manner of the ancients by simplistically assuming that our mountain or valley, our tradition or culture, or even our race or planet is at the center of the universe. By making such an assumption, the ancients were able to endorse their roots and traditions (3) without denying transcendent and universal significance for themselves (2) or their beliefs (1). For us moderns the situation is more complicated. We are now told that to have roots in a tradition or culture is to see the world from a limited perspective or point of view and that all of our beliefs are historically and culturally conditioned by this rootedness, so that none can have universal significance. Thus the spiritual center falls apart: roots are particular and local, absolute values are universal; and never the twain shall meet. It seems that we must choose, as Richard Rorty aptly puts it, between "Solidarity and Objectivity," between roots and universality.[16] We cannot have both, as the ancients did in their simplistic way.

To recapture the spiritual center would be to overcome this opposition—between the particularity of our perspectives and the universality of our aspirations—not in the simplistic way of the ancients, but in some other way suitable to the present age. To accomplish this, as Kolakowski sees it, the most difficult and pivotal task is a reassessment of the modern rejection of absolute values. About this, he says:

> To sneer at "absolute values" has been extremely easy . . . since the Enlightenment managed to convince us that all human beliefs about good and evil are culturally and historically relative, and that mankind had already suffered enough from struggles between various religions and doctrines whose adherents, on all sides, were deeply convinced of being the only privileged carriers of the absolute truth. Humanist skepticism, with its dismissal of "absolute values," forged a powerful weapon against the fanaticism of sectarian strife. (p. 150)

Belief in absolute values has often been associated with authoritarianism and fanaticism, two evils that the Enlightenment relentlessly opposed. Even today many fear talk of absolute values as an invitation to authoritarianism and fanaticism, or even totalitarianism: to admit absolute values is to open the door to kooks of every known variety who are ready to commit atrocities in the name of their special access to absolutes. Enlightenment thinkers, like Voltaire, fought prejudice and superstition in the belief that anyone who can make you believe absurdities can make you commit atrocities. The twentieth century also knows that danger. The problem with absolute values is that people who think deeply know how hard it is to find them, while those who do not think deeply too often believe it is easy to find them—and think they have already done so. This gives the edge to the fanatics who are certain they have the truth.

Because of its association with fanaticism and authoritarianism, many people today would prefer to avoid the expression "absolute value" altogether. But this fear is misplaced and I think it should be resisted. It is based on the common association of what is "absolute" with what is "certain," a disastrous association that has created all kinds of confusion in modern discussions of value, as we will see in chapters 2 to 4. The term "absolute," as it will be used here, is simply the opposite of "relative." It means "valid for all persons, times, or points of view," as opposed to what is "relative," or "valid for this or that person, or time, or point of view, but not for all." Absolute values can therefore also be called "universal," since they hold true for all persons in all situations (though we will see in chapter 3 that they are universal in a special way). You can believe in absolute values in this sense of what is good from every point of view without supposing that your beliefs are certain, much less that you have the right to impose them authoritatively on others. Belief in them therefore need not imply fanaticism or authoritarianism. As Kolakowski suggests in the same essay, to reject the possibility of absolute values merely to ward off fanaticism or authoritarianism may be a case of throwing the baby out with the bathwater.

This is especially true if relativism is our concern. For "relativism," in the broadest sense in which we will be using the term, is simply the rejection of absolute values. It is the view that all judgments about what is good or evil, right or wrong, are valid only from some particular points of view, but not from all. No judgment about good or evil, right or wrong, says the relativist, can be valid *period*, without qualifying "for whom," or "when," or "from what point of view." This is quite simply a denial that any values are absolute. Sometimes "relativism" is given stronger meanings than this. For example, it is sometimes said to be the claim that no view is any better than any other. Such a "vulgar relativism," as Bernard Williams has called it, is easily defeated because it makes an absolute claim about all views for which it lacks the grounds.[17]

But it is a mistake to think that by refuting such a vulgar relativism we have disposed of the worries that lead to relativism. For relativism in the broader sense of a denial of absolute values is not easily defeated by facile philosophical arguments and it is the view that haunts the modern intellectual landscape.[18] Even this broader relativism cannot be proven, of course, but the temptation to believe it will be strong wherever doubts exist about the possibility of grounding absolute values without falling into fanaticism, authoritarianism, totalitarianism, or some other "ism" that the modern world has come to fear.

DISCUSSING ETHICS

Before we begin to address these doubts in chapter 2, I want to add a word of caution. Not a few people are skeptical about the practical significance of theoretical discussions of ethics. How will ideas save us, goes one objection, when the secret police come to the door?[19] Or, one hears that ethical argument will not have any effect on the Hitlers, Stalins, or other genuine evildoers of the world, who are the causes of our problems and who need instead a better upbringing or, failing that, a prison cell. Such thoughts are correct up to a point, but they entirely miss the larger picture.

The first of many confusions people have about ethics concerns the value of thinking about it. Ethical argument is not primarily directed at those who are bent on doing evil. It is directed in the first instance not at bad people, but *at good people whose convictions are being drained by intellectual and moral confusions*. Ideas matter, though we cannot wave them like a talisman to convert the guilty or ward off the secret police. Rather, they are needed in difficult times to strengthen the conviction and dedication of well-intentioned people, who can then go out into the world to heal the troubled, to undo poor upbringings so far as they can, and to change things politically so that the secret police will not come to the door.

A second confusion is to think that, while the bad will not be affected by ethical argument, the good do not need it. Some may think that all the "good people" need to motivate them are edifying sermons and stories to pique their moral consciences, not ethical arguments. But this is also dead wrong, if their convictions are being tested by intellectual challenges and moral confusions. If ethical doubts are based on intellectual problems, as they often are, they cannot be removed simply by appealing to emotions or to people's existing consciences, which they may be questioning. This simple truism is easily forgotten because the "spirits of the times"—expressed by the media and commercial interests—tend to transform all thoughtful issues into matters of feeling. By saying that good people need only sermons and edifying stories to pique their consciences, one unwittingly joins forces with those relativists and skeptics who say "it is all a matter of how you feel." As regards moral conviction today, it is *not* all a matter of how you feel; intellectual doubts run too deep to be dispersed by mere edifying thoughts and stories.

So let us concede that ideas cannot directly convert evildoers or ward off the secret police. They will not grow in a desert. Yet they matter, if planted in fertile ground—in the minds of well-intentioned persons who may then over time turn the desert into a garden. Ideas can only work their way upon the evils of the world indirectly through people who care. We all know such people. But in an age threatened by moral confusion, the problem is that even the best may lack conviction, not knowing what to believe; so that the fertile ground may dry up and turn into desert. (The ecological loss of fertile topsoil throughout the world's agricultural regions is a timely model of what is happening to the moral landscape.) Such a circumstance is well described in one of the great poems of the century, Yeats's "The Second Coming":

> Things fall apart; the center cannot hold;
> Mere anarchy is loosed upon the world,
> The blood-dimmed tide is loosed, and everywhere
> The ceremony of innocence is drowned;
> The best lack all conviction, while the worst
> Are full of passionate intensity.[20]

If absolute values are rejected to ward off fanaticism, we must beware of the opposite danger feared by Kolakowski, Smith, Bellah, Bloom, Milosz, Solzhenitsyn, and many others: a relativism, skepticism, or nihilism in which the spiritual "center cannot hold" and "the best lack all conviction." Our collective task is to find a way to avoid these extremes.

2

The Ends Principle

PLURALISM AND UNCERTAINTY

To lose moral innocence in the modern sense of the *Perelandra* story is to be troubled by two things: *pluralism* and *uncertainty*. Being troubled by pluralism means recognizing the possibility that there are many correct senses of right and wrong (some people are required to live on the fixed land, but others are not) and so there may not be one true or absolute right or wrong. This is the Tower of Babel problem.

Now we are often told that pluralism, or diversity of points of view, does not of itself show that there are no absolute values. The mere existence of competing points of view is compatible with the fact that one of them is right and the others mistaken. This observation is true enough, but it does not go very far toward relieving uneasiness about relativism, if we are also uncertain about how to show which of the competing views is right. In other words, it is not pluralism alone that causes problems about relativism, but pluralism *plus* uncertainty about how to resolve disagreements between conflicting points of view. The two together conspire to erode convictions about the truth of one's own beliefs, just as they did for the woman on Perelandra. In Nietzsche's image, recognizing a thousand different tribes beating to a thousand different drums, we become the first people in history who are not convinced we own the truth.[1]

The uncertainty that conspires with pluralism is actually based on a deeper philosophical problem. If we confront a plurality of conflicting points of view, how can we show that any one of them is the absolute or correct one? To argue that our own view is the right one we must present evidence. But the evidence will inevitably be collected and interpreted from our own point of view. If the debate is about good and evil, the critical evidence will include our views about good and evil, which are not going to be accepted by others who have major disagreements with our point of view in the first place. For this reason, there is a tendency to go around in circles when defending absolutes. The circularity may not always be as evident as "The Bible is absolutely right because it says so" or "I am absolutely right because I believe I am," but it seems that circularity will emerge in some form or another because we are faced with the task of defending the absolute status of our point of view *from* our point of view, which, it seems, is going to beg the question and fail in principle.

This problem of circularity lies behind those popular intellectual trends, mentioned in chapter 1, which make much of the fact that we must always see things from a particular conceptual framework or cultural tradition, and therefore can never climb out of our framework or tradition to see things from an absolute or neutral perspective above the fray. How can it be shown that our point of view, or any other, is the right one and that all competing views are wrong, when we must assume the basic presuppositions of a particular, and therefore limited, point of view in order to support our claims?

OPENNESS

In this chapter I want to address those who are troubled in this way by pluralism and uncertainty, but who also have not given up the possibility of believing in absolute values or the search for them. They have lost moral innocence in the sense of the *Perelandra* story, but they are not yet willing to succumb to relativism or skepticism in ethical matters.

Ordinary persons in such a situation often have the following thought. They think to themselves that since it seems impossible to demonstrate that their view is the right one from their point of view (because of the circularity problem), and since everyone else seems to be in the same condition, the only proper attitude for everyone to take is an attitude of "openness" or tolerance, not passing judgment on other points of view from one's own. Judgments about good and evil, right and wrong, they reason, are personal matters and should be made for ourselves only and not imposed on others without their consent. Is it not true that many of the evils of the past—persecutions and wars, slavery and injustice, exploitation and oppression—have come from the opposite attitude of persons believing that they have absolute right on their side? "Evil takes root," Russian poet Joseph Brodsky has said, "when one man begins to think he is superior to another."[2]

This line of reasoning seems natural to many persons in the face of pluralism and uncertainty, especially those who have been brought up in free and democratic societies. But it is often disparaged by theorists and philosophers. Allan Bloom thinks such an attitude is perverse.

"Openness," he says, "and the relativism that makes it the only plausible stance in the face of . . . various ways of life . . . is the great insight of our time. The point is not to correct the mistakes and really be right; rather it is not to think you are right at all" (p. 26). Bloom thinks such an attitude of openness—an "openness of indifference," as he calls it—is the scourge of our times, infecting society, education, and young people in perverse ways because it creates an indifference to objective truth and absolute right.

Now if Bloom were correct about the consequences of this line of reasoning which ordinary persons are tempted to follow—from pluralism and uncertainty to openness or tolerance—then the results might be as perverse as he thinks they are. But I want to argue that he is wrong about where such a line of reasoning leads. Ordinary persons who think this way when faced with pluralism and uncertainty are on to something important. Their reasoning does not lead to an "openness of indifference," nor to many of the other consequences that trouble Bloom, but rather to the conclusion that some things are universally right and others universally wrong. Persons who reason in this way may not have thought out what they want to say as clearly as they should, but their instincts are sound and not perverse as Bloom charges. To realize why this is so is an important step in the search for absolute value.

FROM PLURALISM AND UNCERTAINTY
TO RELATIVISM?

Let us put the thinking of these people under a microscope. They begin with (1) pluralism and uncertainty, and they think that the plurality of points of view and our uncertainty about what is right suggest that we should (2) take an attitude of openness or tolerance to other points of view. On Bloom's account, this attitude of openness leads them to assume that no point of view can be absolutely right; each can only be right from its own perspective. And this is (3) relativism, or an "openness of indifference," which he thinks is perverse.

But neither (1) pluralism and uncertainty nor (2) an attitude of openness (nor the two combined) implies (3) relativism. Recall that a pluralism of points of view merely suggests the possibility that other views are correct; it does not demonstrate that they are. And uncertainty means only that we cannot know for sure that ours or any other view is the absolutely right one. It does not demonstrate that there is no right one, much less does it demonstrate the vulgar relativist view, mentioned in chapter 1, according to which no view is any better than any other.

In other words, pluralism and uncertainty challenge belief in absolute values, but do not rule out their possibility. This elementary point can be obscured by the confusion, mentioned in chapter 1, between "absoluteness" and "certainty." The assumption often made is that absolutes are what we must know for certain, or infallibly—what we cannot be mistaken about. But an absolute right or truth, as we said, is something that is right or true for everyone (from all points of view); it is universal. And nothing in this definition implies that we, or anyone, could not be mistaken about what is or is not an absolute right or truth. The real issue is whether we can have good reasons for believing in (at least some) universal values or truths despite not being certain. For we have learned that certainty is an elusive ideal in all areas of human inquiry, including those that are considered by many to be the most reliable, such as the natural sciences. If good reasons for belief can be sought in other areas of inquiry without demanding certainty, then we have the right to ask whether there can be good reasons for believing in absolute values without demanding certainty.

To summarize, we have been arguing that (1) pluralism and uncertainty do not necessarily imply (3) relativism, though they challenge belief in absolutes. But Bloom also argues that many people go from pluralism and uncertainty to relativism by another route. Pluralism and uncertainty suggest to them that the proper attitude for everyone to take is (2) an attitude of "openness" or tolerance to other points of view—that is, not assuming knowledge that any view (including one's own) is superior to others and can be imposed on others. And this step to openness, he thinks, does lead to relativism.

Once again, however, the implication fails. We can be open and tolerant to other points of view while believing that some views are better than others and even while believing that one is absolutely correct. An attitude of openness may mean only that we are uncertain which is the correct view and would like to find out. "Openness" need not imply an "openness of indifference." It may only indicate a humble recognition that we are not in certain possession of the truth and thus are willing to learn from others.

Probably many people have made the mistake of thinking that an attitude of openness or tolerance required them to believe in relativism in one form or another. What I doubt is that *all* persons who react to pluralism and uncertainty by suggesting openness and tolerance are guilty of this mistake. Many of them have simply reasoned from (1) pluralism and uncertainty to (2) openness, without mistakenly going on to assert (3) relativism. They had the insight that pluralism and uncertainty somehow suggest that we should take an attitude of openness and tolerance to other points of view, but that was as far as they were willing to go.

THE SEARCH FOR TRUTH

And if they only go this far, I think there is an important truth in their insight, if we can only learn to understand it properly. Bloom acknowledges that openness need not imply an openness of indifference, but he is so blinded by the dangers of relativism that he fails to appreciate the positive role openness can play in the search for absolute value. If openness is wrongly thought to imply relativism, it can have perverse consequences. But conceived in another way, it can be the key that unlocks the door to absolute value.

Why would anyone think an attitude of openness or tolerance to other points of view was a proper reaction to pluralism and uncertainty, if they were not interested in defending relativism? I suggest the following answer. In the face of pluralism and uncertainty an attitude of openness might simply be a way of finding out which is the correct view among the competing alternatives by keeping your mind open and not assuming from the start that yours is the right view. Rather than being a prelude to relativism, an attitude of openness may actually be a way of *searching for truths about value* beyond one's own limited point of view.

Those who are troubled by pluralism and uncertainty, but who have not yet given up the search for absolutes, may reason in the following way. Because of pluralism and uncertainty, they may say, the normal way of finding absolutes is blocked: you cannot position yourself within one point of view and demonstrate from that point of view that it is absolutely right and every other point of view wrong. But if this normal route to absolutes is blocked, there may be another route. Instead of taking up one point of view and trying to prove that it is the right one, try this: assume an attitude of openness and tolerance toward all points of view in order to find thereby some absolutes that will stand up to critical scrutiny. Since no point of view can be proved from the start by its adherents to be the right one for everyone, assume *as an initial stance* that none should be presumed right for others who disagree with it or imposed on others who disagree with it against their wills. Try to sustain this stance to the degree possible as an ideal of action and see what happens.

There is no faulty argument for relativism here. Relativism is not being assumed. For all one knows, some points of view or ways of life may be absolutely better than others. One is simply keeping one's mind open on the subject and assuming that anyone who wishes to find the truth should do likewise. Nor is it assumed that this general attitude of openness is *the* right attitude to take in the final analysis. As a matter of fact, it will turn out not to be the right attitude. But one finds this out only by taking it as an initial stance, by opening one's mind to other points of view and seeing what happens. The idea is: "Open your mind to all other points of view in order to find the truth." But the idea is not: "The truth is that you should open your mind to all other points of view." It turns out that you cannot open your mind to all other points of view. Openness of mind is the initial attitude in the search for truth, but the "openness of indifference" or relativism is not the final one.

Here is another way of putting the essential idea. Rather than assuming the impossible burden of proving yourself right and everyone else wrong, assume an attitude of openness to other points of view in order to *allow others to prove themselves right or wrong.* By taking such an attitude you lift from yourself the burden of proof and distribute it to everyone equally. You are not entirely off the hook, for you still have the burden of proving yourself right or wrong; and we will see that this is burden enough for anyone.

AN ALTERNATIVE PATH TO ABSOLUTES

Philosopher Jerry Fodor has said that the process of discovery in the history of ideas often takes the form "Let's try looking over here" when we haven't been successful looking elsewhere. Modern conditions of pluralism and uncertainty present problems for traditional approaches to absolute value. The suggestion I am making here is that we try something new. At this point it is only a suggestion, a "thought experiment" that we will undertake. But the starting point of openness for the experiment is not arbitrary. We choose openness as an alternative search procedure, first, because it takes seriously the conditions of pluralism and uncertainty that have thwarted other attempts to find absolute value, and, second, because it focuses attention on the fact that what we are searching for is absolute value, that which is good from all points of view. If there are many competing points of view (pluralism) and we are not certain which is the correct one (uncertainty) *and* we are searching for what is good from all points of view, we should open our minds to all points of view in order to find out what each has to contribute to the universal good.

The remarkable thing is that if we perform this thought experiment—as we will do in the present chapter—if we put this attitude of openness into practice as an ideal of action from which we are to depart as little as possible, we find that we arrive at universal norms of human behavior that conform in a surprising way to a broad range of everyday ethical intuitions. In short, we come up with an ethical view characterized by a rich content and historical precedents, one that accounts for commonly recognized exceptions to moral rules as well as the rules themselves.

The question will then naturally arise as to why this remarkable result should have come about and what the experiment means. Is it possible that there are deeper ethical motivations for taking the attitude of openness in the first place that account for the results of the thought experiment? This question will be addressed in later chapters, especially chapter 4, when such deeper motivations are explored. But if these motivations do in fact support the attitude of openness, then the ethical results arrived at in this chapter will be among their consequences.

Since the attitude of openness is not put forward as the final truth, but only as a way of finding the final truth, the reasoning to follow may also be described as "dialectical" in the manner of Socrates: let someone take up a stance or a position without claiming it is the final truth, criticize it, hone it in response to criticism, criticize it, hone it, and so on. This is how we will proceed.[3]

STEP 1: AN IDEAL OF ACTION

The first step in this search procedure is taken when, in the face of pluralism and uncertainty, we assume an attitude of openness or tolerance to other points of view, governed by the idea that "no point of view (including one's own) should be presumed by its adherents to be right for others who disagree with it or imposed on others who disagree with it against their wills." We are to take up this attitude as an ideal of action, trying to sustain it to the degree possible, and see what happens.

Let us recall the reason for starting this way. It is to lift from ourselves the burden of proving our view right and others wrong and *to let others prove themselves right or wrong* by their actions. This is why we let them act in accordance with their own views, and do not allow our view or any other view to be imposed on them against their wills. The whole idea is to "get beyond" our limited point of view and let others be heard in the interests of finding out what is good or valuable in general, not just from our point of view.

The second step in the search occurs when we try to act upon this initial attitude of openness and find it cannot be consistently followed. It turns out that you cannot open your mind to all other points of view, a result that has important implications for ethics. But it will take a few sections to show why this is so and I need to clarify a few things first.

To begin with, something must be said about the much-used expression "points of view." We defined pluralism by noting that there are many competing points of view and have talked about being open to other points of view. But how should we understand these points of view? As a first try, let us say that the "points of view" of persons are defined by their beliefs, desires, intentions, hopes, preferences, and other psychological attitudes, which together tell us what they believe about the world and what their "values" are. By the values of persons, we mean what they care about and what is important to them. In other words, such things as what they desire, like friends, social approval, or meaningful work; what they enjoy, such as sports or music or trips to the seashore; their goals or purposes (for a career, for example, or in a marriage); their images of happiness or success; the excellences of achievement they admire and their highest ideals (justice, democracy, and so on).

Understanding "points of view" and "values" in this way, we can better understand what the initial attitude of openness amounts to. It requires a certain *respect* for the points of view of others governed by the principle that "no point of view (including one's own) should be presumed by its adherents to be right for others who disagree with it or can be imposed on others who disagree with it against their wills." And this means respecting the *values* of others in the above sense, that is, allowing them to pursue their purposes, desires, and images of happiness without interference, rather than imposing one's own purposes or desires upon them against their wills.

This looks very much like an ethical principle of sorts, which indeed it is; and anyone familiar with the history of ethics can think of several notable principles to which it bears a resemblance. Some versions of the Golden Rule come to mind ("Do unto others as you would have them do unto you"). Those who know more of the history of ethics will also be reminded of the second formulation of Immanuel Kant's Categorical Imperative, which tells us to treat all persons as "ends in themselves" and not as "mere means to our own ends."[4] But we should not identify the attitude of openness at this stage with any historical ethical principles. First, the fit is not exact. Second, the attitude of openness is not meant to be a "final" ethical principle, but only a first step in a dialectical argument leading to such a principle. We are going to see that it fails as a candidate for a universal principle.

Nonetheless, the resemblance of the attitude of openness to traditional ethical ideas is significant; and Kant's language of "ends" and "means" can be used to express the starting point. The attitude of openness can be translated into the language of "ends" and "means," if we say that to treat persons as ends (in themselves) is to respect their points of view, and hence their values (as the attitude of openness requires), thus allowing them to pursue their purposes, desires, and images of happiness without interference. And to treat them as means to our ends would be to impose our purposes or desires upon them, forcing them to do what we want against their wills. The attitude of openness could then be expressed by saying that persons should act in accordance with a principle similar to Kant's, which I am going to call the

> Ends Principle*: Treat every person in every situation as an end and never as a means (to your or someone else's ends).

This formulation creates a principle of action from the original idea of openness—that "no point of view (including one's own) should be presumed by its adherents to be right for others who disagree with it or imposed on others who disagree with it against their wills." Despite its similarity to Kant's famous imperative, this principle is not meant to be the same as his or any other traditional ethical principle. It is designed for a different purpose: to capture the attitude of openness which is only an initial attitude taken in a search for truth, not the final answer.

STEP 2: THE BREAKDOWN OF THIS IDEAL

We are now ready to take the second step, which is to show why this attitude of openness cannot be consistently followed as an ideal of action. There are situations in life (many of them, in fact) in which it is impossible to treat all persons as ends—that is, with respect for their points of view and values—as the Ends Principle and the attitude of openness require. These situations are typically ones in which some person or group is already treating some other person or group as a means by coercing, harming, or manipulating them. If you are walking down the street and witness a man attempting to rape a woman and there is something you can do to stop it (by physically intervening or seeking help), then you have entered a situation of this kind. If you do something to prevent the rape, you are not allowing the rapist to live in accordance with his point of view without interference; you are not treating him as an end. But if you just "walk on by" and do nothing, you are not allowing the rape victim to live in accordance with her point of view without interference; you are not treating her as an end, or with respect. Openness or tolerance to *all* points of view is simply not possible in this case.

Some people argue that by walking on by in such a situation you do nothing wrong, since you are not doing something positive to harm the victim. But the Ends Principle does not allow such a legalism. For if thrust into such a situation, however unwillingly, you either choose to not respect the assailant's point of view (by trying to stop him) or the victim's point of view (by walking by). You cannot have it both ways. If you can do something about the situation and yet walk by, you will not be respecting the woman's point of view. She would certainly view it that way: indeed, if she were to see you walk by, the look in her eyes would tell you that you were not respecting her point of view. When pirates under the command of William Kidd attacked Philadelphia in the eighteenth century, pillaging and raping, some of the resident men with pacifist leanings would not protect their women. They were in effect allowing the pirates to pursue their goals in life without interference, but not granting this same freedom to the women—respecting the pirates but not their own women.

The case is similar with those New York residents who witnessed the well-known assault and murder of Kitty Genovese near their apartments and never called the police. The public did not expect that these witnesses (many of whom were aged) should have taken on the killer directly. That would have probably meant two or more deaths rather than one. But the witnesses were faulted for not doing what they *could reasonably have done* in the situation, that is, call the police or otherwise try to get help. They were expected to do what they could have done in the situation because, failing that, they would not be respecting the victim. We might ask Kitty Genovese about this, if we could.

So there are situations in life in which, when you are thrust into them, you cannot treat everyone as an end, *no matter what you do;* and thus it turns out that you cannot open your mind to all other points of view in all situations. Mae West once said, "When faced with a choice between two evils, I always choose the one I haven't tried yet." That is scarcely good moral advice in such situations. But advising openness or tolerance to William Kidd's pirates or the assailant of Kitty Genovese does not seem better.

THE MORAL SPHERE

To see what ought to be done in such conflict situations, we need a general way of talking about them. Let us define a *moral sphere* of life as a situation in which everyone *can* treat everyone else as an end; in other words, the moral sphere defines a space in which the Ends Principle can be followed by everyone. This is an ideal sphere of action, which clearly may not always obtain in the real world. In the situations we have described, the moral sphere has "broken down," and it is no longer possible to treat everyone as an end. One must choose, but on what basis?

To answer this question, we must return to the starting point. The original attitude of openness was assumed as a search procedure. We were to see what could be learned about how to act toward others by trying to sustain this attitude *to the degree possible* in every situation. (In other words, be open as much as possible if you wish to find whatever truth about these matters is to be found.) Now when the moral sphere breaks down, we cannot be completely open. We cannot respect every point of view. The task, then, is to determine which choice (between not respecting the rapist by thwarting him or the victim by walking on by) comes closest to sustaining the ideal of respect for all in these imperfect conditions. Neither choice does it to the letter because someone's point of view will not be respected. But by choosing not to respect the rapist's point of view—by trying to stop him—we are doing something to sustain the ideal of respect for all that we would not be doing if we just walked by. First, we are attempting to restore the moral sphere by thwarting the one whose actions broke it, which means we are trying to restore conditions in which the ideal of respect for all *can be followed once again* (for that is what the moral sphere is). Second, by thwarting the rapist we also sustain the ideal by trying to do something to deter others who might break the moral sphere in the future, thereby preserving conditions in which the ideal can be followed by others.[5]

Thus by thwarting the rapist we *sustain the ideal of respect for all to the degree possible* under adverse conditions when it cannot be literally followed. And we do this in two ways: by attempting to *restore* the moral sphere in the present and *preserve* it in the future whenever it has broken down. In a familiar phrase, by choosing to respect the victim and not the rapist, we serve the ideal "in spirit" when it cannot be served to the letter. It has been said that ideals are like the stars to the ancient mariners, in the sense that while we never reach them, we chart our course by them. This is an appropriate image, for it is our persistence in trying to sustain the ideal to the degree possible when we cannot reach it that leads to an answer about what to do in adverse circumstances.

But some might object that to stop the assailant we (or others) must use violence and so employ the same forbidden tactics that broke the moral sphere in the first place. This looks like restoring an ideal (treating everyone as an end) by breaking or violating it. "Two wrongs do not make a right," people say, or they say "the end does not justify the means."

But here lies a very common moral confusion. We are indeed violating the ideal of treating everyone as an end by stopping the assailant and restoring the moral sphere. But remember that we are in a situation in which it is *impossible* not to violate that ideal *no matter what we do*. The defining characteristic of moral sphere breakdown is that it is no longer possible to treat everyone as an end. The only choice we have is about *who* will be treated as a means, the guilty or the innocent, not whether someone will be. And our choice of the rapist is in the service of the ideal—restoring it by stopping the one who is breaking it and creating the impossible situation.

Similarly, a good end does not usually justify a bad means. But in cases of moral sphere breakdown, the means (treating someone's point of view disrespectfully) is something we must do, no matter what we do. So the justification for treating someone as a means in such cases does not come from the end, but from the fact that we cannot do otherwise. What the end tells us is that it should be the guilty party who is treated as a means, not the innocent party, for this choice comes closest to serving the ideal when it cannot be served to the letter.

But is it always so easy to determine who broke the moral sphere and who is the "guilty" party? The answer is obviously No, and we will look at some harder cases later. But even in simple cases, like rape and assault, where it is wise to get one's ethical bearings first, skeptics might raise a question. They may point out (grotesquely) that while the rapist is thwarting the woman's interests and purposes by force, she is also thwarting his by forceably resisting. The impossible situation, such critics might say, has arisen because of a mutual conflict of points of view. On what grounds, then, do we treat the parties asymmetrically, calling one guilty and the other innocent? Grotesque as this objection is, it points to the important issue of how to determine who broke the moral sphere—an issue that increases in significance as ethical situations become more complex.

The immediate reaction is to say that the rapist acted first, and so initiated the conflict that broke the moral sphere; the woman merely reacted. This is part of the story, but not the whole of it.[6] To fully understand moral sphere breakdown, I suggest that we have to bring in the additional notion of a "plan of action" or "life-plan." Suppose the woman, when she was assaulted, was leaving work and planned to go shopping and then return to her home. Her plan of action for the day is quite different from the rapist's because it could have been carried out without her treating someone else as a means. His plan of action, by contrast, included forcing his will on some woman or other, should he care to, even in the face of resistance. In other words, his life-plan was by its very nature a "moral sphere breaker," while hers was not. This is an important asymmetry that accounts for our saying that he broke the moral sphere. She did indeed resist once the trajectories of their life-plans crossed, but it was the nature of his trajectory (life-plan) that initiated the breakdown. Our stopping him, as a consequence, is not just a matter of restoring the moral sphere in the present, but of deterring him and others from following similar (moral-sphere-breaking) life-plans in the future.

STEP 3: A REVISED IDEAL

Now let us stand back to consider what all this means. The original attitude of openness or tolerance to all other points of view spelled out by the Ends Principle does not pass critical scrutiny. One cannot treat *every* person in *every* situation as an end and not as a means. We learn this by imagining situations in which one tries to follow the attitude of openness to the letter and finds that it cannot be consistently followed.

Yet the original attitude of openness was Bloom's "openness of indifference"—treating every point of view tolerantly without qualification. We now see that such a position is impossible and cannot be maintained. When we restore the moral sphere by treating the rapist as a means, we are effectively saying that the rapist's point of view or way of life is *less worthy of being respected* in this case than the victim's. We are making judgments of better and worse among ways of living and acting (among life-plans). Ironically, though we started with an attitude of openness, we do not end with an attitude of openness. Quite the contrary: we get the result that some views are better than others, more worthy of respect, and some less worthy.

And so it is with all the Hitlers, Stalins, murderers, rapists, oppressors, exploiters, and other evildoers of the world. We do not have to say their points of view are just as good as everyone else's. By their actions, they place themselves outside the moral sphere, so to speak (in which everyone can be treated as an end), and make their ways of life less worthy of respect than others. To start with an attitude of openness is simply to treat them as innocent till proven guilty, and then *let them prove themselves guilty* by their actions. The mistake is to suppose that we must maintain an attitude of openness (of indifference) to everyone. We cannot do this. The ideal which tells us that we should normally respect others also tells us we should not do so in some cases.

Letting others prove themselves less worthy of respect by their actions may seem to suggest waiting till they actually break the moral sphere before acting to restrain them—which would be disastrous in many instances. But this is not so. For we have seen that the goal is to *preserve* the moral sphere when it is endangered in addition to restoring it when it has already been broken. Deterring those who intend to break the moral sphere is as much a way of maintaining the ideal as restoring it after it has broken. But this reasoning, of course, can also apply to cases in which someone has not yet broken the moral sphere, but is about to. Those who read Hitler's *Mein Kampf* in the 1930s could see what his life-plan entailed and they had every right to prevent him by force, in the interests of preserving a moral sphere, when they saw he was about to carry it out. (Though we know in fact that many leaders of the time could not believe Hitler meant what he said.) Most such cases of preemptive action are difficult to decide upon because one must have good evidence that a breakdown is going to occur. But the general principle of preemptive action is a part of the ideal of preserving the moral sphere in the future.

Finally, the argument of the preceding sections shows that the Ends Principle, which expresses the attitude of openness in imperative form, cannot be an *absolute* ethical principle, because it cannot be followed in every situation. We have, in dialectical fashion, subjected it to critical scrutiny (counterexample) and found that it does not stand up. There are numerous examples (rape, murder, theft, assault, oppression, exploitation, and so on) which show that it cannot be followed in every situation. But having recognized this fact and criticized the principle, we can hone it into something that may come closer to the absolute principle we seek.

> *Ends Principle**:* Treat every person as an end and not as a means (to your or someone else's ends) *whenever possible*. When it is not possible, strive to sustain this ideal to the degree possible, by choosing those actions that will best restore and preserve moral spheres (in which everyone can be treated as an end).

TRADITIONAL ETHICAL COMMANDMENTS: LYING, CHEATING, AND SELF-DEFENSE

This revised Ends Principle, along with the new *qualified* attitude of openness that it implies, has tremendous scope as a potential ethical principle. Not only does it allow us to count as inferior and less worthy of respect all of those whose purposes and points of view would have them do violence to others—from ordinary assailants and rapists to ruthless dictators and warmongers—it also covers many other forms of behavior that are covered by traditional moral rules, like the Ten Commandments: Thou shall not kill, steal, lie, and so on.[7]

Take lying. To lie to others in order to get something out of it for yourself, or in order to harm them, is normally to treat them as a means to your own ends. It is not to respect their desires and purposes and is therefore in violation of the Ends Principle. But just as many strands of Jewish, Christian, and other religious traditions have allowed exceptions to the rule "Thou shall not kill" (for example, in just wars or in self-defense), so many have countenanced exceptions in rare cases to "Thou shall not lie." An old example that teachers of ethics often use is this. Suppose a woman is living on a farm in Nazi Germany during World War II and hiding a Jewish family on her property. The Gestapo come to the door and ask whether she is hiding a Jewish family. Should she lie or not? Many people see this as a genuine moral dilemma. Their heritage says "Thou shall not lie," yet they are inclined to think that here is a case where lying may be the right thing to do.

What does the revised Ends Principle say? The woman in this case is in a situation similar to that of the passerby in the rape example. The Gestapo is just as clearly intending to harm the Jewish family as the rapist is intending to harm his victim. The woman who is hiding the Jewish family cannot respect both points of view in such a situation. If she tells the truth to the Gestapo, she treats them as an end, not interfering with their purposes, but she allows the Jewish family to be treated as a means. She may protest that she herself did not directly do harm to the family. But this is like the passerby in the rape example protesting that he himself did not perform the rape. If he walks by when he could have helped, the look in the rape victim's eyes would tell him that he was not respecting her point of view. And similarly, if this woman tells the truth to the Gestapo, the look in the eyes of the Jewish family members as they are dragged away would tell her that she chose to respect, not their point of view, but that of the Gestapo.

She cannot have it both ways. Someone will not be respected *no matter what she does;* her choice again is only about *who* it will be. And, for the same reasons given in the rape case, it is the ones whose life-plan broke the moral sphere—the Gestapo—who should not be respected. In other words, she should lie. The same principle—the revised Ends Principle— which tells us that in *most* instances lying is wrong, also tells us that in *some* instances it is the right thing to do, just as the principle tells us that while violence is usually wrong, it sometimes must be used. The same is true if someone forced you to sit down to a game of cards and threatened to harm your family if you lost. Cheating, like lying, is usually wrong because it involves treating someone else as a means. But in this instance it would be right to cheat in any way you could.

The same reasoning also shows why self-defense is often cited as an exception to moral rules against using violence. If a thief approaches you in an alley with a lead pipe in hand, the moral sphere has broken down because someone is going to be treated as a means—either you or him—no matter what you do. The case is very much like the rape and

Gestapo examples except that in this scenario you are playing the roles of both victim and third party. Your choice is not about whether someone will be treated as a means in the situation, but about who it will be. And the same reasoning as in the other examples tells us that it should be the one whose plan of action initiated the conflict—the one who has broken the moral sphere and created the situation in which the ideal of respect for all could not be followed. You can physically resist the attack, just as you can physically restrain the rapist when you are a third party witnessing a rape.

Self-defense has often (though not universally) been regarded down through history as an exception to the general rules against killing or harming others. Persons can defend themselves against attack, and so can nations; there are just wars of self-defense, it is said. Our reasoning supports these conclusions. The same principle (the revised Ends Principle) which tells us that killing, harming, lying, or cheating are usually wrong, also tells us that they may sometimes be right when the moral sphere breaks down.

EXCEPTIONS TO MORAL RULES AND
THE LIMITATIONS OF RELATIVISM

I noted in chapter 1 that one of the symptoms of lost moral innocence (as in the *Perelandra* story) is the recognition that many of the traditional moral commandments learned in childhood (about killing, lying, stealing, and so on) have exceptions. Once exceptions are admitted, confusion and disagreement set in about where the line is to be drawn in making exceptions, and doubts arise like those that bothered the woman on Perelandra: if others can do it (make exceptions), why can't I?

It is interesting that the revised Ends Principle answers questions about exceptions in the same way that it answers questions about openness and relativism. It tells us the line on exceptions is to be drawn exactly where the line between better and worse points of view or ways of life is to be drawn: at the point *where the moral sphere breaks down.* Those who, by breaking the moral sphere, create situations in which we cannot treat everyone as an end, place themselves outside the moral sphere and thereby make their ways of life less deserving of respect than those who remain inside the moral sphere. But breakdown of the moral sphere is also the point where exceptions to the rules appear. We use force to restrain the rapist, we lie to the Gestapo, or we cheat those who have threatened our family, because by their actions they have placed themselves outside the moral sphere and we restrain them in order to restore that sphere.

Two problems connected with the loss of moral innocence are thereby addressed together. By reacting to pluralism and uncertainty with an attitude of openness, we do not arrive at the relativist view that every way of life is as good as every other, but instead at the view that some are less worthy of respect than others; and in the same way we see where to draw the line on exceptions to moral rules and why such a line is necessary. It is of interest also that the exceptions are not handled in an ad hoc manner, as if we were to add to our "thou shall nots" an endless string of exceptions to meet every new problem. To the contrary, the line between the rule and its exceptions arises naturally from trying to apply the original ideal—treat everyone in every situation as an end—and finding that it is impossible in some situations. The line on exceptions is drawn at the point at which this impossibility occurs, where the moral sphere breaks down. The revised Ends Principle therefore covers the content of many traditional moral principles and their exceptions at the same time.

STEP 4: MORAL SPHERE BREAKDOWN AND ITS RULES

This point about exceptions also shows that when the moral sphere breaks down, it is not the case that anything goes. There are still moral rules to be followed, the first of which, we found, is "Thwart the guilty, not the innocent." We are now in a position to see that the same line of reasoning which led us to say we should thwart the guilty when the moral sphere breaks down suggests another rule: "Use minimum force to restore the moral sphere." The rapist must be restrained. But neither bystanders nor the police have the right to shoot him through the heart if he can be subdued with less force.

This second rule is based on the same considerations that led to the "Thwart the guilty" rule. By using minimum force to restore the moral sphere, we treat the guilty party with as much *residual* respect as is consistent with the fact that we must restrain him. In this way, we come as close as possible to serving the ideal of treating all persons as ends, when the Ends Principle cannot be followed to the letter. The reluctance to shoot the assailant through the heart, if less force will do, is an example of trying to sustain the ideal (of respect for all) *to the degree possible* in a difficult situation, even as we restrain him. In the same vein, one could say that jailed criminals retain some rights and should be afforded some measure of respect as persons, even though they have forfeited the full measure of respect. The revised Ends Principle thereby slices through two confusions. One confusion is that criminals and victims are owed equal respect in all situations (since both are persons). The other confusion is that the guilty in situations of moral sphere breakdown are owed no respect at all.

JUST WARS AND RULES OF WARFARE

These rules ("Thwart the guilty" and "Use minimum force") also have relevance to questions about warfare and conflicts between nations. Long-standing traditions in Western culture and in other cultures have allowed for "just wars" under certain conditions for example, in cases of self-defense, or when coming to the aid of another nation that has been unjustly invaded. But this does not mean, according to these same just war traditions, that when warfare breaks out, anything goes. Most nations accept moral constraints on war, many of them embodied today for the international community in the so-called Geneva Conventions. If we consider the rules of just warfare embodied in these international conventions—for example, rules against harming innocent noncombatants, against indiscriminate saturation bombing, against killing the enemy when one can take prisoners, and so on—it can be seen, I think, that the rules of "thwarting the guilty" and "using minimum force" are operating behind them, just as we would expect. *Innocent* noncombatants are to be treated with respect and combatants are to be treated with as much *residual* respect as is consistent with the needs of battle (as in the case, for example, of rules protecting prisoners of war or mandating medical care for captured enemy soldiers).

This hardly means that questions concerning just wars and rules of warfare are easily answered. As with any general principle, applying the revised Ends Principle to particular cases is fraught with difficulty because the relevant facts may be too many, or unknown, or ambiguous. But this is no argument against the principle. Its aim is to tell us what kinds of facts to look for (who broke the moral sphere? how much force is necessary to restore it?) if we are to decide the moral issues. No principle can supply us with the facts themselves or with all the answers; and this is especially true in cases of warfare. Books on the ethics of warfare, like Michael Walzer's *Just and Unjust Wars*,[8] show how many ambiguities are involved in trying to decide particular cases. For the United States and the other Allied nations, World War II was one of the clearest cases of a just war in this century. The aggressions of Nazi Germany and Japan were examples of breaking the moral sphere as clear as one can find in the tangled annals of warfare. Many on the Allied side have consequently called it the "Good War"—not "good" really, but a just war from their point of view.

By contrast, the Vietnam War (or "conflict," as it was officially called) was riddled with ambiguities for most Americans. I won't review the tangled arguments for and against the Vietnam conflict here, but an important insight about it can be derived from our discussion of the Ends Principle and the rules of war. It follows from our reasoning that there is likely to be moral consensus in a nation about what is a just war when aggression is obvious and the moral sphere has clearly broken down, when it is possible to identify the guilty party without ambiguity, and when it is reasonably clear how to proceed to restore the moral sphere by using minimum force. By contrast, if some of these things are ambiguous and hotly debated, as in the case of Vietnam, moral consensus will be hard to attain and it will be difficult to prosecute a war. Some will want to fight, others will not; many who do fight will do so uneasily—without the same confidence and commitment of the soldiers of World War II. If there is a lesson here it is this: beware of fighting ambiguous wars, those on which you cannot reach moral consensus, for they will tear your society asunder.

The recently concluded war in the Persian Gulf throws further light on these principles. So long as the Bush administration tried to justify intervention in order to preserve the flow of oil from the Middle East, or to preserve jobs back home, its arguments rightly did not make much headway with the American people. The arguments that really turned the tide of public sentiment had to do with throwing the aggressor, Saddam, out of Kuwait (supplemented by descriptions of atrocities against Kuwaitis by Iraqi soldiers), as well as protecting Saudi Arabia and Israel from Saddam's possible further aggression. Considerations such as these, it turns out, are supported by the revised Ends Principle. Counterintervention to free a nation unjustly attacked is a case of *restoring* the moral sphere when it has broken down (the international analogue of coming to the aid of the rape victim), and intervention to protect other nations endangered by potential aggression is a case of *preserving* the moral sphere when further breakdown is possible. Moreover, identifying the guilty party (the one whose life-plan initiated the breakdown) was never in doubt in the Persian Gulf War: Saddam was everyone's perfect villain.

This left the question of "minimum force" in dispute. Would sanctions have done the job against Iraq with minimal costs, or was war necessary? Once started, was the war stopped too soon to defuse the aggressor's power? The jury is still out on these questions (and others, such as whether Saddam was coddled by the Bush administration in the years prior to the war). The issue of sanctions was debated by the U.S. Congress before the war in one of its least superficial debates of recent memory. The uncertainty of sanctions and the swiftness of the war settled the question for most people. But the aftermath, with Saddam still in power and the brutal suppression of Kurdish and Shiite rebels, has reopened it, along with the question of whether the war was brought to an end too soon. These issues will continue to be debated. But, insofar as they are treated as ethical issues of warfare, and not merely as issues of power politics, I think we can see the relevance for their resolution of the revised Ends Principle, moral sphere breakdown, and the rules "Thwart the guilty" and "Use minimum force." Applying these same rules shows why the Persian Gulf War, despite the lingering questions that still surround it, was less ethically ambiguous for most Americans than Vietnam.

PERSUASION AND COERCION: PACIFISM AND NONVIOLENCE

While our argument obviously does not support the pacifist view that war and violence are wrong in *all* situations, it does throw some positive light on pacifism. For it supports the idea that pacifism is the right moral stance *inside the moral sphere,* where everyone can be treated as an end. Against extreme pacifism, the point that needs to be made is that, in the real world, the moral sphere often breaks down and violence may be necessary to restore a situation in which unsullied moral action is possible once again. If, out of pacifist motives, men allow pirates to assault and rape women, they have not avoided a world in which someone is treated violently as a means. They have merely chosen that it be the women and not the pirates who are treated violently. If a moral principle, like the revised Ends Principle, allows violence in some instances, this need not mean there is something wrong with the principle. It may mean only that there is (often) something wrong with the world.

The difficulties of an extreme pacifist position are clearly indicated by the story I once heard from Quaker friends in Philadelphia, the story of a Quaker farmer who caught a thief in his chicken yard. Aiming a shotgun at the thief, he said: "Sir, I do not want to harm you, but I advise you to run, because you are standing where I am about to shoot."

We may use the language of the Quakers, or Friends as they prefer to be called, and say that the moral sphere is the sphere of *friendly persuasion.* Friendly persuasion is always to be preferred to coercion wherever it is possible, because it treats others as ends, allowing them to freely choose from their own point of view. Thus, friendly persuasion belongs inside the moral sphere, coercion outside it. So long as we agree to discuss with others, rather than forcing our views upon them, we respect their points of view and the moral sphere obtains. This is the preferred situation; but the moral sphere can break down, and friendly persuasion must sometimes give way to coercion.

Nor should we confuse friendly persuasion with the manipulative persuasion that is so pervasive in modern societies, through advertising, public relations, propaganda, and other means—a persuasion whose aim is not to respect others and treat them as ends, but to use them as means to the persuader's ends. The Quaker notion of friendly persuasion is a useful one in this connection, because "persuasion" pure and simple has a bad sound for many people today, since it calls to mind manipulative persuasion. By saying that the moral sphere is the sphere of friendly persuasion, we are saying it is the sphere where the values and choices of persons are respected for their own sakes (as "ends in themselves") rather than one in which they are manipulated or used as means by others. Outside the moral sphere we have not only coercion, but also more subtle forms of manipulative persuasion and exploitation.

Returning to pacifists, they have something important to tell us, even if we cannot go all the way with them. Though violence can sometimes be justified by virtue of moral sphere breakdown, humans are prone to jump to violence too quickly as a means of resolving social conflicts, thereby assuming too quickly that the moral sphere has broken down. We should try our best to conceive of other means first. This is an extension of the "Use minimum force" rule. It is also the lesson of nonviolence movements in the twentieth century pioneered by Mohandas Gandhi and Martin Luther King, Jr.

Nonviolence movements are important moral experiments, according to the revised Ends Principle, because they attempt to sustain the moral sphere "to the degree possible" in imperfect conditions by invoking friendly persuasion rather than coercion. We often use more force when less force would do. But how do we know how much is needed unless we experiment with less? It is therefore a moral imperative to try nonviolent methods where they *may* work, even if, in the end, there are limits to nonviolent methods, as to pacifism.

What we may call "moral progress," as opposed to technological or other kinds of progress, might be defined as expanding the moral sphere so that it encompasses more and more areas of human life—so that the domain of friendly, or moral, persuasion expands and that of coercion and manipulation contracts. Believers in nonviolence may be viewed as contributing to that moral progress by showing us that non-coercive methods can work in areas of life where it was never before thought possible.

Gandhi called his experiments with nonviolence his "experiments with truth."[9] If we need scientific experimentation for technological progress, then why not moral experimentation for moral progress? It is the only way our moral sensibilities will catch up to the technological advances of modern civilization.

THE GOLDEN RULE: TWO VERSIONS

Readers may have suspected from the first statement of the Ends Principle that it has something to do with the so-called Golden Rule ("Do unto others as you would have them do unto you"). Indeed, it does. But we have to be careful. There are at least two historical interpretations of the Golden Rule, one of which is very close to the Ends Principle as we have finally stated it, the other far from the Ends Principle indeed.

Yet the connection between the Ends Principle and the Golden Rule is significant, for the Golden Rule has been endorsed in one form or another by many of the major spiritual traditions of mankind. Here are a few examples.

> *Christianity:* "All things whatsoever ye would that men should do to you, do you even so to them: for this is the Law and the Prophets." (Matthew 7:12)
>
> *Judaism:* "What is hateful to you, do not to your fellow men. This is the entire law: all the rest is commentary." (Talmud, Shabbat 31a)
>
> *Hinduism:* "This is the sum of duty: Do naught unto others which would cause you pain if done to you." (*Mahabharata* 5:1517)
>
> *Buddhism:* "Hurt not others in ways that you yourself would find hurtful." (Udana-Varga, 5:18)
>
> *Islam:* "No one of you is a believer until he desires for his brother that which he desires for himself." (Sunnah)
>
> *Confucianism:* "Surely it is a maxim of loving kindness: Do not unto others that you would not have them do unto you." (*Analects*, 15:23)
>
> *Taoism:* "Regard your neighbor's gain as your own gain and your neighbor's loss as your own loss." (*T'ai Shang Kan Ying P'ien*)
>
> *Zoroastrianism:* "That nature alone is good which refrains from doing unto another whatsoever is not good for itself." (Dadistan-i-dinik, 94:5)

The negative formulations of Confucius's *Analects* and several of the others ("Do not unto others . . . ," "Hurt not others . . .") are sometimes said to express the "Silver Rule," but the general thrust is very much the same as the traditional Golden Rule ("Do unto others . . ."). We do not go wrong if we take them as expressing the same principle.

The astonishing thing about these historical formulations of the Golden Rule is the number of them which add that this rule is "[the sum of] the Law and the Prophets," or "the entire Law: all the rest is commentary," or "this is the sum of duty." If this were true, and the revised Ends Principle did in fact express the Golden Rule, it would encapsulate the Law of many traditions, or the sum of duty. We have already seen how the revised Ends Principle can cover traditional commandments of the Mosaic law not to kill, steal, lie, and so on, as well as their exceptions, and this is suggestive.

But what about the claim that there are two versions or interpretations of the Golden Rule, only one of which is expressed by the Ends Principle? On one version of the Golden Rule, which might be called the "narrow version," doing unto others as you would have them do unto you would mean allowing them to pursue their values without interference, so long as *they share your values,* or so long as they have the "right" values *as you see it.* If one tribe believes it is right to plant corn, but not to hunt buffalo, then they will allow all their neighbors to plant corn, but not to hunt buffalo, which is exactly how they themselves would want to be treated by their neighbors. But their neighbors may not want to be treated that way at all if their values are different—if they are buffalo hunters, for example, and not corn planters. Under this narrow version of the Golden Rule, doing unto others as you would have them do unto you, you will satisfy others only so long as they share your values. Otherwise, it is a recipe for conflict and war.

By contrast, a second or "wider version" of the Golden Rule says that if you want to be allowed by others to pursue *your* values, then you should allow them to pursue *their* values, *even if their values are different from yours.* This version is similar to the Ends Principle, so long as exceptions are made for moral sphere breakdown. If we add these exceptions to the wide version of the Golden Rule, or suppose they are required to consistently uphold the Golden Rule (as I suspect they are), then we can say that the Ends Principle is a modern version of the wide interpretation of the Golden Rule.

The Golden Rule is one of the great products of the Axial Period of human history, that crucial ancient period of spiritual enlightenment for mankind described in chapter 1. Many of the formulations quoted at the beginning of this section (from Buddhism, Hinduism, Confucianism, and so on) stem from this period. I said in chapter 1 that we have entered an age at the end of the twentieth century in which much of the traditional spiritual heritage of mankind is being questioned. Yet it may not be wise to throw all the old wisdom away, and one piece of ancient human wisdom we especially should not abandon is the Golden Rule.

Yet even as we retain it, we must be aware of the two interpretations—the narrow and wider versions—that have woven their way through history and are still confused by many persons. While we should retain the ancient wisdom embodied in the Golden Rule, we must exercise modern wisdom in interpreting it. We know that the first or narrow version is not likely to have been the interpretation of most of the ancient framers of the Golden Rule, since following the narrow version would most likely lead to war and hate, not the peace and love that they intended. The narrower version of the Golden Rule might have seemed natural to people who believed they could confidently show that their point of view or way of life was absolutely superior to others. But the modern loss of moral innocence and the resulting problems of pluralism and uncertainty have blown that confidence away for most of us.

The proper interpretation of the Golden Rule for those of us who live after the modern Fall is, I think, the second or wide version, which corresponds to the revised Ends Principle. It is the version that results from a search for absolute principles which takes pluralism and uncertainty seriously. We have bitten too deeply into the fruit of the tree of knowledge of good and evil to go back to the narrow version. The best expression I have ever read of the suppositions that underlie the wide version of the Golden Rule and the revised Ends Principle is a statement attributed to the great Sioux Indian chief Sitting Bull, who is best known for his confrontation with General Custer at Little Big Horn. He is reputed to have said to government agents in 1883, "If the Great Spirit had desired me to be a white man, he would have made me so in the first place. He put in your heart certain wishes and plans, in my heart he put other and different desires. Each man is good in his sight. It is not necessary for eagles to be crows."[10]

BREAKDOWN WITHOUT A GUILTY PARTY: HEROISM AND SACRIFICE

Can we always locate a guilty party when the moral sphere breaks down? The answer is No, and this answer brings us to the final steps in our discussion of the Ends Principle. It may be difficult at first to imagine situations of moral sphere breakdown in which there is no recognizable guilty party, but such situations comprise another important dimension of the ethical life.

Let us begin with a striking example that conveys some lessons about all such cases, before we turn to other examples. Suppose the moral sphere has broken down because of a natural disaster not caused by any human agent. For example, a ship has sunk in a storm and ten men are in a life raft that can only safely sustain eight. Two of them are not going to be treated as ends (are not going to have their purposes or desires fulfilled), but no one of them is guilty. Or, suppose that four men are in an airplane that is going down with only three parachutes. These are situations in life where things have turned really bad. The moral sphere has broken down, and not everyone can be treated as an end, but there is no identifiable guilty party.

Let us focus on the airplane example, and suppose, to make it as hard as possible, the men know that each of the three parachutes will only sustain one man: if two men share one parachute both will die. What should the four men do? This is not a question about what they *might* do. They might get into a brawl over the three parachutes and settle the matter by force. But, while it might come to that eventually, our question is whether there are any "ethical" options left to them before force prevails. What are the ethical constraints, if any, in such difficult situations of moral sphere breakdown where no one is guilty?

The clue here is to proceed in the same general manner as in earlier cases. When the ideal of treating everyone as an end is threatened, we should strive to *sustain the ideal to the degree possible under imperfect conditions*. In the earlier cases this meant restraining the guilty with minimum force. What does it mean when there is no guilty party?

A number of options spring to mind for the men in the airplane. The first possibility is that one of them might volunteer to sacrifice himself and become a hero. Our intuitions tell us that this would be an ethically favorable solution if it could come about. Buy why? Because if someone voluntarily took this heroic step *the moral sphere would be restored,* since everyone would then be treated with respect—the three who parachuted and the volunteer who acted out of his own free will. No one would have been coerced. Heroic acts often restore the moral sphere in this way—and so maintain the ideal—and they do so when the world has deteriorated to desperate conditions so that maintaining the ideal is at its most difficult. Heroism is more than duty requires, *yet it serves the ethical ideal.*

But let us make the airplane example even more difficult. No one volunteers to be a hero; they all choose to survive. Are there any moral options remaining now before they merely fight it out? Most people who reflect on such situations sooner or later come up with the suggestion that, at this point (where all else has failed), they should perhaps draw lots or flip coins. The suggestion has merit, but again we should ask why it seems such a natural option. The answer, I believe, is once again found in the notion of sustaining the ideal of respect for all to the degree possible in imperfect conditions. Someone is going to die against his will, but deciding by lot means that all will be treated with respect in the process of deciding who it will be. No point of view will be treated as privileged or superior, which is the nearest they can come at this extreme to the ideal of respect for all when the ideal cannot be followed to the letter. (And, of course, the ideal cannot be followed to the letter in the last analysis, because the lottery loser will not be treated equally.) If choosing by lot seems appropriate in extreme conditions like this, I believe this is the reason why. Centuries ago Aristotle noted that choosing by lot would be the fair way of resolving some difficult issues in society that could not be fairly resolved in any other way.

But what if, as a final step in the downward spiral of events, the loser in the choice by lot panics and does not agree to abide by it? Then we really have reached a state at which force is all that remains. Harsh as it may seem, the other three men could be acting ethically if they restrained him or even threw him out, if they must do so at this point. But this is only because they have reached a point where, by following a fair procedure to decide who would die, they have done as much as they *can* do in the situation to retain the moral ideal of equal respect for all. The idea that we should do as much as we can do in a situation (for example, the witnesses to the Kitty Genovese murder should at least have called the police) is an aspect of the idea that we should *depart as little as possible from the ideal when we cannot follow it to the letter.*

STEP 5: LEVELS OF THE MORAL SPHERE

Such cases lead us to a final revision of the Ends Principle. Examples of moral sphere breakdown can be summarized in terms of the following diagram.

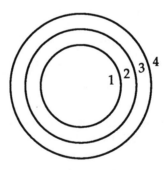

Level 1 is the "moral sphere," the sphere in which everyone can be treated as an end.

Level 2 is where the moral sphere has broken down and there is an obvious guilty party. Not everyone can be treated as an end at this level, but it is not the case that anything goes. There are still rules at level 2—stop the guilty and use minimal force—which express the idea that one should maintain the moral sphere to the degree possible where it cannot be maintained to the letter.

 · Level 3 includes the cases just discussed in which the moral sphere has broken down, but there is no guilty party. Here again, someone will be treated as a means, but we must strive to decide who it will be by the fairest possible procedure (for example, choosing by lot, if it comes to that), which again amounts to maintaining the ideal of respecting all parties to the degree possible in a bad situation. In general, as we move away from the ethical center, we try to retain as much of it as possible.

Finally, level 4 represents the situation in which the lottery loser refuses to abide by the decision. At this level, all moral options have been exhausted and force prevails. Level 4 represents the most de-graded of moral states, which Thomas Hobbes in *Leviathan* called the "state of nature," a state of war of "all against all."

Extreme pacificists say that violence or force is *never* justified in human affairs. An opposite "might-makes-right" doctrine says that violence and force are *always* legitimate means of resolving human conflicts. Pacifism would be right if the moral sphere never broke down, in other words, if the world were always at level 1. Similarly, the might-makes-right doctrine would be correct if the world were always at level 4—if the state of nature, or war of all against all, prevailed. What is wrong with both these views is that the world is not always in one or another of these extremes. When the moral sphere breaks down the pacifism of level 1 fails, but we do not move immediately to the "anything goes" situation of level 4. Ethical options are not that simple. There are constraints at the levels between 1 and 4—restraining only the guilty, using minimum force, seeking the fairest resolution of conflict—that must be exhausted before the state of nature prevails.

STEP 6: CONFLICTS OF INTEREST AND THE ENDS PRINCIPLE

Level 3 breakdowns of the moral sphere extend far beyond the life-and-death examples of the airplane and the life raft. Any everyday situation in which people's goals or interests conflict with one another so that not all of them can realize their goals is a level 3 situation. Such "conflicts of interest" are clearly very common in everyday life. One man wants peace and quiet, while his neighbor wants to play the trumpet; two countries lay claim to the same disputed territory; a husband wants to play cards with his friends while his wife wants him to visit her parents. "The ends of men are many," as Sir Isaiah Berlin puts it, "and not all of them are compatible with one another."[11]

The moral sphere is about to break down in such conflict-of-interest situations because someone's desires or purposes are going to be thwarted. Yet (as with the airplane and raft examples) no one is guilty *as yet*, if no one has yet attempted to impose his or her will on the others. What resolution is suggested in regard to such everyday level 3 situations? The airplane example provides clues. Departing as little as possible from the ideal of treating everyone as an end in such situations means trying to find a fair compromise, or as fair a compromise as possible, because "fairness" in such situations means respecting the ends or points of views of all parties to the degree possible. Ideally, what is suggested is a negotiated solution in which each party would agree to yield something out of respect for the other's desires. The trumpet is played in the daytime when the neighbor is at work or the countries split the disputed territory.

Yet we know that many real-world disputes are not so ideally resolved. Ideal solutions to level 3 conflicts stay as close as possible to the original goal of treating all with respect, but disputed objects cannot always be divided equally like pieces of a pie. The biblical story of King Solomon and the baby claimed by two different women reminds us of this truth. Indeed, the biblical story is meant to remind us of the pitfalls of conflict of interest, or level 3, ethical situations. More often than not they cannot be resolved by the parties themselves face to face; emotions run too deep or there is a suspicion that one or another party is not bargaining in good faith. When these things happen "second-best" strategies must be employed. One might have to appeal to third-party arbitrators, or judges, or juries, to resolve conflicts of interest, or perhaps majority vote, or even, in some cases, settle the matter by lot. But in all cases one is striving to stay as close as *possible* to the ideal of respect for all when it cannot be perfectly realized.[12]

Majority vote is an interesting example of a "second-best" strategy that tries to do this when other methods fail. Accepting the majority decision will produce an unhappy minority which does not get its way, so it is not an ideal solution. But democratic theorists have argued that, in many social situations, majority vote is the fairest way to resolve conflict because it comes as close as possible in imperfect conditions to respecting the voice of each person equally.

Adding level 3 conflicts to the ethical picture provides us with a final revision of the Ends Principle in terms of our four-level diagram.

Ends Principle: Treat every person as an end in every situation and not as a means (to yours or someone else's end) *whenever possible* (level 1). When this is not possible because the moral sphere has broken down, strive to sustain the ideal of treating every person as an end to the degree possible in imperfect conditions. This means, when there is a guilty party (level 2), restrain the guilty and use minimal force to restore and preserve the moral sphere, and when there is no guilty party (level 3), seek as fair a compromise as the situation allows, one that respects all persons involved to the degree possible.

REVIEW OF THE ARGUMENT

While this revised Ends Principle (which might also be called a modern version of the Golden Rule) has large scope as a guide to moral action, it also has limitations. It is not the whole or final answer to all ethical questions, as subsequent chapters will make clear. But I think it is part of the answer—at least a first step through the moral maze, whose image in chapter 1 was the ancient Tower of Babel.

To summarize the argument of this chapter: We were to undertake a thought experiment that began by assuming an attitude of openness in the face of pluralism and uncertainty. By doing so, I suggested, we would not end with relativism, or an openness of indifference, as Bloom supposed. Rather, we would arrive at general norms of human behavior that remarkably conform to a broad range of everyday ethical intuitions. We would arrive at an ethical view with considerable scope and content, and with historical precedents—for example, with similarities to the Golden Rule, whose origins lie in many of the great cultural traditions of humankind.

The question then naturally arises of why this surprising result should have come about and what the thought experiment of this chapter ultimately means. I suggested that we would not be able to completely answer that question until chapter 4, when deeper motivations for starting with an attitude of openness are explored. (Meanwhile, some intervening steps are needed and will be explored in the next chapter.) But in this chapter we already have the beginnings of an answer to what the thought experiment means. The attitude of openness was a response to pluralism and uncertainty. Since the traditional method of searching for absolute values was blocked, we looked for an alternative. The attitude of openness was suggested for two reasons: first because it took seriously the conditions of pluralism and uncertainty that have thwarted other attempts to find absolute value, and second, because it focused attention on the fact that it is absolute value—what is good from all points of view—that we are searching for.

Starting in this way with openness, we did not arrive at the conclusion that every view was as good as every other one, but at the conclusion that some ways of living and acting were less worthy of respect than others. Yet, paradoxically, we found this out only by initially opening our minds to all points of view and *trying to sustain such an attitude to the degree possible in imperfect situations*. It is the persistent striving to maintain this ideal in the face of obstacles and conflicts that leads to ethical insight. Openness thus serves as a path to the truth, but not as the final truth itself. As I said, the idea is "Open your mind to all other points of view in order to find the truth," not "The truth is that you should open your mind to all other points of view." Rather than leading to relativism, openness becomes the key that unlocks the door to absolute or universal value.

Why "absolute" or "universal" value? Because the argument of the chapter purports to show that *any* persons who start with the attitude of openness and try to sustain it, as we have done throughout, will arrive at the revised Ends Principle (or wide version of the Golden Rule) as the resulting principle of action. If this is so, then the principle will hold for *all* persons, *if* the attitude of openness is the right place for them to start in the search for ethical truth. This final "if" brings us back, of course, to the issue that must be pursued in subsequent chapters about deeper motivations for starting with the attitude of openness. But if there are such motivations, then the ethical results arrived at in this chapter will be among their consequences.

The ultimate consequence of such a search procedure for ethical understanding concerns *our own way of life*. Since the moral sphere may encompass more than one way of life (even though others may lie outside of it), the thought experiment of this chapter need not narrow the "right" ways of life to one. In particular, the argument does not show that ours is the only right way. In fact, our way of life or point of view may not even be within the contracted circle, *if we break the moral sphere*.

In other words, the rightness of our way of life is no different than the others; it depends on how we act. So when I said earlier that we should assume an attitude of openness in order to allow others to prove themselves right or wrong, I added that we are not entirely off the hook, for we still have the burden of proving ourselves right or wrong; and we will see that this is burden enough for anyone. It is indeed burden enough—for the "proof" is not carried out in theory alone, but in how we live.

VALUES CLARIFICATION AND MORAL EDUCATION

To conclude this chapter and pave the way for the next one, I want to mention one last consequence of the argument we have been summarizing: its relevance for *moral education*.

One of the social consequences of relativism decried by Bloom and other critics cited in chapter 1 is the prevalence of a method of moral teaching in the schools called "values clarification."[13] This method is based on the premise that, in a democratic climate of value pluralism, none of us has *the* right set of values to pass on to other people's children, so that teachers in the schools must instead focus on the means by which people come to have and accept values. Through group discussion, in which the teacher remains nonjudgmental, young people are supposed to express and discuss their differing values in order to come to a better understanding of their own values, to self-acceptance, and to respect for the values of others. Advocates of such a method of values clarification say it is the only way the schools can go about teaching values in a pluralistic society, while critics insist that it is a royal road to relativism and indifference. Such a method, the critics say, is more likely to lead to the belief that no view of right or wrong is any better than any other, so long as it feels good to the one who "accepts" it.

Suppose we look at this controversy through the lens of the present chapter. The values clarification method is clearly a reaction to conditions of pluralism and uncertainty about values, or a response to the Tower of Babel; and it starts where we started, with an attitude of openness. Its advocates share the view of those ordinary persons I described at the beginning of the chapter who had the insight that openness was the proper response to pluralism and uncertainty. Bloom thought this insight, if carried through, would lead to relativism, and he and other critics think the same of the values clarification method in the schools.

But advocates and critics of values clarification both fail to realize that the attitude of openness breaks down where the moral sphere breaks down. This breakdown in turn leads to the revised Ends Principle, which *is* judgmental, and tells us that some things are universally right or wrong and some ways of life more worthy of respect than others. If we start with openness, as the values clarification method does, we cannot end by asserting that every view is as good as every other view. To the contrary, we must end up by saying that some views are better or worse than others for anyone who starts with openness. Realizing this, the clarification of values can take place in the schools, but it would presuppose a framework of absolute or universal rights and wrongs defined by the Ends Principle and attendant ideas of moral sphere breakdown, which emerge from its starting point.

This theme applies to moral education at all levels, including the home. As children are bombarded through the media with different points of view from all over the global village, parents may say this:

Be open if you wish to other points of view. This may be a correct attitude *to start with* if you want to find the truth. But just remember that this attitude does not mean anything goes, ethically speaking. Quite the contrary, trying to sustain an attitude of openness leads to the conclusion that some things are really right and other things wrong, and some ways of living are really better than others.

And incidentally, some of those things that are really right or wrong are signified by those tired old commandments you have heard about. Don't kill or lie. Don't steal or cheat. Don't be unkind or inconsiderate or cause harm unnecessarily or be unfair. Don't treat others as means to your own ends, unless you are forced into it by their actions. And when you must, when the moral sphere breaks down, do what you can to restore and preserve conditions in this world where respect for others can flourish once again using minimum force and as fairly or justly as conditions allow. To love rightly is to recognize that you cannot love everything equally—except in a perfect world—and the world is often imperfect. But even where you cannot love equally in an imperfect world, you can love well by striving to restore and preserve conditions in which mutual respect can flourish once again.

The same theme applies to higher education as well, to the universities, where openness (of mind)—academic freedom—is a way of life. The message here is once again that the cherished openness of the universities does not lead to relativism or indifference. If we try to sustain openness to the degree possible as regards values, we will be led to the conclusion that some ways of life or points of view are objectively better or worse than others. This is not an argument against freedom of speech or thought, which are implied by the original attitude of openness. It is an argument against being indifferent to the dangers that moral-sphere-breaking ways of life will be put into action. Even as we allow the most distasteful kinds of opinions to be heard, we need not stand by mutely testifying to the doctrine that no point of view is any better than any other. The commitment to openness in the universities is ultimately an *ethical* commitment.

In *On Liberty* John Stuart Mill expressed the belief that by maintaining a condition of openness and allowing all points of view to be heard, the truth would emerge. Mill consciously echoed John Milton's well-known lines: "Let her and Falsehood grapple; whoever knew Truth put to the worse in a free and open encounter."[14] The argument of this chapter is a version of that claim: by being initially open to all points of view, the "ethical" truth emerges that some ways of life and points of view are more worthy of respect than others.

3

The Human Quest

ETHICS AND RELIGION

Even if the path to universal or absolute values taken in chapter 2 is adequate, we cannot rule out the possibility of other paths. In this chapter and the next (and in chapter 7) we will explore alternative paths to absolutes that have had a long history in human thinking and may have something further to offer us.

For most ordinary persons who think about paths to absolute value, religion is the first alternative that comes to mind. Prior to the modern age the search for absolute value was invariably linked to religion and still is by most people. The norm throughout human history was to think of religion and ethics as inseparable, so that one learned the correct religious view and then accepted the ethics put forward by that religion. ("If God is dead," as Ivan Karamazov put it, "everything is permitted."[1])

This connection between religion and ethics may still be true, but one of the themes of chapter 1 was that we can no longer simply assume its truth or view the relation of ethics to religion in the simple ways of the past. For the pluralism and uncertainty of the times affect religion as well as ethics. In a world of conflicting religions, the same problems of uncertainty and circularity that arise for ethics also arise for religion, problems of showing one religious point of view right and others wrong. To ignore these problems is to extend an invitation to the authoritarianism and sectarian strife of which the Enlightenment warned us. If a new Axial Period is upon us, one of its themes would surely be that religion has become part of the problem of pluralism and uncertainty, rather than the simple solution it was traditionally thought to be.

One does not have to take a dismissive attitude toward religion to say this. All one has to concede is that the whole question of religion and its relation to ethics has become more complicated and problematic in the present age, so that we can no longer appeal to religion as the immediate and simple solution to the problems of absolute value, as people could do in the past. For this reason, I am going to postpone a discussion of religion and its possible relation to ethics until chapter 7, that is, until after we have explored other approaches to universal or absolute value and to value in general.

HUMAN NATURE AND THE GOOD: NATURAL LAW, BIOLOGY, AND ANTHROPOLOGY

Most readers are likely to think of another obvious path to universal or absolute value we have not yet touched upon, a path that has played an important role in human history, often in connection with religion, but sometimes separately. Suppose that beneath the diversity of human cultures and beliefs about good and evil we could discern some features and needs that are common to our *human nature*. Despite cultural and individual diversity, we humans have many common biological, psychological, and social traits. Perhaps one could find other absolutes by looking for the universal human characteristics we share amid cultural and individual diversity.

The values arrived at by this path might also address limitations of the Ends Principle mentioned at the end of chapter 2. The Ends Principle tells us to respect other ways of life, but does not offer more-particular direction about the best way to live. What is the content of the good life over and above the requirement to treat others as ends and not means to *our* ends? The search for the universally human amid cultural diversity might provide some of these specifics. It might tell us that, given what human beings are, some forms of life are better for them than other forms. The Ends Principle focuses on our person-hood (the fact that we are intelligent beings capable of moral agency), but to know *how* to live we also have to think about other aspects of our humanity.

This manner of searching for absolutes by way of the universally human is, of course, very old. It was the favored path to absolute value of the ancient philosophers and sages who wrote many of the great books of Western and non-Western cultures. One aim of ancient thinkers, like Plato and Aristotle, was to identify those universal traits that defined human nature, so as to discern the common ends or goals sought by all humans. To realize such ends or goals would then bring human fulfill-ment, which Aristotle called *eudaimonia*—a term usually translated into English as "happiness," though scholars warn us that he did not mean by it merely a subjective feeling of satisfaction, but something like "living well and doing well," "flourishing," or "being fulfilled."[2]

This pattern of searching for absolutes by way of the universally human continued into the medieval and later periods of Western culture. The aim was to identify a universal human nature which would tell us about the common ends or goals that all humans seek. A life that brought fulfillment of these goals would then be the good life for humans. This pattern in turn became the basis for what are now called "natural law" theories of the good and the right, still defended by some thinkers.[3] Natural law in this case does not mean the laws of physics, but moral laws governing human behavior that define the right way to live. They are called "natural" because they are supposedly grasped by understanding the nature of human beings and the ends that humans naturally seek.

But this alternative path was not merely the favored ancient way of searching for absolute values. It is also one that has emerged in twentieth-century biology and anthropology, especially during the past forty years. In anthropology it was a reaction to earlier studies that emphasized diversity of cultures and even relativism. At the end of the nineteenth century and the beginning of the twentieth, when modern anthropology was emerging as a respected discipline, field studies of primitive cultures were being made throughout the world. One of the reactions to these studies was sheer amazement at the diversity of human cultures: unusual social forms, rituals, sexual practices, and so on. This was obvious fodder for the popular imagination, and books, like Ruth Benedict's *Patterns of Culture* (1931), that stressed cultural diversity were widely read.[4]

A by-product of the emphasis on human diversity was the tendency of many thinkers (including anthropologists themselves, like Benedict, W. E. Sumner, E. Westermarck, and M. Herskovits) to infer value relativism from this anthropological diversity.[5] Benedict argued, for example, that what was normal (or abnormal) for one culture was not necessarily normal (or abnormal) for another, and therefore what was right and wrong for one was not necessarily right or wrong for another. We have already seen the limitations of such reasoning: the mere existence of cultural diversity does not show that relativism is true. Benedict and other value relativists were clearly going beyond the evidence. But their views and the mounting evidence of their anthropological colleagues about the diversity of cultures posed an increasing threat to belief in absolute values as the century wore on.

To make matters worse, many anthropologists felt that scientific objectivity required that they merely describe and explain the functioning of cultures and not pass judgment about which had the right values for all cultures. They also believed that objectivity especially required that they not be ethnocentric—that they not assume their own culture (for example, Western culture) had the correct or more advanced view, and other cultures were "primitive" in a pejorative sense. Paradoxically, their commitment to scientific objectivity prevented them from saying that *any* cultural values, including their own, were absolutely true, or true for all.

In the post–World War II period many anthropologists began to worry about the emphasis on diversity in their discipline and its contribution to belief in relativism. The Nuremburg trials in which Nazi leaders were accused of crimes against humanity provoked some of these worries. Nazi officers defended their role by saying that they had merely done their duty as it was understood in the society in which they lived. If we extend to Nazi society the relativist view that normality and right differ from culture to culture, it is difficult to counter such a defense.[6] Talking about crimes against humanity required a greater focus on universal human values. Noted anthropologists, like Clyde Kluckholm, argued that their discipline had been focusing too much on cultural diversity.[7] It was time to right the balance and search for "cultural universals." In more recent times these anthropologists have been joined by ethnologists and sociobiologists (to be considered later) who have been stressing the importance of common biological traits for understanding human values.

In summary, the alternative path to absolutes we are going to consider in this chapter—the search for universal human traits—has two important precedents. It was the favored path of traditional philosophers who sought to understand human nature and "natural law," so as to define the good life for humans. And it is the path taken by anthropologists, biologists, and other modern thinkers who have been searching for cultural universals based on common biological, psychological, and social human traits.

EXISTENTIALISTS, CULTURAL RELATIVISTS, AND SOCIOBIOLOGISTS

Not everyone, by any means, believes this is a promising path to absolute values. There is a strong countertendency in twentieth-century thought to disparage and discredit the search for ethical absolutes by way of the universally human. Existentialist philosophers have argued against the traditional view that one could determine how to live by discerning a common human nature or human essence. Human beings, they said, are characterized above all by a freedom to choose different values and ways of life. They "make themselves," as Jean-Paul Sartre put it, and are not predesigned with an existing human nature so that all will flourish in the same way.[8] There might be some common biological or psychological traits for all humans, but, given our freedom to choose, it turns out that these common traits are not sufficient to tell us what is the right way to live among the many we may choose.

In a similar vein, there have been criticisms of the anthropological search for cultural universals. The critics, who include noted anthropologists like Clifford Geertz, argue that the cultural universals which their anthropological colleagues have found—for example, that all human societies have family and kinship structures, rites of passage, sexual restrictions, and divisions of labor—are so general that they cannot resolve difficult questions about ethical relativism.[9] Geertz's conclusion is similar to the existentialists' conclusion: there may be common psychological and social traits of humans, but given the diversity of cultures and our freedom to choose, these common traits are not sufficient to tell us what is the ethically right way to live among the many we may choose.

Similar criticisms are made of biologists who have tried to draw ethical conclusions from biological data. The evolutionary criterion of survival of the fittest is often regarded as the most universal of all human values, but attempts to draw ethical conclusions from it (beginning with the doctrine of Social Darwinism at the turn of the century) have been much debated.[10] Survival among humans often has more to do with sheer power and cleverness in the use of power than with considerations we normally regard as ethical. Some of the longest lasting human cultures have been based on slavery, subjugation, and other cruel practices.

In recent decades a new breed of so-called sociobiologists have introduced further sophistication into the debates about ethics and biology by emphasizing the idea that altruistic behavior plays a more important role in evolution than was previously believed.[11] But the ethical critics of sociobiology—of whom there are many—argue that the kind of altruism sociobiologists describe extends only to one's genetic kin (those who share the individual's genetic endowment) and to others who can return some benefit to one's kin. Such altruism is ultimately based on self-interest, the critics say (the "selfish gene" rather than the selfish individual), and cannot be the basis for a genuinely ethical or moral perspective.

THE SEARCH FOR A COMMON HUMAN NATURE

Despite the critics, I do not think we should too hastily dismiss the search for absolutes by way of the universally human. The twentieth-century distaste for thinking about moral matters in terms of human nature or natural law or universal human traits is a reaction against ancient modes of thought that has gone too far. The critics are right to some extent: this path cannot give us everything the ancient thinkers believed. But it has much to teach us.

I think the search for a common human nature needs to be continued, but with three qualifications. First, we should not be overly concerned that some individuals or groups can manage to survive without the common human traits one might identify as ethically relevant. For we are not looking for human traits that pertain to survival alone, but rather for those that are conducive to "flourishing," or leading the most fulfilled or fulfilling kinds of lives. Second, we should not make a fetish of the requirement that the ethically relevant human traits we are seeking be completely universal human traits and provably so, rather than merely *common* human traits. If the vast majority of human beings have needed friends and friendship, we should not be overly concerned if a few unusual persons should turn up who survived and even thrived without the need of friends. The reason is that if we are seeking direction about how to live, it is enough to know that human beings commonly need certain things. For we can reason that *since we are human, there is a high probability that we need these things as well for a fulfilling life.* Thus, by all means, we should look for universal traits, but not dismiss those that are merely common, for they too can tell us much about how to live.

Third, and finally, I think that we should recognize that the search for common human characteristics will disappoint us to some extent in the search for moral or ethical absolutes. In particular, the search for cultural and biological universals cannot take the place of the Ends Principle and cannot resolve the ethical dilemmas that the Ends Principle resolves, as we will see later in this chapter. Consequently, the search for cultural and biological universals cannot replace the path to absolute values taken in chapter 2 or the one to be taken in chapter 4, and this is a point of no small importance. But I think the search for a common human nature can serve as a supplement to these other paths, providing direction about the human pursuit of happiness.

HUMAN SOCIETIES

It will be helpful to begin by simply listing some of the ethically relevant uniformities or near-uniformities of human culture and life that have been suggested in recent decades by cultural anthropologists, sociobiologists, ethnographers, developmental psychologists, and others. That way we can get a sense of the kinds of things that have been in the running for the "universally human" before trying to make sense of the evidence.

There is a considerable amount of material here that is too often ignored by modern ethical theorists. To ease reference and later discussion, I will group these common features into several distinct categories.

Structural Features

As Kluckholm and other cultural anthropologists have argued, the needs and characteristics of human biology and social organization impose constraints on all human societies. Among these needs and characteristics are the existence of two sexes, the helplessness and dependence of human infants, ordinary life spans, the presence of individuals of different ages and abilities and the basic needs for food, clothing and shelter.[12] James Thurber once remarked that "dogs are raising families of their own before the first anniversary of their birth, and so it goes among all animal species save man, whose young are practically no good at all until they have wobbled around the house for almost a quarter of a century."

As a consequence of these social needs, all human societies have (1) a *division of labor* and a *division of social roles* to satisfy basic needs for food, shelter, and so forth. All have (2) *families* (the nuclear family with its strong maternal and other bonds is a near-universal), all place importance on (3) *kinship relations,* and all have (4) *rules and taboos regarding sexual relations* (the incest taboo seems to be universal, though its exact form differs). They need to live in a (5) *healthy environment* and therefore have provisions for sanitation and the like. All have (6) *moral codes* (though the contents of the codes differ), and all value (7) *courage or bravery* since societies must be protected from threats to their existence coming from natural disasters or enemies (though, again, they may define courage or bravery differently). All have (8) *rites of passage* (from youth to adulthood, for example) *and other rituals.* (The great ethnologist Konrad Lorenz has noted that very little in human behavior is unritualized and that entirely unritualized behavior, such as scratching or picking one's nose, is often regarded as obscene.)[13] In addition, each society has some (9) *leadership hierarchy* and/or provisions for making social decisions, and each has (10) *shared symbols and values,* embodied in *myths* or other beliefs, which provide social solidarity and give meaning to their shared life.

Basic Value Experiences

Human beings also share certain kinds of experiences that are invariant across cultures and have an intimate connection to views of good and evil. We might call them *Experiential Uniformities*. It is no accident that humans in general have a favorable attitude to such experiences as joy, gladness, pride, delight, sensory pleasure, elation, enchantment, amusement, enjoyment, ecstasy, comfort, contentment, peace of mind, exhilaration, euphoria, and others, all of which might be called (11) *basic value experiences*. Nor is it an accident that they share an unfavorable attitude to such (12) *basic disvalue experiences* as sadness, sorrow, displeasure, pain, suffering, boredom, fear, disgust, annoyance, disappointment, grief, shame, embarrassment, depression, revulsion, frustration, loneliness, humiliation, terror, anxiety, despair, and others.

There is something so fundamental about these human experiences that it seems gratuitous to ask why humans generally think that some of them are good and others bad. A clue about why it seems gratuitous was provided by the philosopher Baruch Spinoza in the seventeenth century: it is through having such basic value and disvalue experiences that we come to distinguish and define good and evil in the first place.[14] Such experiences are like windows through which value first enters into our human world.

As an illustration of this, consider the opening lines of Schiller's poem "Ode to Joy," which Beethoven set to music in his Ninth Symphony: "Joy, beautiful spark of the gods, Daughter from Elysium."[15] The image suggests that experiences like joy are sparks of light in an otherwise dark world that give us some intimation of what the good is. By contrast, the first of the Buddha's Four Noble Truths presupposes that all evil is suffering of one form or another: pain, sorrow, frustration, loneliness, despair, and other basic disvalue experiences. The fact that we define the terms describing these feelings and emotions in value-positive and value-negative ways is a reflection of the fact that humans first understand and define what good and evil mean in terms of such experiences.

Yet such experiences only give us the first word on what is good and evil in human life, not the last word. As Spinoza also pointed out, joy or gladness can be evil if it is taken in the suffering of others, and pain and grief can be good if they are means to the attainment of some higher end, like inner peace or virtue. So we first learn what good and evil mean by having such experiences, but then find that they can be overridden when placed within a broader vision of human life.

Nonetheless, though they may be overridden, such basic experiences are panhuman and remain important for our understanding of good and evil. There may be other intelligent creatures in the universe of different species than the human who do not have such experiences and who come to know good and evil differently. If there are such creatures, they would have very different forms of life and sensibilities than ours; and what was good for them might not necessarily be a human good. But the existence of such alien creatures would not change the fact that the human good is defined in some measure by such basic human value experiences.

Social Values

In an interesting book entitled *The Biological Origins of Human Values* George Pugh has attempted a synthesis of the contemporary biological and ethnological data regarding human values.[16] He discusses some of the basic value and disvalue experiences, noting that many of them are manifested in common facial expressions across cultures. There are distinguishable facial expressions in humans for fear and anger, joy and sorrow, disgust and shame. And he adds that this fact suggests that such emotions express social values—they are to be communicated or expressed to others. He then goes on to link these basic values to other social needs and desires that biological and ethnographic evidence suggest are common to the human species.

Here are some of these additional values, which we may classify along with Pugh as *Social Values*. Human beings need to be (13) *nurtured and loved when young*. This is as clear a candidate for a human universal as one can find, rooted in the helplessness and dependence of the human infant, and well documented in other primate species. Pugh adds that humans also generally desire the (14) *approval of their peers*, (15) *social acceptance* and the (16) *admiration* of others for their accomplishments, and they also crave (17) *love, sympathy, and affection* from others. According to the distinguished historian of ideas Arthur Lovejoy, the moral philosophers of the seventeenth and eighteenth centuries classified these four desires under the heading of the desire for "approbation for others" and regarded their satisfaction to some degree as essential to the fulfilled human life.[17] In *The Descent of Man* Darwin argued that the universal human desires for approval and sympathy were the primary reinforcers of morality.[18] (We will see later why such desires are not sufficient, as Darwin thought, by themselves to account for morality. But they are important to it and, as he suggested, they seem to be panhuman.)

Other instinctive social motives in humans mentioned by Pugh include (18) *gregariousness* and the desire for *conversation*, (19) *enjoyment* of *humor*, (20) *the cultivation of friendships*, and (21) *the desire to work with others in cooperative enterprises toward common goals*. We have already mentioned the first and third of these. Regarding the others, the human enjoyment of humor has several roots, according to Pugh. It relaxes tension and contributes to human solidarity. But, in addition, since the essence of humor is incongruity with established patterns of thinking, humor also serves a cognitive function, making us more flexible and less rigid in our ways of thinking (a likely source of insight into why humorlessness and inflexibility of thought often go hand in hand).

The last of the above four features, the desire to work with others in cooperative enterprises, is also widespread in humans and probably has roots in the hunt and other collective efforts as early humans. The enjoyment taken in team sports, playing in an orchestra, building something together, and so on, are distinctively fulfilling and generally desired by humans. And the extensions of this desire are especially important, including the desire to be part of a (22) *community* of persons who share a meaningful form of life and the desire for (23) *roots*, which Kolakowski referred to as "an historically defined sense of belonging" to traditions that give meaning to the past and purpose to the future. Both of these are connected with the needs for human solidarity mentioned under the Structural Features of human societies, and they underwrite the ancient view expressed by Aristotle that man is a social animal.

Virtually all human societies have striven to maintain a sense of community and roots, and those societies that have failed are exceptions which, so to speak, prove the rule. The best illustration in modern anthropological literature of the consequences of failing to satisfy these needs is the now-famous story of the Ik tribe of Western Africa told in Colin Turnbull's *The Mountain People*.[19] When the Ik were forced off their land by encroaching settlers, their tribal traditions and sense of community collapsed. When Turnbull encountered them they were living a dismal existence in which selfishness was the prevailing motive. Children were put out to fend for themselves after the age of three or four. Food was routinely snatched away from the older and weaker members of the tribe and they were left to die. What happened to the Ik was not entirely their fault. But it illustrates the consequences of entirely losing "an historically defined sense of belonging" to a community of persons with collective goals. Not surprisingly, the Ik did not survive for very long after Turnbull encountered them.

Egoistic Motives

Pugh would be unfair to the biological and anthropological evidence if he did not add that the Social Values just mentioned are balanced in the human makeup by other, less-benign *Egoistic Motives*.

In addition to the human desires for social acceptance, sympathy, and common goals, he notes that humans also have a desire for (24) *dominance* that has deep biological roots. Sociobiologists trace it to the drive to maximize reproduction of one's genes. But whatever the source, it plays important social roles and is deeply embedded in primate behavior generally. Dominance essentially means being at the top of whatever hierarchies exist in one's social group, so that others defer to you. The desire for it lies behind natural human desires for (25) *power or control* over others, drives (26) *to be competitive* and *to excel* or *be superior* to others in achievements and possessions (fame, wealth, and so on), and human (27) *aggressive and territorial instincts,* which have been much discussed since the appearance of Konrad Lorenz's well-known study, *On Aggression.* [20]

Ancient religious writers would have assigned these egoistic motives to our "fallen" human nature. But, for better or worse, they have to be viewed as part of the total picture of human nature, if the biological and anthropological evidence is to be taken seriously. The ancient view was that human beings are naturally neither wholly good nor wholly bad by ethical standards. They are somewhere between the angels and the beasts, torn between social motives, on the one side, and selfish ones, on the other. ("When I'm good," Mae West said, "I'm very good, but when I'm bad, I'm even better.")

The idea that human nature is torn between social and egoistic motives is another piece of ancient wisdom that stands up well to the modern evidence. Ways of life that presuppose too optimistic or too pessimistic views of human goodness will usually go wrong. The optimistic ones will be utopian at first, the pessimistic ones authoritarian. But both will end up being tyrannical. One of the lessons of twentieth-century politics is that utopian schemes of the left or the right—however idealistically they begin—either collapse or turn harshly authoritarian, human nature being what it is. In politics, as one wit said, friends may come and go, but enemies accumulate.

Miscellaneous Traits: Expression and Meaning

To the above list of cross-cultural characteristics, Pugh and other writers add a number of other *Miscellaneous Traits* that are not easily classified, though many have to do with human desires to be expressive and to understand and give meaning to the world around us. Thus humans also generally desire (28) *meaningful work;* (29) *making or creating things;* (30) *expressing themselves* through dress, painting, storytelling, dance, and dramatic performance; and they desire (31) a certain measure of *freedom or autonomy* in their expressive and creative activities (though the degree of individual autonomy required differs dramatically from culture to culture). In addition, human cultures have (32) an *appreciation of artistic expression* in others—an *aesthetic sense*—and *standards of taste* (though standards and artistic forms are also culturally variable).

In connection with these traits, Rom Harré remarks that, while many of the patterns of human culture have direct utilitarian aims—the securing of food, shelter, territory, and so forth—a substantial proportion of human behavior of even the most ancient human cultures serves *expressive* ends.[21] Humans have a need to express what they feel and to define publicly what they are. Moreover, as Harré points out, this expressive need is so great that many cultures (even so-called primitive ones) devote as much attention to expressive aims as to their utilitarian aims. As soon as basic utilitarian needs are fulfilled, they turn to expressive activities.

The storytelling and expressiveness of humans serve other purposes of a more intellectual kind. Human cultures have a need to (33) *understand and explain the world* around them—initially, says Pugh, because information is necessary for survival and out of a distaste for ambiguity. But eventually they are driven to (34) *explain the meaning of their existence in terms of myth, ritual, and beliefs about their origins and destination.*

Clearly, this last need is connected in most human cultures with religious beliefs. But the question of whether religion is a cultural universal seems to be in part a matter of definition. If "religion" is defined too narrowly, so that it accords with only one tradition (for example, monotheistic belief in a personal God), then it is not universal. But if it is defined broadly, as by Eliade and other historians of religion, as a way of life involving practices and rituals and presupposing beliefs that assign to human life purposes that transcend the individual and the biological, then a case can be made for saying that religion is universal in human cultures prior to the modern age. The qualification "prior to the modern age" is important. If we are now entering a new Axial Period, provoked by relativism, skepticism, and nihilism, then the future of religion is an open question, though recent worldwide trends suggest that the human needs which lie behind religious beliefs are not easily dismissed. (We will return to this issue in chapter 7.)

HUMAN FLOURISHING: FAMILY AND ENVIRONMENT

Even though incomplete, this list should persuade us that we humans have an impressive number of traits in common. One could continue to debate whether many of them really are universal. But, as I said earlier, the object of our search was not to discover the conditions for mere survival, but those for human "flourishing." The issue is not whether humans can get by if one or another of the desires on this list remains unsatisfied, but whether humans would live a better life if a substantial number of them were satisfied. The existence of many common traits or desires not only tells us something about human nature, but provides us with more than a few guidelines about the ways of life that are most likely to be humanly fulfilling.

We have already seen, for example, that the mix of Social and Egoistic motives in the human makeup suggests that social and political schemes that are based on too optimistic a view of human sociality or too pessimistic a view of human selfishness are unlikely to succeed. This is, in fact, one very good argument for democracy (as we will see in chapter 6). George Will quotes an unnamed wit as saying of democracy that human beings are just good enough to make it possible and just bad enough to make it necessary. The considerable truth in this remark comes directly from the mix of Social and Egoistic motives in the human makeup.

But there are many other lessons in the above list of human traits. For example, take two of the needs listed that are as close to being universal as any others: (13) the need of humans to be loved and nurtured when young, and (5) the need to live in a healthy environment. Any flourishing human society should give priority to sustaining those social structures, especially the family, that provide love and nurturing to the young, and any such society should give priority as well to the quality of its physical environment.

Both these priorities seem self-evident, yet we can easily lose sight of them. It is ironic that in recent American history conservatives have made "family issues" a matter of central concern but have tended to turn a deaf ear to "environmental issues," while liberals have done the opposite—stressing environmental issues, while (until recently) saying little about family issues. It is becoming increasingly clear that both sides have been shortsighted, because we are dealing here with two equally fundamental needs for human well-being. A severely abused child (whose need for love and nurturing when young is not fulfilled), or one whose brain has been impaired by eating lead paint or by inhaling asbestos (whose need for a healthy environment is not fulfilled) is not going to get a fair chance to exercise liberty or to pursue happiness. So we can hardly say we are committed to the values of life, liberty, and the pursuit of happiness if we are not prepared to give social and political priority to those things that are preconditions for the enjoyment of the basic rights. We might call such preconditions for the enjoyment of basic rights "prerights"—the most prominent of which are a healthy family life and an unpolluted physical environment.

How do we lose sight of the overriding importance of such pre-rights in social debates? Usually, because we become fixated on certain values to the exclusion of others. (This is what Kolakowski calls the "idolatry of politics.") Thus American conservatives usually put a high priority on business and free enterprise, and we know that environmental concerns are usually "externalities" from the business point of view—in other words, a royal pain in the neck—often incurring costs with no compensating profits. By contrast, the liberal emphasis on freedom of expression often blinds liberals to the needs that families have for social support in the moral education of the young. In each case something could be said for the values emphasized, but not for the exclusive focus on them. For example, the free enterprise system, on which conservatives fixate, is a most efficient economic instrument for satisfying certain needs and desires on our list—from (1) an efficient division of labor for the accumulation of human necessities, to (21) cooperative enterprise, (26) excelling at competitive tasks, (29) creating things, and (31) freedom or autonomy. The case for a free economic order could be, and has often been, made in terms of such traits. But such a case would make free enterprise only one human good that has to be balanced against others—including the essential needs for healthy families and a healthy environment.

COMMUNITY, ROOTS, AND SOCIAL VALUES

In a similar manner, many other traits on the list tell us something about flourishing human societies and lives. The human needs for (31) community, (32) roots, and (21) cooperative activities with common goals have been at the core of much recent social criticism of the corrosive effects of unrestrained individualism in modern free societies. The lesson of such works as *Habits of the Heart* and other jeremiads mentioned in chapter 1 is the lesson of human costs incurred when persons feel they are losing a sense of community, roots, and shared values. This is also the theme of currently popular "communitarian" trends in ethical theory and social philosophy.[22]

An especially poignant example of the loss of two other items on the list—(14) approval by peers and (15) social acceptance—is provided by Ruth Haynes's recent study of immigrants from India who live and work in the cane fields of the Fijian islands.[23] Suicide rates among these Indian immigrants are very high, especially among women under thirty, as a consequence of traditional Indian practices and the special circumstances of life on the islands. "Daughters," says Haynes, "tend to be undervalued in much of Indian society, and may even be seen to be a liability . . . where they are reared by the parents only to be 'married-off' at some expense in their teens." Young brides become the property of their husbands, are subject to their in-laws' whims, and are virtually on trial until they bear children, especially sons. When one adds the special circumstances of Fiji, where in the rural areas the young women cannot reach their families of origin and cannot receive emotional support when distressed, the suicide rate soars. These suicides of young women are cries in the darkness, signaling that some fundamental human needs are going unmet in such a social environment.

Indeed, few would deny that a flourishing human life will involve satisfaction of a substantial number of the common human needs and desires on our list: love and nurturance when young, a healthy environment, a greater balance of basic value experiences (like joy and pride) over basic disvalue experiences (like boredom, loneliness, and anxiety), social acceptance and the approval of others, meaningful work, the opportunity to exercise talents in creative and cooperative enterprises, friendship, roots, self-expression, excellence of achievement, a measure of autonomy, and so on. The mix of these goods may be different for different persons, but this only shows that there can be different kinds of "good lives" for humans (making a place for the existentialist point that humans are characterized by the freedom to choose different values). Such freedom is compatible with saying that the common human traits identified provide substantial guidelines for defining human well-being and the pursuit of happiness.

CULTURAL UNIVERSALISTS VERSUS CULTURAL RELATIVISTS

Yet critics continue to insist that, for all one may learn about the human good by inquiring into human nature, this approach will fall short of giving us the ethical universals or absolutes we seek and will not, in the end, succeed in refuting ethical relativism. We can see why many believe this by looking first at the anthropological critics of the search for cultural universals. Earlier in the chapter, anthropologists like Clifford Geertz were cited as arguing that the cultural universals which their anthropological colleagues have found are so general they cannot resolve difficult questions about ethical relativism. Their point can be understood by looking at the first two categories of common human traits we have listed, Structural Features and Experiential Uniformities.

All societies may have (1) a division of labor, say critics like Geertz, but how they divide labor differs dramatically from an ethical point of view. Some actually practice slavery or exploit different classes in society. All societies may have (2) nuclear families and (3) kinship structures, but these too differ, and many are exploitative, for example, of women. All societies may have some (8) rites and rituals, but some of the rituals involve human sacrifice or other cruel practices. All societies may have (6) moral codes and (7) value bravery, but their moral codes and ideas of brave action differ, and some are quite cruel and immoral by our standards. Ruth Benedict describes the case of the Kwakiutl, a northwest American Indian tribe that exhibited the following custom. When the chief's sister was accidentally killed in a canoeing accident, the chief was grieved and felt he had to atone for her death by taking his warriors to a neighboring tribe and killing several innocent people. Having done this, as Benedict describes it, his grief lessened and he felt much relieved.

This story illustrates the central point of critics like Geertz: the cultural universals in question are too general to tell us much about what is ethically right or wrong. For each of the structural universals (family structure, division of labor, kinship, and so on) there is variability in how it is culturally realized, and among the variations we find behavior ranging all over the ethical spectrum, from kind and generous to cruel and vicious. Citing the fact that all human cultures have these structural universals does not tell you what the right and wrong variations are. But the ethical disputes usually lie in the variations.

The same thoughts apply to other categories of common human traits, like the Experiential Uniformities. Let it be granted that the fulfilled human life will certainly include a greater balance of such basic value experiences as joy, gladness, pride, pleasure, amusement, and the like, over such experiences as boredom, loneliness, frustration, and anxiety. But this tells us little about how absolutely good in the moral sense such a life would be. The joys may be in the misfortunes of one's enemies, the pride or elation in one's dominance over others, and amusement in the ineptness and frustrations of others. The search for sensory pleasures also can be notoriously selfish and exploitative. Again, Geertz's point is that these experiential uniformities are too general to resolve the difficult ethical issues. The variability is in the objects of our joys and pleasures, and in this variability lie the ethical disputes.

EGOISM AND ALTRUISM:
SENSIBLE KNAVES AND CLASSIST AMORALISTS

The third of our categories of common human traits, the Social Values, seems more promising for ethical purposes. As I mentioned earlier, many influential thinkers of the past (as well as more ordinary mortals) have looked to the social values for human motivation toward morality. Approval from others, social acceptance, desires for admiration and for love, sympathy and affection, gregariousness, the need for friends, and desires for community and roots would seem to motivate us toward living moral lives of respect and concern for others. Do we not tell our children to be honest and generous if they want to have friends, be loved and admired, find social acceptance and a sense of belonging? We do, of course, but if that were all we did we would not have gone beyond appeals to their self-interest. And that is part of the problem of appealing to the Social Values for ethical absolutes.

The other part of the problem is that the Social Values are balanced by the Egoistic Motives, desires for dominance, control, power, and superiority (in fame, wealth, and so on). We are back to the point that a clear-eyed picture of human nature would not paint us as wholly unselfish or selfish, wholly angel or beast, but somewhere in between. Granting this divided human nature, the problem is that individuals might seek healthy doses of approval and love, gregariousness, and friendship from a few other people in order to satisfy their social needs, while otherwise living lives of selfish accumulation of dominance, power, wealth, fame, or pleasure. David Hume memorably referred to persons who live this way as "sensible knaves." In the modern jargon, they are enlightened (that is, calculating) egoists. Many of them may also be "free riders" or "freeloaders," persons who make use of the good intentions of others or the benefits of society, while seeking their own advantage by cheating and manipulating others whenever they think they can get away with it.

By whatever name, this selective playing on both sides of the fence (the social and the egoistic) is one of the most common patterns of immorality in human life. When children see their parents and other adults being kind to those close to them, but ruthless or deceptive to others, the children begin to sense hypocrisy and their moral education is in trouble.

Another class of persons who satisfy the Social Values, but remain immoral, are those whom philosopher Kai Nielsen calls "classist amoralists."[24] They align themselves with a certain class or group in society which they regard as superior (aristocrats, upper social classes, a race or ethnic group). Unlike sensible knaves or free riders, classist amoralists are not merely out for themselves and their individual interests. They have a genuine commitment to their class or group and will follow a moral code in behaving toward their own kind. Strictly speaking, they are not egoists. Yet, as Nielsen points out, they are amoralists, because their concerns for others extend only to their own class, which might in fact be exploitative of other classes thought to be lower down on the social, ethnic, or racial register.

Sensible knaves, enlightened egoists, free riders, and classist amoralists show why appealing to the Social Values in the human profile will not by itself provide an adequate foundation for ethical or moral beliefs. Such persons can satisfy the Social Values—approval from others, social acceptance, friendship, community, and roots—yet they do so only *selectively* within a limited circle or group or class or nation, while satisfying their egoistic motives by treating others outside their circle immorally.

SOCIOBIOLOGY AND RECIPROCAL ALTRUISM

This selective application of acceptance and affection coupled with egoistic behavior is a common pattern of immorality in human life precisely because it allows persons to satisfy both egoistic and social needs. Traditional moralists would have said it is the primary manifestation of our fallen human nature. Modern sociobiologists account for it in a different way. A few remarks about this now-influential modern biological view will also help to show why the Social Values do not get us to ethical absolutes and why there is a gap between modern biological images of human nature and traditional views about ethics.

Sociobiology is defined by its leading proponent, E. O. Wilson, as "the systematic study of the biological basis of all social behavior."[25] Sociobiologists, like Wilson, Richard Dawkins, and Richard Alexander, argue that altruism, or concern for the good of others, plays a more significant role in the process of evolution than was previously supposed by evolutionists. They have made altruism a legitimate object of study for biologists; but the altruism that sociobiologists talk about is limited in scope. The reasons are clearly stated by Alexander in *The Biology of Moral Systems:*

> [N]atural selection has apparently been maximizing . . . survival by reproduction of genes . . . [but] this includes effects on copies of their genes, even copies located in other individuals. In other words, we are evidently evolved not only to aid the genetic materials in our own bodies, by creating and assisting descendants, but also to assist . . . copies of our genes that reside in . . . relatives. (pp. 2–3)

According to sociobiologists, individuals assist their genetic relatives because close relatives (and, to a lesser extent, distant relatives) share some of the same genetic material. This is sometimes called "kin selection" and it gives altruism, or concern for others, a role (at least to some degree) in the evolutionary process: helping to raise a niece, finding a brother a job, protecting and sacrificing one's well-being or even one's life for family, kin, or clan.

But such altruism will be limited in scope because it extends only to one's genetic kin. Why would unrelated people help each other? The sociobiologists' answer is to add the notion of "reciprocal altruism" to that of "kin selection." If we aid our neighbors when they are in need, then even if they are not related to us they are more likely to aid us or our kin when we are in need. This is "reciprocal altruism": You scratch my back and I'll scratch yours. Individuals and extended families will have more success reproducing and increasing the success of their genes if they engage in such reciprocal altruism. Hence, evolution favors it, according to the sociobiologists.[26] Indeed, they point to the well-known fact that throughout nature whole species of plants, insects, and animals live in symbiotic relationships mutually assisting each other's survival.

But kin selection and reciprocal altruism are still limited in scope if we stick to a merely biological perspective. They extend to one's genetic kin and those that can help one's genetic kin, and no further. In an older idiom, altruism on such a basis extends only to "kith and kin" ("kith" being an earlier English word for "friends"). So it is appropriate for a sociobiologist like Dawkins to speak of "selfish genes" rather than of selfish individuals. Sensible knaves, free riders, and classist amoralists can be reciprocal altruists to some people, and probably will be, while acting cruelly or selfishly to other individuals or groups.[27]

A DISTINCTION BETWEEN UNIVERSAL AND ABSOLUTE ETHICAL VALUE

These arguments point to the fundamental reason why the search for universal human needs and desires—however much it may tell us about the good life for humans—falls short of giving us ethical absolutes. The reason is that *persons can be selectively concerned with attaining their natural human needs and desires—including social values—by caring only whether they, or select groups to which they belong, fulfill these needs and not caring about other persons or groups outside their favored ones.* To be thus concerned with your own (or your group's) pursuit of happiness and not that of others is the essence of immorality as we ordinarily conceive it. Yet it is consistent with persons satisfying natural human needs for themselves (and those they care about).

This selective caring shows why we have to distinguish between "universal human values," on the one hand, and "universal or absolute ethical values," on the other. Such a distinction is one of the most difficult to grasp in all of ethics, and most textbooks rarely do justice to it.

But it is also one of the most important distinctions. Perhaps the easiest way to illustrate it is to say that universal human values—like living in a healthy environment or being loved and nurtured when young—are things that everyone needs for personal happiness. Ethical absolutes, by contrast, have to do with *whether all other people should value or care about our personal happiness.* Egoists and amoralists can admit that all humans would be happier if they lived in a healthy environment and were loved and nurtured when young. But they see no reason why they ought to value or care about the personal happiness of you or me or others, if we happen to be outside their circle or group and their social needs can be otherwise satisfied. (They may live in a comfortable suburb while you and I live on a toxic waste dump.)

If a human need, like being loved and nurtured when young, is universal, then we can say:

> *Universal Human Value:* For *all* humans, their being loved and nurtured when young is good for them (and those who care about them).

Yet, though it is universal, such a value may still be *relative* so long as it is only good for (or from the point of view of) the person who is loved and nurtured and those who care about him or her. To make it an absolute value, it must also be true that

> *Universal or Absolute Ethical Value:* For *all* humans, their being loved and nurtured when young is a good *period,* that is, a good that should be acknowledged by *all* persons from *all* points of view (whether or not other persons happen to care about them or not).

This claim is doubly universal, and it is the second universality ("good . . . from all points of view") which makes the good nonrelative, or absolute. It is not wrong to assume that absolute value is universal (as we have done throughout the book), so long as we recognize that it is universal in a special way, namely, that it should be acknowledged as good from all points of view. Nor is it difficult to see why this special kind of universality is crucial for *ethical* value. Egoists and amoralists may recognize your personal happiness as a relative good for you (and my personal happiness is a relative good for me, and so on for all humans), making it a universal human value. But they do not view your personal happiness as an absolute good that they and others should recognize and respect.

In this sense, an absolute good is like an absolute truth. If a statement like "2 + 2 = 4" is absolutely true, then it is true *period,* and thus true from everyone's point of view, whether or not everyone recognizes it. One tribe may say it is true and another that it is false. But this does not mean it is true for the first tribe and false for the second. If it is an absolute truth, the tribe that says it is false is mistaken. So it is with an absolute good. If *your* being nurtured and loved when young is an absolute good, then it is not just good from your point of view (or from the points of view of those who happen to care about you). It is good from every point of view, whether or not others recognize it or care. Those who fail to recognize it, like the egoist or the amoralist, are simply mistaken.

In the case of the Indian chief who took his warriors to a neighboring village and killed several innocents to expiate his sister's death, if we assert the absolute value of the lives of those people who were killed, we are saying that it is true from everyone's point of view that their lives were valuable and should have been respected. The Indian chief clearly did not believe this. They were expendable to him, usable as means to his ends. But if we assert their absolute value, we are saying that he is mistaken. They are not really expendable from his or anyone else's point of view, whatever he thinks. This is what the revised Ends Principle and the wide version of the Golden Rule assert—the absolute value of the victims, whether the guilty recognize it or not, which is more than recognizing that staying alive is good from the victim's own point of view.

When we say that every human life is precious—so that if an innocent child suffers, that is bad from everybody's point of view, whether anybody happens to know about it or cares about it—we are asserting an absolute value. When Christ said in more figurative language "if you have done it to the least of these . . . , you have done it to me" (Matthew 25:45), he was communicating the absolute value of all creatures. And when utilitarian moral philosophers say that everyone's pleasures and pains are to count equally toward the "greatest good of the greatest number," they are asserting an absolute value. For they mean to say that this is so from every point of view, whether everyone admits it or not.

IMPORTANCE AND LIMITS OF THE SEARCH FOR THE UNIVERSALLY HUMAN

This is how the "selective caring" of the egoist and the amoralist show that there is a gap between universally human values, on the one hand, and universal or absolute ethical values, on the other. The universally human tells us what we all need to attain happiness. But the absolute tells us that our attaining happiness has worth that goes beyond our personal interests and the interests of those who care about us and *should be recognized by everyone.* This explains why the search for the universally human can teach us so much about the human good and human happiness without giving us ethical absolutes—why it can supplement, but cannot take the place of, principles like the Ends Principle or the wide version of the Golden Rule.

It also explains why the attempts of the classical philosophers to derive ethical absolutes from "natural law" or human nature, or modern attempts to derive them from biology or anthropology, must fall short of giving us ethical absolutes, however much they tell us of importance about the human quest for happiness (and even if they do find some universal human values). The chief limitation of all natural law theories, old and new, is a failure to fully appreciate the gap between the universally human and the ethically absolute.[28]

In summary, we set out in this chapter on an alternative path to absolutes—to look for the universally human amid cultural diversity—to search out a common human nature we may all share despite differences of beliefs and values in the modern Tower of Babel. We found this path rich in insights about human needs and value, about good societies and the good life for humans. Those in the twentieth century who scoff at the idea of a common human nature have underestimated the importance of this path. The common human needs and desires we have discussed place important constraints on the kinds of lives that are likely to lead to human happiness and fulfillment. Not anything goes. Some ways of life and some social systems are objectively better at fulfilling basic human needs than others.

But we have also found that this path by itself cannot lead to absolute value and it can only supplement, not replace, the role played by the Ends Principle or the Golden Rule. It gets us only to the universally human and beyond that is a gap to the absolute which is hard to bridge. Human nature as it turns out is a mixture of the good and the bad, angel and beast, Social and Egoistic motives—an ancient piece of wisdom we do well to conserve. What we want to believe is that this mixed being we are, neither all good nor all bad, nevertheless has absolute value in the nature of things and is not just expendable. To get this, we may have to be more modest and more daring at the same time.

4

Objective Worth

AN ELUSIVE GOAL AND AN ALTERNATIVE PATH

In this chapter we pursue yet another path to absolutes, which combines features of those followed in chapters 2 and 3, but goes beyond both. By the end of the last chapter you may have been getting the impression that absolute value is an unusual object of inquiry, not easily attained. Even if we knew all there was to know about human nature, we would only have reached *universal human* value, not *absolute* value in the ethical sense. I think we ought to take this impression very seriously, for absolute values, whether ethical or of any other kinds, are indeed strangely elusive, so much so that we should be wondering whether the search for them can be like any ordinary search or inquiry.

To be sure, we know in a literal sense what absolute value is. We have a definition: something is an absolute value if it is good or right *period*. That is to say, it is good from the point of view of the universe (which is sometimes called the absolute point of view) and is therefore universally good or right from every other point of view, even though it may not be recognized as such from every point of view.

So much for definitions. Unfortunately, they are purely formal and do not tell us much. They do not tell us what sorts of things might count as absolute values or how we are to search for them. What is this good *period*, or the absolute point of view, and how are we to determine it? Sometimes it is called, in Hilary Putnam's phrase, the "God's-eye point of view,"[1] which is a clue about how one traditionally went in search of absolute values. Find out who was speaking from the divine point of view—a sacred book, a prophet, a church, or an inspired person—and then whatever they said about the good and the right would represent the absolute point of view. But this is where today's pluralism of voices and points of view—the Tower of Babel—enters the picture. Which voice is expressing the divine point of view, the Bible or the Quran,

New Testament or Old, the Granth of the Sikhs or the Bhagavad-Gita of the Hindus, this church authority or that, this prophet or another? Perhaps, as Plato suggested centuries ago, we must first have some knowledge of the absolute good in order to determine which of the competing voices is really speaking from God's point of view.[2]

We are back to the old familiar circle that led us to have doubts about the traditional way of searching for absolutes. The idea of good *period*, or good from every point of view, is elusive because—finite creatures that we are—we can only take up *some* point of view as our own, or at least only a finite number of them. It seems that what the God's-eye point of view may be, or indeed whether there is one, is something that is known to us only "through a glass darkly."

The alternative path to absolutes to be explored in this chapter will also address the question raised at the end of chapter 2 about the deeper motives for taking the path of openness. In the face of pluralism and uncertainty, why continue to search for absolute values at all rather than simply succumbing to relativism, skepticism, or nihilism? And if we do continue the search, what justifies taking the path of openness as we did in chapter 2? Even if the argument of chapter 2 is valid, might we not have begged the question against relativists, skeptics, and nihilists by starting with openness?

This question in its various forms is deeper than the questions posed in previous chapters because it takes us to the root of things as far as the ethical quest is concerned—to the very nature of the search for absolute values. With deep questions of any kind, including this one, the tendency is to stare mutely into space, not knowing what the answer is, or even what a proper answer would look like. Philosophers call this condition "wonder" and it is supposed to be the first stage on the path to wisdom (though often it is also the last stage). When we are struck mute by deep questions, it is almost always because we have exhausted the kind of inquiry we have been engaged in. We have come to the ground floor of some line of reasoning and find there is nothing else to say of that kind. But this is often a clue that we have to look at the matter in a new way. We have to break one mold of thinking and substitute another.

SEARCHES IN THE REALM OF ASPIRATION: QUESTS

I want to suggest that the search for absolute values is a different kind of search than familiar ones. It is within what may be called the "realm of aspiration." If there is a new Axial Period upon us, I suspect this may be one of its most important lessons.

Our ordinary image of a search is something like this: We have lost our keys in the yard and are looking for them, in the grass or in the garden. We know what we are looking for—the keys—and we will recognize them when we find them. But some searches are more complex than this. The ancient explorer Pythias went in search of the land of the midnight sun (the arctic regions where the sun does not set) not knowing whether there was any such place to be found. Or physicists may search for things like faster-than-light particles or magnetic monopoles, not knowing whether any such things exist. Yet even in these more complex searches, where the object sought may not exist, Pythias and the physicists have ideas about the kinds of evidence that will tell them when they have found what they are looking for.

Now consider yet another kind of search: A knight goes into the trackless forest in search of the Holy Grail. He is told by the wise men that it is a beautiful golden chalice of a certain description, and that it is the Holy Grail of legend. His search requires every bit and more of the skill of Pythias or other explorers, and he faces as much danger. Moreover, so far as the knight knows, the golden chalice that the wise men describe, like the land of the midnight sun, may not exist at all, or at least may not be in the forest where he is searching for it. So far there is similarity with the other searches.

But let us now assume that while the knight will know when he has found the golden chalice described by the wise men, if it is there in the forest at all, he cannot know whether this golden chalice *is really the Holy Grail* of legend rather than a fake, even if he should find it. This is a complication we do not have in the case of the keys or of Pythias or of the physicists. In one sense, the knight will know that he has found what he was looking for (the golden chalice), but in another sense he will not know whether he has found it (the Holy Grail). Yet, for all that, his search may be successful. He may in fact find the Holy Grail, though he cannot be certain he has found it.

The knight's search, we could say, belongs to the realm of aspiration, which means it has the following characteristics. He (1) aspires to (or desires and seeks) something of great importance (the Holy Grail), (2) whose attainment is imaginable or possible, but not assured. There are (3) actions he can perform, or a search he can undertake (seeking the golden chalice in the forest), which he has reason to believe may lead to the goal—(4) not guaranteeing its attainment—but (5) necessary in the sense that failure to undertake these actions or this search (for the golden chalice) would mean for him abandoning hope of attaining the cherished goal (the Holy Grail).

Searches in the realm of aspiration can be called "quests," to use the language of the great legends and myths of mankind like that of the

Holy Grail, which often have so much to teach us about the important things in life. Such searches can be as arduous and require far more skill than ordinary searches; and like ordinary searches, they may even succeed. The difference is that the searchers can never be certain they have succeeded even when they have succeeded—at least not in the sense in which when you find your keys lying in the grass, you know you have succeeded in your search, or when Pythias gets to a place where he can sit in the sunlight at midnight, he knows he has found the land of the midnight sun.

ASPIRATION AND THE QUEST
FOR SCIENTIFIC KNOWLEDGE

Now searches in the realm of aspiration may seem like tenuous and wistful things, but the surprising fact is that, if we view human searches and inquiries in a certain way, we can see that many of them are ultimately in the realm of aspiration: they are quests. This has been a challenging realization of certain strains of twentieth-century thinking. For example, there are scientists who aspire to find the real truth about the nature of the universe and its laws, and most think that modern theories of relativity and quantum mechanics are the closest we have so far come to discovering such truth about the fundamental laws of physics. Yet they are also ready to admit that these theories, as we presently have them, may not be the final truth; current theories may be altered by future evidence and superseded by better theories.

So it is now commonplace to say of scientific theories that they are hypotheses, more or less well supported by past experience, and subject to further tests by future experience. In fact, it is said to be a virtue of scientific inquiry that its theories are, as Sir Karl Popper has said, in principle falsifiable by experimental evidence—not in the strong sense that they can be definitely shown to be false, but in the sense that there is always the possibility of further evidence turning up in their favor or against them.[3] They take a risk. This is said to be a virtue because it shows that science is an activity of critical inquiry. It is not authoritarian or dogmatic, but always open to new evidence.

Yet if this is true, there is another side to the story. If scientific theories are always open to new evidence, then none of them can be certain—which places the scientific search for the final truth about nature in the realm of aspiration. Scientists may in fact find the final truth to which they aspire, but they can never know they have found it *even when they have found it*. This idea was expressed centuries ago by an obscure thinker of the original Axial Period, the Greek philosopher Xenophanes:

The gods did not reveal from the beginning
All things to us, but in the course of time,
Through seeking, men find that which is the better.
But as for certain truth, no man has known it,
Nor will he know it; neither of the gods. . . .
And even if by chance he were to utter
The final truth, he would himself not know it.[4]

Not all scientists may view their enterprise this way, but for the many who do their view puts the scientific search for the truth of nature firmly into the realm of aspiration.[5] It turns scientific inquiry into a quest, without in the least diminishing its rigor and discipline. Scientists cannot be assured that if they do all the right experiments and subject their theories to all the available evidence, they will have found the truth of nature. But they have every reason to believe that if they do *not* do these things, they will not have found that truth. And such conditions have all the earmarks of the realm of aspiration. The scientists (1) aspire to something of importance (the truth about nature) (2) whose attainment is possible but not assured. In addition, (3) there are things they can do that they have good reason to believe will lead to the goal (consider all available evidence, do experiments, find the best available theory, and so on)—(4) not guaranteeing its attainment—but (5) necessary in the sense that for them to cease doing these things would mean abandoning hope of attaining the goal. They do not know that their best available theory (the golden chalice) will be the final truth about nature (the Holy Grail), but they can be reasonably convinced that if they do not strive to find the best available theory they will not find the truth about nature.

This example should make clear that aspiration is far more than hope, though it involves an element of hope. You can hope for something while idly sitting in an armchair and doing nothing about attaining it. Aspiration, by contrast, involves an often arduous quest for what we desire and seek. The point of the Grail legend and other mythical quests is precisely to emphasize the self-discipline, skill, character, and effort needed to persist in the attainment of cherished goals and high ideals; and so it is also with the discipline and skill of scientific inquiry. Searches in the realm of aspiration are not for the faint of heart or weak in spirit.

The term "aspiration" is an appropriate one for such quests. It signifies an "outflowing of the spirit" to some higher goal, but also a development of the spirit in the quest for that goal. It comes from the Latin *aspirare,* which literally means "to breathe forth," but also "to have a fixed desire or longing for something" and "to seek to attain it." The term has a different root than the Latin term for "hope" (*spes*), which Cicero defines as merely "the expectation of good" (*spes est expectatio boni*).[6] Hope is a part of aspiration, as we see from condition (5) above, but only a part. It leaves out the effort and the search, the element of questing.

DOUBT AND CERTAINTY: MYTH AND ILLUSION

There is another way to illustrate how aspiration lies behind the quest for human knowledge, of which the quest for absolute value is a part. Nearly every beginning student of Western philosophy learns about René Descartes's view that we can doubt the existence of almost everything, even of what we experience with our own senses.[7] Descartes supposed that everything might be a dream or that we might be deceived by a powerful Evil Genius who has created the illusion of a world in our minds when no world actually exists. The point of his unusual speculations was to prove that we could not in this way be made to doubt everything. For if you or I so doubted, we would still *be there* doubting and being deceived. Each of us would be thinking, and therefore could at least infer his or her own existence: "I think, therefore I am" ("*cogito, ergo sum*").

I suspect Descartes is right about this last conclusion, but I won't debate it here. It is his other idea I want to focus on, the idea that everything else we experience might be a dream or a global illusion or a deception. This possibility appears altogether fanciful and not worth a moment's reflection; it seems to be fit only for the imagination of philosophers or science fiction writers. But in such fancy there often abides a kernel of wisdom. One is reminded of Wittgenstein's comment that "to solve the problems of philosophers, one has to [learn to] think even more crazily than they do."[8]

In fact, Descartes's problem of global dream or illusion—a problem that stands at the very beginning of "modern" Western philosophy—is the expression of deep ancient themes of human consciousness in a mythical form. The global illusion theme is very old. It is expressed in the Hindu Upanishads where this world is said to be *maya*, or illusion, and it is expressed playfully by the ancient Taoist philosopher Chuang-Tzu who asked his students whether he was a Chinese philosopher dreaming he was a butterfly or a butterfly dreaming he was a Chinese philosopher.[9] "Trickster" gods who create illusions are a commonplace of the mythologies of Africa and other continents and convey similar lessons.

What is their message? At least a part of the message is that any search for what is really the case from the point of view of the universe cannot attain certainty. It is a warning about human pride. Any such search lies in the realm of aspiration. We seek and we *may* find. We can never be sure we have succeeded, but we can believe that if we have not done our best to eliminate errors and mistakes, we will not have succeeded. We think, for example, that there are three chairs in the room next to us. So we go into the room and look to make sure we are not in error. The philosophers and mythmakers tell us that the chairs might be an illusion and the room itself a dream; and they may be right for all we know. (About dreamers it is said that it takes one to know one.) Yet if you want to know what is really in the room, what else can you do but go and look? Then at least you will know that in *your* dream there are three chairs in the room and not two or four or eight. And what else can scientists and other inquirers do but try their best to eliminate error by careful reasoning, observation, and repeated experimentation, and then trust that their result is the reality?

This was Descartes's solution to his own problem: do your best to make your ideas and perceptions clear, and trust that you are not deceived. He put his trust in God. But all inquirers in the realm of aspiration must trust that they are not deceived, whether they invoke God or not. (The ancient Greek word for "belief," *pistis,* literally means "trust.") This is one lesson to be learned from our collected myths and philosophical puzzles about global illusion.

So it is with the search for absolute values. Since it is a search for what is really good or evil, right or wrong from every perspective, not simply our own perspective, it belongs to the realm of aspiration and we may speak of it as a quest, "the ethical quest." Searching for absolute values is akin to the scientists' search for the final truth about the universe. It is aspiration on the same grand scale and with the same pitfalls. We can never know we have attained the final goal, but unless we do our best to get our ideas clear and our hearts set right, we have every reason to believe we will not attain it.

Yet while they are akin, the scientific quest for the truth about the physical universe and the ethical quest for absolute value must also be different in some ways, since they have different objects. To this problem we now turn.

OBJECTIVE WORTH, PART 1: ALAN THE PAINTER

What is the object of the search for absolute *value?* What do we seek when we undertake a distinctively ethical quest? That object is not likely to be anything simple, to be sure, but I think we can give it a name. I call it "objective worth." To illustrate what is meant by objective worth and why we humans aspire to it, let us consider a few simple stories.

The first is about a fellow we will call Alan the painter. Alan has been ill and depressed, so much so that a rich friend concocts a scheme to lift his spirits. The friend arranges to have Alan's paintings bought at the local art gallery by a number of his agents using assumed names for $10,000 apiece. Alan mistakenly assumes that his paintings are being recognized for their artistic merit by knowledgeable critics and collectors and his spirits are lifted.

Now let us imagine two possible worlds involving Alan. The first of these imagined worlds is the one I have just described in which Alan thinks he is a great artist, and thinks he is being duly recognized as such, but really is not. He is being deceived. The other imagined world is a similar one in which Alan has many of the same experiences, including the belief that he is a great artist. But in this second world he *really* is a great artist and *really* is being recognized as such; it is not merely that his rich friend is deceiving him to lift his spirits. Finally, let us imagine that in both these worlds Alan dies happily because he believes that he is a great artist, though only in the second world was his belief correct. In the first world he was deceived.[10]

We begin to understand what objective worth is all about when we ask whether it should make any difference to Alan which of these worlds he lives in, given that he believes he is a great artist in both and does not feel less happy subjectively in one world than in the other. To say that there is an important difference in value in the two worlds for Alan *even though he would not know it and would feel equally happy in both,* is to endorse a notion of *objective* worth. One of the consequences of this notion is that a person's subjective (or felt) happiness cannot be the final measure of value, since Alan feels just as happy in both worlds. To understand what objective worth means to Alan, we would have to tell him the story of the two worlds and then ask him which one he would rather live in. And if he answers, as we might expect, that he would prefer to live in the second (undeceived) world, this will show that objective worth, rather than merely subjective happiness, means something to him as it does to most of us. Consider how demeaning it is to say of someone, "His painting, or music, or scientific work, or whatever, is objectively worthless, but so what? He is having fun (feels happy) doing it, and that is all that counts."

Of course, we can imagine a third world in which Alan is deceived by his friend as in the first world, but finds out he is being deceived. And that world is clearly the worst of all three posited, since in it Alan is horribly deflated and more depressed than ever. But the fact that the third imagined world is the worst of the three for Alan in no way changes his judgment that the first world where he is deceived (and never knows it) is worse than the second world where he is not deceived. And this shows that objective worth means something to Alan.

Subjective happiness without objective worth (as in the deceived world) is deficient even though the two together are the best of all.

Notice that to make judgments about the objective worth of these worlds, Alan must step back from his immersion in them and view them *objectively*, from outside both. From inside the first and second worlds (that is, from his subjective point of view) things look pretty much the same to him, since he believes he is a great artist in both worlds and dies happily believing this in both. It is only when he takes what Thomas Nagel has called the "objective viewpoint," imagining himself standing outside the worlds, viewing them as a whole and knowing that he was deceived in one but not the other, that he can judge their comparative objective worth.[11] This is what gives point to the expression "objective worth."

Now there are modern skeptics who say that the subjective view from inside the worlds is the only one Alan, or any of us, can ever really have. It is therefore irrational for him to worry about the objective worth of his paintings. What does it matter to Alan, they might say, if he never knows he was deceived so long as he dies as happily in the one world as the other? What difference can other, merely imagined worlds make to him if they are never realized? But I suggest to you that it is an important fact about human beings that other imagined worlds do "strangely concern us" as the poet Rilke says.[12] We are creatures of fantasy and myth and storytelling for a reason. And it is another important fact about us that we can step back and take the objective view of such imagined worlds, for therein we come to recognize the objective worth of things—their absolute value.

These modern skeptics are trying to tell us that subjective experience is the only and final measure of value, and it might be so if we were like beasts, thoroughly immersed in our own immediate experiences and not capable of taking the objective view outside our experienced world. But we are capable of taking such an objective view and we can perfectly well understand how Alan could be right to say, "The undeceived world would be better for me, even if in the other world I would never know I had been deceived." This is to acknowledge objective worth.

OBJECTIVE WORTH, PART 2: *SOLARIS*

The story of Alan tells us something about objective worth, but not all we need to know. Here is another story that shows a further dimension of this complex notion.

The Polish writer Stanislaw Lem has written a fascinating novel about a planet called "Solaris" (which is the book's title) covered by a sentient ocean with astonishing powers.[13] Among other things, this living ocean can conjure up what seem to be real figures from the past of its human visitors who are studying the planet from laboratories built above the ocean. In the case of one of these visitors, the story's hero, the ocean conjures up the figure of his long-dead ex-wife. At first, he believes she is resurrected. They renew their affair, trying to change some of the traits that pushed them apart; they make love, converse, and review the past. But then a fearful thought begins to dawn on the hero: the wife image is not a real person. It is a simulacrum reconstructed by the planet's mysterious ocean out of his own unconscious mind and memories. It is a far more elaborate dream than he himself could conjure, but a dream nonetheless.

Now this realization is crushing for the hero, as it would be for most of us. Why? Because, among other things, he realizes his ex-wife is not really resurrected. Their relationship had not really been renewed at all. And it is not just that this is a sad thing for him, as when Kierkegaard says that despair over the loss of something is really despair over the loss of oneself.[14] No, it is not just that. He loved the woman and he wanted her to be alive for *her* sake. A theme favored by Saint Augustine was that to love anything (as God loved us in his view) is to want it to *be*.[15] I have always thought this to be one of the most profound of metaphysical insights because it connects objective reality and objective worth: to love something, anything, is to want it to *be* real.

If the hero did not care about the objective reality and objective worth of what he loved—if he cared only about his own pleasures—he might have continued to find the phantom wife just as good a companion as the real wife. In every visible way the phantom wife was a simulacrum of the real wife: same voice, same features, same traits of character, same ways of acting, an equally enjoyable sex partner. In some ways it would have been better if he had gone on being deceived. But this would have been to look at the situation from his own selfish point of view. Since he truly loved his lost wife, he cared about more than that: he cared about whether she was real and was grieved to find she was not. Like Alan, he could not say it was just as good to be deceived, because he was having just as much "fun" with the phantom wife and this is all that mattered. As with Alan, he cared about more than his subjective satisfactions. But unlike Alan, it is not the objective worth of his paintings that concerns him, but the objective reality of someone he loved; and this is another aspect of objective worth.

This story contains another lesson. It shows how objective worth is related to our "inner life," as we might call it, of consciousness and feeling. The figure conjured up by the ocean is not the real wife, though in every outward aspect it is *like* the real wife. What is missing is on the inside. The phantom wife lacks the inner life of consciousness and feeling of the real wife, experiencing him from her point of view. When we love another, what we want to be real is not just the outer shell, the public self, but the inner self, the subjectivity of the other—what Gerard Manley Hopkins wonderfully calls the person's "inscape."[16] Otherwise it is not the person, but a mere simulacrum. Such concern for the inner life of others, their inscapes, is another way in which the concern for objective worth enters our lives.

TWO DIMENSIONS OF WORTH: RECOGNITION AND LOVE

These two stories—of Alan and the man on Solaris—bring to our attention the two dimensions of objective worth:

> To have *objective worth* is (1) to be *worthy of respect or recognition with praise* from all points of view and (2) to be *worthy of love* from all points of view.

Alan's story demonstrates the first of these dimensions. By favoring the world in which he is not deceived about the real worth of his paintings, he demonstrates the desire that his accomplishments be worthy or deserving of "respect or recognition with praise" from others.

To say that this worthiness or desert is objective is to say that anyone from any point of view who accords him such recognition is right to do so, while anyone who refuses to accord him such recognition is wrong not to do so. It does not mean that he actually gets the respect he deserves from all others. Actual recognition from others is a more complex matter because it depends on their worth as well as our own. The problem with honor and esteem by others is that it requires an audience fit to render it, as Alfred North Whitehead says. Actual recognition or esteem by others is also a good, but, like Alan, we show our concern for objective worth when we favor the recognition of those who know or who are sensitive enough (about painting in Alan's case) to be "fit to render it." They provide us with the more reliable evidence of the objective worthiness of our accomplishments.

The *Solaris* story shows the other dimension of objective worth— the worthiness to be loved. The desire for objective worth in this sense is the desire to be worthy of the kind of love bestowed on the ex-wife by the hero of *Solaris*. We sometimes describe this as the desire to be loved for ourselves alone (for our own sakes) and not merely for what we have accomplished or what we can do for others (reciprocal altruism), not merely as the phantom wife might be loved as a sex object or a conversational partner, but as the real wife was loved. The hero wanted the real wife to *be*, and the mere fact that she was not there to enjoy and share with him was a sorrow greater than the loss of his own subjective enjoyment alone could be.

This is the kind of love we accord our children when we desire their continued existence and happiness without any strings attached. It is what the Western tradition has called "agape," borrowing the Greek term to mean the selfless love of others without admixture of personal gain. And it is the kind of love we desire to have from those we love, for example, our children, even after we are dead. To say whom one loves in this way, as Roland Barthes has put it, is to testify that they have not lived and often suffered for nothing. Their lives and their sufferings are remembered, pondered, and justified.

ABSOLUTE VALUE AS UNIVERSAL DESERT OR WORTH

What makes objective worth an *absolute* value is that it is the worthiness to be recognized and loved in these ways from every point of view, and this means that anyone from any point of view who accords such recognition or love is right to do so, while anyone who refuses to accord it is wrong not to do so. What we see in such a notion is that absolute value does not have to be actually recognized *in* every perspective in order to be good *from* every perspective. Focusing on worthiness therefore allows us to compare absolute value to absolute truth, as we did in chapter 3. If it is absolutely true that the earth is a spheroid and not flat, then this is true from every point of view. It does not matter that some primitive tribesmen or modern flat-earthers do not believe it. If it is absolutely true, they are simply mistaken. The absolute truth does not require universal consensus.

This point is important enough to dwell on a little further. Some people despair of finding absolute value because they think it requires finding something on which *everyone* from *every* point of view can be brought to agree. And they despair of ever finding such a thing, especially about value, because we are all different in our valuings. But once we realize that absolute value is a kind of objective worth we can see that actual universal consensus is not what we are looking for. The *worthiness* to be praised and loved by all is not the same thing as actually being praised and loved by all. It is no argument against the absolute value of Bach's music that tone-deaf persons cannot appreciate it, any more than it is an argument against the truth of 23 + 21 = 44 that it cannot be appreciated by people who cannot count higher than 10.

A poem by Jack Gilbert has always stuck in my memory because it illustrates this point so well. Recall that in the Greek myth Orpheus went down into hell to rescue his love Eurydice by distracting her beastly keepers with his beautiful music. Gilbert imagines Orpheus descending into the depths of hell, out of the clear light of day—confident of the powers of his music to sway anyone who should hear it. In the myth itself, Orpheus succeeds in his mission of swaying the beasts, but Gilbert asks us to imagine a different scenario. What if our Orpheus should reach those depths and there, encircled by the "closing beasts," and preparing his lyre, should suddenly realize "they had no ears?"[17]

What if, indeed? If the beasts had no ears this would certainly be a blow to Orpheus's plan of freeing his beloved Eurydice from them. But would it tell against the objective beauty of his music that these earless beasts were not swayed by it? No more than it tells against the truth of 23 + 21 = 44 that it cannot be appreciated by mathematical illiterates. Or no more than it would tell against the fineness of a portrait by Rembrandt that a person with impaired vision could see it only as a blur.

The same is true of worthiness to be loved. Your worthiness to be loved does not depend on whether everyone loves you, or even upon whether everyone *can* love you. It certainly does not depend upon whether a Hitler or a Stalin or a Jack the Ripper or a Vlad the Impaler might or could have loved you. The problem with winning their love has more to do with their fitness to render it than your worthiness of it, just as Orpheus's problem of winning the praise of the beasts has more to do with their fitness to render it than the worth of his music. If absolute value is a kind of worth or desert in this sense, then we can understand how it can be universal (deserving of praise and love from all perspectives) even though it is not universally recognized in all perspectives.[18] Like absolute truth, absolute value does not require universal concensus.

GLORIA EST CLARA NOTITIA CUM LAUDE

We have distinguished two aspects of objective worth, represented by the stories of Alan and the man on Solaris: worthiness for recognition with praise, and worthiness for love. There are other traditional names for the first of these aspects, represented by the Alan story. Most of us want to be deserving of recognition, respect, and praise for our accomplishments and achievements, whatever they be, from artistic endeavor like Alan's and other worldly accomplishments, to being a good parent or friend or colleague, or even simply being a good person. The desire for what the eighteenth-century philosophers called "approbation" by others, is well grounded in the human makeup, as we found in chapter 3. We see it in children, whose desire for praise in their accomplishments is nearly inexhaustible and its fulfillment so necessary to their healthy development.

Another ancient name for this first aspect of objective worth is "glory," which the medieval philosopher Saint Thomas Aquinas, following Saint Ambrose, described in this wonderfully succinct definition: *"Gloria est clara notitia cum laude,"* Glory is clear recognition with praise.[19] Aquinas is discussing God when he formulates this definition and he endorses the medieval view that God is that being who is deserving of glory in the highest (*in excelsis*) and deserving of love in the highest. In short, God was conceived in those religious times as the paradigm of objective worth, the being who is deserving of the two aspects of objective worth—love and glory—in the highest degree. We humans, according to those same medieval thinkers, could only hope for a smaller measure of such worth, but if our task was the imitation of God (*imitatio Dei*), as they held, then we too should seek (insofar as we are capable) to be worthy of love and worthy of glory. In other words, we should seek objective worth.

It is sometimes said that in the Christian tradition love supersedes glory and all other aspects of worth; all glory goes to God. This is true in one sense. Love is the supreme value in Christianity. But in another sense it is superficial to say that worthiness for glory has no role in the Christian view (or in other religious views). To say that all glory goes to God is a corrective against human pride and the relentless seeking of honors, esteem, and praise in this world, which may come from an audience unfit to render it, or may not accord with one's actual worth. But the *worthiness* for glory in the sense of clear recognition with praise is quite another thing. This is worthiness from God's point of view, the absolute point of view—or, in other words, in religious terms, worth in the eyes of God—and that certainly should be desired from a Christian view or any theistic view. Actual glory is indeed downplayed in the Christian and other religious traditions, but I think it is a mistake to say the same for the worthiness of it. The real connection between worthiness for love and worthiness for glory is in fact very complicated, as we shall see.

TWO ASPECTS OF THE SELF: THE BACH CRYSTALS

The two aspects of objective worth—worthiness for love and glory—are also connected to two aspects of the human self. Glory (clear recognition with praise) is connected to what we might call the outer or public self, the roles, projects, accomplishments, and achievements that (like Alan and his paintings) we identify as ours and want to be worthy of recognition by others whether or not we get it. Whereas love (as we saw in the *Solaris* story) is connected to the inner or private self, to the inner life of consciousness and feeling that Hopkins called the inscape. In reality, each of us is only one self, with inner and outer aspects, and we must use our imagination, as in the *Solaris* story, to think of the inner and outer aspects separately. But it is important to use our imagination in this way if we are to fully understand objective worth. It helps us understand why objective worth has these two aspects corresponding to the two aspects of the self.

Consider the case of Johann Sebastian Bach. He lived a fairly modest existence as a court musician and organist while composing some of the greatest music of the Western tradition, receiving a measure of worldly glory few humans attain. Suppose, however, that during Bach's time noblemen discovered a set of amazingly complex crystals made of an unknown substance that spontaneously produced polyphonic music equal to Bach's. Music critics could not distinguish the compositions of these Bach crystals from Bach's own music. We might imagine the aristocrats of the time to be a callous lot who then lost all interest in Bach the man. The crystals produced all the beautiful music they could desire and they did not have to feed and clothe the crystals as they had Bach and his large family. Bach was out of a job.

For such aristocrats Bach would have been valuable only for what he produced. His music was worthy of recognition with praise, but it was not important that *Bach* produced it. It could just as well have been produced by a fellow named Schmidt or Muller, or even by some organic crystals, so long as it was beautiful music. Glory can be impersonal in just this sense, but love cannot be so. The achievements and accomplishments of the public self are interchangeable. They can always be imagined to be the achievements and accomplishments of someone or something else. The phantom wife may be a praiseworthy conversationalist and sex partner, and in this sense her deeds are interchangeable with those of the real wife, but she herself is not.

Love is directed not just at the public self, but at the inscape as well, and this is unique. One cannot exchange it for another without loss. If Bach were put out of a job by the miraculous crystals he might say, "The nobles seemed to care about me, but all they really cared about was what I could do for them." And this is certainly not how we want to be conceived of by others, as mere instruments or means to their satisfaction, like servants who are expendable if a cheaper equivalent could be found. As Kant says, anything for which there is no equivalent in value has not only value, but also *dignity*.[20] This shows the ethical connection between human dignity, the uniqueness of the individual, and the worthiness to be loved. It shows how dignity is grounded in objective worth.

Glory attaches to what is universal, love to the particular. In desiring objective worth we desire to be worthy of both. In the nobles' callous behavior, Bach sees that they would have cared about the accomplishments of Bach, but not that these were the accomplishments *of Bach*. This is one way in which glory and love are related, but not the only way, as we shall see.

WORTHINESS FOR LOVE

How do we determine what is truly worthy of glory and truly worthy of love, how do we determine what has objective worth? This question brings us back to the notions of quest and the realm of aspiration with which we began this chapter, for these notions contain the germ of an answer.

Let us look at love first. How do we know we are truly worthy of love from every point of view without qualification? The first part of an answer is that we cannot *know* this in the sense of having certainty about it any more than the scientists know that they have the final truth about nature or the knight knows he has found the authentic Holy Grail. We aspire to it, which means that while we cannot guarantee attainment, there is something we can do to seek it. Scientists cannot be assured that if they do all the right experiments and subject their theories to all the available evidence, they will have found the final truth. But they have every reason to believe that if they do not do these things, they will not have found the final truth; and so it is with the knight and the search for the Holy Grail.

So it is also, I suggest, with most of the really important things in life, and that includes the worthiness to be loved. They are matters of aspiration. It is beyond our human capacity to do something that will guarantee we are worthy of love from every point of view in the universe. Yet there is something we can do, if we *aspire* to such absolute value— something which, if we do not do it, we will not be worthy of love from all points of view. That something is to love all others; we can ourselves manifest agape. This loving all others will not guarantee our worthiness to be loved by all others, but it is that without which our worthiness to be loved cannot be absolute.

Why? Recall that in chapter 3 I said that the essence of immorality was that persons could be selectively concerned with attaining their natural human needs and desires by caring only whether they, or the select groups to which they belonged, fulfilled these needs, and not caring about other persons or groups outside their favored ones. This was the problem with egoists, sensible knaves, free riders, and classist amoralists, all in their different ways. Egoists care only for themselves, classist amoralists for their group, but both will exploit others beyond themselves or outside their groups.

Now anyone who acts this way cannot be unqualifiedly worthy of love from all points of view because there is no reason why the exploited other persons or groups should love them. If one group enslaves another, then the enslaving group is not worthy of being loved from the point of view of the enslaved, and therefore the enslavers are not worthy of being loved from all points of view. The Indian warriors who killed innocent neighbors may have been loved by their children, families, and other members of their tribe, but there is no reason for their being loved by the seven innocent people they killed to atone for the death of the chief's sister. "If you have done it to the least of these you have done it to me" (Matthew 25:45). In other words, if you are not worthy of love from all perspectives—even those that seem too insignificant to matter—you are not worthy of love from the absolute perspective.

OBJECTIVE WORTH AND THE ENDS PRINCIPLE

Therein lies the connection between objective worth and ethics or morality. It comes through the worthiness to be loved. If the essence of immorality is being solely concerned about attaining our natural needs for ourselves or our group while exploiting others, then the essence of morality is not being so selectively concerned and not exploiting others in this way.

But that is precisely what the revised Ends Principle and the wide version of the Golden Rule counsel us to do: to treat all others with respect or dignity, as ends and not means, even if they are different than us in their values or ways of life and even if they are not our natural kin or not the objects of our natural affection. Recall that a little earlier we linked dignity to the worthiness to be loved. Dignity is related to our uniqueness as persons, to the idea that there is nothing equivalent with which we might be replaced, as the Bach crystals replaced Bach. Love in the sense of agape is directed at what has dignity in just this manner, the particular, unique person—like the real wife on Solaris whose inscape was irreplaceable.

To treat someone as an end in the sense of the revised Ends Principle is to treat them as unique and irreplaceable in just this way, not as something one uses (as a means) for one's own ends, as the phantom wife might be used for pleasure, but as someone whose inner point of view is important in its own right. To state Saint Augustine's theme that loving someone is wanting them to *be* means that we love them for their own sake, as the hero of *Solaris* loved his real wife. This is why, when applying the Ends Principle in chapter 2, we had to ask what the other person's values were and not assume their values were the same as ours, or impose ours on them. To treat them as ends was to look at the situation *from their point of view*, not just from ours. We should now see that this requirement is grounded in the idea of loving them for their own sakes, and not just for our sakes, which is a requirement for being worthy of love in return.

Thus, the revised Ends Principle and the wide version of the Golden Rule are grounded in the desire to be absolutely worthy of love, to have objective worth; and this provides an answer to the second question posed at the end of chapter 2, that deep question with which we began this chapter: in the face of pluralism and uncertainty, why should we persist on the path of openness that led to the Ends Principle, rather than merely succumbing to relativism, skepticism, and nihilism? The answer is that the argument of chapter 2 was a quest for absolute value. The traditional path to absolute value was blocked, but we did not for that reason forsake the quest; instead, we looked for alternative paths. The path of openness was tried because it took pluralism and uncertainty seriously and highlighted the fact that it was absolute value—what was good from all points of view—that was sought: if you want to find out what is valuable from every point of view, then keep your mind open to every point of view. But now we see that there was also a deeper motive: if you want to be worthy of love from every point of view, then you must love others—not exploit them or use them as means to your ends, but treat them as ends in themselves. The point of openness, then, is to let the value that is in others *be* realized. Keeping your mind open to other points of view is now seen as an initial expression of this kind of love; and it is a step on a path to absolute value because it is an attempt to find objective worth by making ourselves worthy of love by all. It is such striving for objective worth and meaning that leads to the Ends Principle and has led so many in history to the Golden Rule.

Yet we also found that treating all others as ends could not be done unrestrictedly. Openness was only a first step on the path described in chapter 2. To love all others unqualifiedly in the sense of the Ends Principle was impossible whenever the moral sphere broke down. But the ideal of loving all—agape—guided us even when the moral sphere broke down. We try to depart from this ideal as little as possible in an imperfect world when we must depart from it to some degree, a goal from which flowed all the ethical implications of the

Ends Principle and its exceptions. In other words, it was the attempt to *sustain the ideal of respect for all to the degree possible under adverse conditions* that brought us to the goal. Like the scientists and the knight who aspire to a goal, we do what we *can* do to uphold the ideal when it cannot be followed to the letter and trust that this will be good enough. This places the ethical task firmly in the realm of aspiration—makes of it an ethical quest, which is an essential part of the broader quest for objective worth in life.

In chapter 3 we argued that the social motives of human beings (desires for approval, social acceptance, friendship, love, and so on) however crucial to morality, are not sufficient to motivate us to be ethical. It may now seem that by emphasizing love in the moral equation we are retreating from that earlier claim. But we really are not retreating, and it is important to see why. The limitation of the social motives, let us remind ourselves, was that we can fulfill our human social needs selectively by getting approval, acceptance, and love from others close to us or in our group while exploiting others outside our circle or group. In this manner, social motives and egoistic motives combine in a destructive way; and this can be true even of the desire for love, which, applied selectively, can be a motive for exploiting others.

What we have added to the social motives in this chapter is the objective view of our existence that was described in the stories of Alan and the man on Solaris, which add the idea of objective worth from all points of view. It is not just the desire for love that is crucial for ethics, but the desire to be objectively worthy of love, and this is a far more complicated notion. It has to do not merely with the category 3 social motives of chapter 3, but also with the human needs of category 5 that are concerned with finding some objective meaning to life that goes beyond personal pleasure. The search for objective meaning is what induces us to take the objective view of our accomplishments and our inner lives; and it is this further need, combined with the social motives, that spurs us to the ethical life.

WORTHINESS FOR GLORY, PART 1: PRACTICES AND INTERNAL GOODS

We asked several sections ago how one determines what has objective worth—what is truly worthy of glory and love? We have answered that question for worthiness to be loved. If the worthiness to be loved is the object of a quest in the realm of aspiration, then its attainment depends upon the degree to which persons undertaking that quest love absolutely and not selectively. Now let us look at glory. The answer in the case of glory will also require that we talk about quests and the realm of aspiration, but some other ideas are also involved, which I will now explain.

Glory, or clear recognition with praise for one's deeds, achievements, and accomplishments, is a cultural notion. It has significance in the context of forms or ways of life that give specific content to the human quest by conferring *meaning* on one's deeds and achievements. Thus, in a surprising way, the desire for glory is also connected to the desire for roots, which was described in the first and third chapters as a historically defined sense of belonging. These features of glory (its connection to culture, history, and roots) are important for understanding objective worth generally. But they are in need of further explanation. What they mean can best be illustrated by borrowing some ideas from Alasdair MacIntyre's widely read book, *After Virtue*.[21]

MacIntyre's view is that the human quest for the good life must be understood in terms of what he calls "practices" and "traditions." By a practice he means a "socially established . . . human activity" through which we strive to realize goods by achieving "standards of excellence which are appropriate to . . . that form of activity" (p. 187). As examples of practices he mentions architecture, farming, physics, medicine, painting, music, chess, football, politics, the making and sustaining of family life, and other arts, sciences, activities, and enterprises through which humans cooperatively seek the good life. It is in the context of such practices that we become worthy of clear recognition and praise for our accomplishments (as Alan desired for his paintings).

Important for understanding this notion of a practice is the distinction MacIntyre draws between "internal" and "external" goods (p. 188). If the violin maker takes pride in his craftsmanship, in producing an instrument with magnificent sound, then he is seeking a good that is internal to the practice of violin making. By contrast, if his interest is in the money or prestige his work will bring him, he is interested in goods that are external to the practice. One can be interested in both kinds of goods, of course, but external goods, like prestige, status, or money, can be realized in many different ways, whereas internal goods are specific to the practice in question: the skills and excellences distinctive of violin making can only be realized by making violins.

There is a moral point behind this distinction for MacIntyre. Like many other modern social critics, he bemoans the tendency of consumer societies to emphasize *external* goods over *internal* goods. The complaints are familiar: doctors who have more interest in the money and esteem of a medical career than in practicing medicine, craftsmen and repairmen more interested in the fast buck than taking pride in their work, politicians who are in government to amass power and influence for themselves rather than to serve the public good, athletes compromised by commercial interests, low-quality films and other forms of entertainment made with more interest in the bottom line than in artistic excellence, fascination with fame and celebrity, often at the cost of not recognizing genuine merit and excellence, and so on.

There is more than mere self-interest in the vague distaste many people have for these trends. Below the distaste is a recognition that such trends represent a confusion of priorities. Societies that so emphasize external goods over internal goods impoverish the means by which humans cooperatively seek the good. MacIntyre points out that "external goods are . . . characteristically objects of competition in which there must be losers as well as winners. Internal goods are indeed the outcome of competition to excel, but it is characteristic of them that their achievement is a good for the whole community who participate in the practice" (p. 188).

More important, an exclusive concern with external goods diminishes our sense of the objective *worth* of things. One always has to ask what external goods like money and power are good *for;* and when they are detached from internal goods the answer is too often that they are merely instruments in the pursuit of personal pleasures and satisfactions. But if all we care about are our own pleasures and satisfactions, then objective worth goes by the board. The pursuit of excellence and genuine worth for our accomplishments takes a back seat and this impoverishes our sense of ourselves and our search for the good. People who exclusively seek external goods often sense this, dimly and unconsciously, in the restlessness with which they seek more and more of what is supposed to satisfy them. What often happens is that they turn the pursuits of external goods like money and power into internal goods by treating these pursuits themselves as practices in which they can excel and be excellent (for example, the businessman who takes pride not simply in the fact that he is rich, but in the effort, skill, and daring which went into his making himself rich). Thus, they think of their worldly success as a measure of their objective worth (their deservingness of clear recognition with praise) for the skill and excellence that allowed them to succeed.

WORTHINESS FOR GLORY, PART 2:
EXCELLENCES, TRADITIONS, AND ROOTS

This common transformation of external goods into internal goods tells us something about the search for objective worth rather than merely pleasure. The search for objective worth in the form of glory, or clear recognition with praise for our accomplishments, is intimately related to the pursuit of *internal goods* that are identified in relation to human practices in which standards of excellence of performance are defined for the pursuit of various ends. The trial lawyer who takes pride in her courtroom skills is operating within a social practice in which standards of excellence are recognized, as is the accomplished chess player or athlete or musician, the businessman described in the preceding paragraph, the chemist who makes a new discovery, or Alan with his paintings.

This does not mean the standards of human excellence in practices are always fixed or clear. MacIntyre emphasizes the idea that practices change and develop, and when they do so they become traditions. "Within a tradition the pursuit of goods extends through generations, sometimes through many generations. . . . the history of a practice in our time is generally and characteristically embedded in and made intelligible in terms of the larger and longer history of the tradition through which the practice in its present form was conveyed to us; [and] the history of each of our own lives is . . . characteristically . . . made intelligible in terms of the larger and longer histories of a number of different traditions" (p. 222). The trial lawyer's standards of excellence are not just connected to the arbitrary rules of today's legal practice: they are embedded in the longer tradition of common law that is supposed to serve the interests of justice, respect for evidence, fair representation, and so on. When the standards no longer serve these goods they are subject to change. The same is true of the musician practicing within the tradition of Western music, or the chemist working within the tradition of modern chemistry. A tradition, as MacIntyre says, is a continuing argument about what is *worth* pursuing.

These features of the search for objective worth through glory explain the not-so-obvious, but important, connection between the desire for *objective worth* and the desire for *roots*. Having roots in the sense of a historically defined sense of belonging is not just a matter of security and solidarity with one's community and one's past—the warm blanket of belonging. It is that, certainly, but it also has to do with the meaning we give to our accomplishments. Beyond the bare utilitarian demands for survival, humans pursue objective worth through glory as beings embedded in cultural and historical contexts that confer meaning on their deeds and achievements.

If we lack roots in practices, traditions, and ways of life, we lack the contexts in which excellences can have meaning. It would be like trying to understand Shakespeare's greatness without the English language, or Paganini's music if there were no violins. Roots provide the soil in which to plant the seeds of glory. The human desire for them is for more than security and solidarity; it is interwoven with the desire to find meaning in life. In this manner, two aspects of what we called the "spiritual center" in chapter 1—absolute value (understood as objective worth) and roots—turn out to be related.

RELATIVISM AND SKEPTICISM REVISITED: ILLUSION AND REALITY

But is there not a paradox here, which seems to be built into the idea of the spiritual center, as we noted in chapter 1? Absolute value and roots (two aspects of the spiritual center) seem to pull in different directions. Absolute value requires that something have value from all points of view, while rootedness implies that we pursue excellence in particular cultural and historical traditions, and hence from particular points of view. How can the pursuit of internal goods and standards of excellence defined by limited practices and traditions have absolute worth? How can our necessarily limited human achievements be deserving of clear recognition and praise from all points of view?

These questions raise the problem of relativism once again in a different guise, now for matters of glory rather than of love. But it is a similar problem; the Tower of Babel still looms. Since everything is seen from a limited perspective or point of view, how can it be that human achievements from any finite point of view, including our own, are absolute? Similar questions forced us in earlier chapters to look at the problem of relativism in new ways and we must do the same here.

In this case, the clues come from reflecting on a deep philosophical issue that was mentioned earlier in this chapter. The problem of the objective worth of excellences defined within particular forms of life is very much like the problem that arose in our earlier discussion of the myths of global illusion. It is often said that when we try to understand the world around us we always see things from a perspective or point of view—we see the way they appear to us—not the way they really are in themselves; we describe them in terms of our own language and ideas, that is, from our own points of view. How, then, can we know the absolute truth about them, that which is true of them from all perspectives, when we can only see them from our own limited perspective?

This problem of how we know the way things really are in themselves is an ancient philosophical problem, but it has become very acute in the late twentieth century. There has been a crisis of confidence across all intellectual disciplines about our ability to answer. Modern skeptics—including the postmodernists and poststructuralists mentioned in chapter 1—have weighed in with the negative conclusion that we cannot answer it because there is no neutral or absolute perspective, no God's-eye view, from which we could grasp the way things really are. Every perspective on reality is just that—a limited perspective—and every account is made in somebody's all-too-limited "language game."

The answer that I think must be given to this skeptical attitude about objective *reality* provides the clue we need to understand the objective *worth* of human excellences and achievements. In the very statement of the skeptical question—how do we know the way things really are in themselves?—trouble and confusion are already brewing. As Hilary Putnam, John Post, and others point out in recent works on this ancient philosophical problem, the question wrongly assumes that there is such a thing as *the* (one and only) way things are, when it is likely there are different ways things are in reality that can be described from different points of view for different purposes.[22]

Think of the history of a city, like New York, over a twenty-four-hour period, as told by a society columnist, an economist, a weatherman, a political reporter, a social historian, the director of sewers and sanitation, and others. Each of them gives us a different description of the city from his or her limited point of view. But which is *the* true picture? What is the *real* New York "in itself"? The oddity of these questions explains why the skeptics seem to have a point. Who could imagine a neutral perspective from which we could describe the city, not from anyone's particular point of view, but from the absolute point of view?

But there is another alternative. Suppose that the real New York is the *summation* of what is correctly described from all the different points of view. It is what is correctly described by the weatherman *plus* the social historian *plus* the director of sanitation *plus* the society columnist and so on. Then it would be true that there is no neutral description of the real city; we would admit that we cannot help but describe the city from some point of view or other. But the absolute or God's-eye view would not be this impossible neutral perspective at all; rather, it would be the summation of all the true statements about the city from all the different points of view. The number of these possible points of view might be infinite, to be sure, but each would tell us something true about the real New York. They would fall short only in not being the whole story. The real New York in itself is elusive because there might always be more to tell about it (like the physicists' goal of discovering the whole truth about nature), and not because we can never describe anything true about it.

This point also emerges in the ancient Buddhist story of the blind men trying to figure out what an elephant is by feeling different parts of it. Each man has a different story to tell depending on whether he feels the legs or the trunk or the torso; and each wonders what this "thing" could really be. They do not have the whole picture of the elephant, to be sure. But this does not mean that they do not have partly right descriptions from their different perspectives, and it does not mean that they are not describing the (objectively) real elephant. They are, but only partially. Their mistake is in thinking that each of them has the whole truth.

Note also that if each person gets his or her description right, then it is true for everyone, not just for that person. If the weatherman correctly describes the New York weather then what he says about the weather is true so far as it goes for everyone else, the society columnist, the sanitation engineer, and so on. It is not true for the weatherman, but false for the society columnist; it is not merely relatively true. If the blind man clutching the elephant's leg correctly describes his part of the elephant, then what he says is true from everyone's point of view even though he only describes part of the elephant. So each correct description may be absolutely true, or true for all perspectives, though it is only a partial description. The mistake lies not in claiming that it is absolutely true, but in claiming that it is the whole of absolute truth.

OBJECTIVE REALITY AND OBJECTIVE GOOD

Turning now to the pursuit of objective worth through glory, we should take this account of objective reality as a clue. Just as there need not be one and only one way things really are in themselves, so there need not be one and only one way to be objectively good or excellent, to be worthy of glory or clear recognition with praise. Bach is excellent in one way, Einstein in another, Michelangelo and Shakespeare in yet other ways—to take some rarely disputed examples. To really appreciate the different ways in which they are excellent requires different modes of understanding and initiation into different practices and traditions or forms of life (classical Western music in the case of Bach, physics in the case of Einstein, and so on). But this is no more an argument against their absolute good, or objective worth, than is the claim that because descriptions of New York or the elephant are always limited to a point of view, they are not descriptions of the objectively real city or elephant. Absolute good may be the summation of all that is excellent in different practices, traditions, and forms of life (music, physics, painting, family life, and so on) just as the absolute truth about the city is the summation of all that is correctly said about it in the various vocabularies of the weatherman, the economist, the social historian, and so on.

The mistake, then, is not to say that the excellence of Bach or Michelangelo or Shakespeare is absolutely good, but rather to say that any one of them alone represents the sum total of absolute good. If the weatherman gets his description of the New York weather right, then his description of the weather is true for everyone, even for those who do not understand the vocabulary of weathermen and can't appreciate its truth. In a similar manner, we can say that if Bach is excellent in his own way, then his excellence is good from every point of view, even for those who cannot appreciate the subtleties of his music, and likewise for Shakespeare and those who cannot appreciate his language. But each represents only a part of the absolute good, not the whole.

Thus, the absolute good does not require a neutral description. Like the absolute truth, it may be the sum of all the finite goods that arise out of different points of view. If the absolute good is elusive, it is because there may always be more ways to be excellent than we have yet explored, just as there are more possible correct ways to describe the city. The absolute good transcends our finite grasp not because we are getting no glimpses of it in small and large examples of human excellence, but because there is always more to grasp.

THE MOSAIC OF VALUE

There is an image that nicely captures this idea of the absolute good as the summation of particular excellences: the image of a mosaic of value. According to the dictionary, a mosaic is a picture or design made by inlaying small bits of colored stone, glass, or other substances in mortar; by extension, it is any kind of complex picture or design that is made up of distinct parts put together to form a whole. Let us view an entire mosaic as the absolute good, while the inlaid pieces or parts are the various excellences attained in different practices and ways of life. The absolute or God's-eye point of view, which is the summation of all the particular points of view, would then be the overall view of the mosaic with its varied parts. The excellences of particular forms of life are very different in kind, like the colored stones or glass of the mosaic, but in the well-made mosaic each part makes an essential contribution to the whole picture; remove any piece and the mosaic is less good. Similarly, to remove particular forms of excellence would be to diminish the absolute good, the total sum of the good of the universe as a whole, just as removing any one of all possible true descriptions will give us an incomplete picture of New York.

According to this image, your importance and mine, insofar as we seek objective worth through glory, is to be a piece of that larger mosaic of value. We have to do it in our own way, with our own talents, rooted as we are in our own forms of life, but if we do it well we may add a piece to the overall good, however small our individual contributions. To seek objective worth is not to try to encompass the whole of the absolute good, but to be a piece of it (however great or small), whose removal would make the whole mosaic less good. This is another perspective on the openness we discussed in chapter 2. *By being open to the degree possible to other points of view, we are ultimately seeking absolute value by letting the value in each point of view come forth and take its place in the mosaic.* To take one's place is to be worthy of glory or clear recognition with praise from the absolute point of view, even though one's finite point of view is not the absolute one.

Because objective worth pursued by way of worthiness for glory is an object of aspiration (like the worthiness for love), nothing can assure us of its attainment. But seeking those excellences available to us in our practices and traditions is that without which we cannot hope to attain it. Like the knight who cannot be assured of finding the Holy Grail but does what he can to attain it by seeking the golden chalice, or the scientists who cannot be assured of the truth of nature, but who do what they can do to attain it by looking for the best available theories, we do what we can to attain objective worth on the love side by manifesting agape and on the glory side by seeking those excellences available to us in the cultural traditions in which we are rooted.

A PROBLEM ABOUT GLORY AND LOVE: THE FAUST LEGEND

This returns us to a final and difficult question that was raised earlier about the relation between the two aspects of objective worth: worthiness for glory and for love. Could we not pry these two aspects apart and seek objective worth by way of glory alone or love alone? This question is especially important for ethics, because if one sought glory alone, one might do it immorally, since ethical action defined by the Ends Principle and the Golden Rule emerges from the love side of objective worth. It seems that this is the fear of religious traditions which tend to downplay glory even though the desire for recognition of one's achievements is as deeply embedded in human nature as the desire for love.

There are many stories of famous people who pursued their own paths to excellence while neglecting their families or cruelly exploiting others along the way. Ethicists like to discuss the case of the French painter Gauguin, who left his family in poverty in order to pursue his quest for artistic greatness in the South Seas islands.[23] But perhaps the most relevant case of the pursuit of glory at the expense of love is the legendary case of Faust, who sold his soul to the devil in order to become the great knower of all the secrets and who cruelly treated others, including a young maiden, along the way. The Faust legend—so central to Western consciousness—is another one of those myths that will not go away because it probes so deeply into the human psyche and the human condition. In this case, the myth touches upon the basic relation of the two aspects of objective worth: love and glory. (You may remember the theme song of one of our more recent myths, which explores the same idea in a distinctively modern medium, the film *Casablanca:* "It's still the same old story / a fight for love and glory. . . . the fundamental things apply / as time goes by.")

Let us look more closely at this problem about the two sides of objective worth raised by Faust and other legends. We said that worthiness for glory or clear recognition with praise from all points of view does not depend on the ability of beings from all other points of view to render such recognition. The earless beasts of Hades could not hear Orpheus's music or Bach's, nor could such music or the paintings of Michelangelo be appreciated by extraterrestrial beings whose auditory and visual capacities turned the music into meaningless noise or the paintings into random squiggles. Yet we also said that if the music of Bach and the paintings of Michelangelo had objective worth, then they were deserving of clear recognition with praise from all points of view, even from the points of view of these different beings. Such beings would be right to render such recognition and wrong not to do so. How can that be, since they cannot possibly appreciate the music or painting in itself?

The answer is that beings can fittingly acknowledge the objective worth of something they cannot directly appreciate if they acknowledge the *objective worth of those beings different from themselves who can appreciate it.* They must be able to say something like this: "We earless and sightless beings cannot appreciate the excellence of Bach and Michelangelo, so we cannot directly see how it adds to the overall good of the universe. But indirectly we can see how it adds to the overall good of the universe, *if* we acknowledge the objective worth of you human beings and other beings who can appreciate such excellence. We would then acknowledge that what we can directly appreciate from our point of view is not all that counts toward the overall good of the universe. Human beings have worth too and some of the objective worth of the universe (some absolute value) flows through them, even if we cannot directly appreciate it. Their good is part of the mosaic too."

This shows how glory is related to love. To say of other beings that what is good *for them* (from their point of view) adds to the overall good of the universe (even if you cannot appreciate it because you do not share their values or sensibilities) is what love, in the sense of agape, is all about. It is to say of another that you want them to *be*, not just because you like them or appreciate what they can do for you, but because their being and their experiences are an essential part of the absolute value of the universe. This is the kind of love that gives point to the Ends Principle, which counsels us to respect and recognize others even if we do not share their values and cannot appreciate their point of view. It is what is signified by loving others for their own sakes.

Consider what it would be like to take the opposite attitude. Robert Nozick has imagined a race of beings so superior to us in intelligence and creative accomplishment that they look upon the experiences and accomplishments of the human race much as we look upon the activities of bacteria or amoebae.[24] To these superior beings, any accomplishments the human race can boast of, including those of Bach and Michelangelo, are insignificant and negligible. The universe would not be significantly worse off from their point of view if human accomplishments did not exist, or indeed if the human race were destroyed.

What would be lacking in this superior race is love in the sense of agape. The experiences and accomplishments of humans are not much *to them* directly. But what counts in the case of love is what those experiences and accomplishments are *to humans*. If humans are worthy of love for their own sakes, then their experiences and accomplishments are worthy of respect and recognition with praise from all points of view whether or not they can be appreciated from all points of view. Their experiences and accomplishments add to the overall good or mosaic—the objective worth or absolute value—of the universe. The love required by objective worth goes out to all, even to those whose worthiness for glory may seem insignificant from our (self-described "superior") point of view; and such love thereby reminds us that even smaller pieces of the mosaic are indispensable to its overall worth. ("If you have done it to the least of these, you have done it to me.")

So, in an unusual way, worthiness for glory from all points of view depends upon the worthiness for love from all points of view. But note that this dependence is indirect. We cannot say that because Gauguin himself was to a degree less worthy of love because of the cruel treatment he accorded his family that therefore his paintings were less worthy of glory. It is a mistake to make artistic merit and other forms of value depend directly on ethics and moral worth. Gauguin's paintings are to be judged by the standards of his art, not his personal life, and there are good reasons to think they are worthy by those standards. Yet sightless beings or those with very different sensibilities than ours can accord objective worth to Gauguin only if they recognize the objective worth of beings who can appreciate Gauguin's work. So the value of Gauguin's work *to us* and to others like us is assured by its artistic merit alone. But this is only relative value. If the work is in addition to have objective worth in the overall scheme of things, this will be because some of those for whom it has artistic merit are worthy of love—their point of view matters even to those who cannot appreciate it. By their worthiness to be loved, these beings raise something up from mere relative value to something of objective worth in the universe.

WINNING THE WORLD AND LOSING ONESELF

This relation of glory to love also has importance for the individual, as we can see from the Faust legend. Faust wanted to attain his full measure of glory and was prepared to do so by forsaking worthiness to be loved by all. He would forsake commitments to others and even to the whole human community, if need be, to fulfill his dream of glory. This is one way of reading his pact with the devil. According to the older versions of the legend, he accomplished much, yet lost all and was destroyed. Because glory attaches to our deeds or accomplishments, it is always in principle "detachable," as we saw in the story of the Bach crystals. Thus, like Faust, we might accomplish much and lose ourselves. In such manner, the nobles cared about the accomplishments of Bach, but not that they were the accomplishments of Bach: miraculous crystals would have done as well. Likewise, our accomplishments might survive in the final picture (the mosaic) if we are not worthy of love, but like Faust, *we* will be lost (like the people of Orwell's *1984*, whose names were expunged from all records as if they had never existed at all).

The original Faust legends were supposed to show that the desire for glory (or "greatness" of some sort) is ultimately empty and motivated by a destructive pride or hubris. Whatever we accomplish, and however great it seems from our limited human perspective, we are invited to see how little it comes to from the overall perspective of things. We are little and the universe is great. The lesson is worth learning. Yet it would be hard to eliminate the desire for glory in human beings without taking away much of what we call their human nature and the motivation for many of their great and good achievements. (This is the problem that seems to have concerned Goethe in his famous later version of the Faust legend.[25]) The oddness of human life without the pursuit of excellences and achievements in addition to love is summed up by W. H. Auden's witty remark: "We are here on earth to do good for others. What the others are here for, I do not know."[26]

The answer to this dilemma is not to deny the importance of the desire for glory but to put it in perspective—to show how, though our lives and accomplishments are indeed little in the broader scheme of things (as the religious traditions wish to remind us), they can have objective worth, they can be indispensable parts of the greater good. We gain this broader perspective, first, by focusing on the worthiness for clear recognition with praise rather than merely on actual recognition; and we gain it, second, by seeking to be worthy of love as well as of glory. Pride is tempered by this broader perspective because we recognize the littleness of our accomplishments and lives, but also their indispensable worth. Humility becomes that virtue which recognizes the connection between glory and love: it recognizes that the objective worth of our achievements cannot be guaranteed by our efforts alone, which can only secure relative worth.[27]

ASPIRATION AND THE ETHICAL QUEST

In summary the ethical quest is a quest in the realm of aspiration and it is part and parcel of the quest for objective worth, for the objective meaningfulness of one's life. As such, it is like the quest for the final truth. The problem with the modern age is not that it has lost its knowledge of objective Truth and Worth. Humans never had such knowledge; they only thought they did from time to time. The problem is rather that we have lost our will to aspire to objective Truth and Worth in the face of uncertainty and without assurances that they exist. Yet I think this is what a new Axial Period will demand of us.

We can understand this demand by reflecting on the three great questions which, according to Immanuel Kant, human beings can ask.[28]

"What can we know?"

"How should we live?"

"What should we aspire to?"

The second question is the ethical one, and for many centuries humans have believed that they could only properly answer it by first determining the right answer to the first question, "What can we know?" Find the right facts about human nature and the cosmos, they said, and you will have an answer to the ethical question. But I think it is a mistake to think that the answer to the second question ("How should we live?") must depend wholly on an answer to the first ("What can we know?"). This was part of the lesson of chapter 3. We simply do not know enough to ground ethics necessarily in human reason and knowledge alone; and centuries of failure in trying to do so have led many to relativism, skepticism, and nihilism.

The answer to Kant's second question—"How should we live?"—must also depend on the answer to the third question, "What should we aspire to?" That which can sufficiently motivate us to be moral in the universal sense required by principles like the revised Ends Principle and the wide version of the Golden Rule is a concern for objective worth, or absolute value, in ourselves and in others. But objective worth, in the form of either worthiness for love or glory, belongs to the realm of aspiration; it is something we can seek without the assurances of attaining it.

This may sound dispiriting at first, until we realize that most of the important things in life are matters of aspiration, not knowledge. All of our idealism about Truth and Justice and Beauty and Worth, our religious impulses about what is genuinely worthy of worship, our philosophical and scientific strivings to find out what really is and what we really are—all these are matters of aspiration, objects of quests. If we find this despiriting, then it is the human condition we find dispiriting. And this is truly a sad thing, for it saps our ability to aspire to anything greater than our own transitory satisfactions.

The spirits of the times that breed relativism, skepticism, and nihilism whisper that because we cannot really know anything ultimately important, we cannot aspire to anything ultimately important. For those who listen to this message the meaning of life shrinks to a very small circle, and they end up living in what Herman Melville in *Moby Dick* calls "an ice palace made out of frozen sighs."[29]

"Aspiration" seems to me just the right word for this radically contingent seeking. From its Latin root, as we saw, it signifies a "going outward of the spirit." The image is of our spirits reaching beyond the finite perspectives we inhabit toward an objective reality and objective worth that are always only partly revealed to us. Yeats wrote that after all his poetry and studies, after all his searching, he had stumbled onto one great truth. It was this: "Human beings can embody the truth, but cannot know it."[30] This expresses the very essence of aspiration, and I think it *is* a great truth. By living in certain ways, by loving and seeking excellences in our various practices and traditions, cultures and ways of life, we may "embody the truth" in the sense of attaining objective worth, without being sure of having attained it.

THE SPIRITUAL CENTER

I want to add a final word on how this account of objective worth relates to one of the themes of chapter 1, the image of the "spiritual center." The modern loss of the spiritual center was defined there, following Kolakowski, as the loss of a sense of (1) absolute value, of (2) the uniqueness and dignity of persons, and of (3) roots, or an historically defined sense of belonging. We have seen in this chapter that these three aspects of the spiritual center are connected by the notion of objective worth. Objective worth connects (1) absolute value to (2) the uniqueness and dignity of the individual by way of the *worthiness for love* (as we saw in the *Solaris* story and the relation of the "inner self" or inscape to uniqueness and dignity); and objective worth connects (1) absolute value to (3) roots by way of *worthiness for glory* (as we saw in the discussion of human excellences within cultures and traditions, which confer meaning on the life of the "outer or public self"). In this way, the three features of the spiritual center come together in objective worth.

If we use the ancient term "wisdom" to designate an understanding of these aspects of the spiritual center, we can say that to be wise requires more than knowledge of facts and of means to ends. To be wise is ultimately to understand what is really *worth loving* and *worth praising* in life—in other words, it is to understand what has objective worth.

5

Public and Private Morality

A NECESSARY DISTINCTION FOR FREE SOCIETIES

One of the most important unmentioned implications of the discussion of ethical issues in chapters 1 through 4 concerns social ethics or public morality. The pluralism and uncertainty of the times, symbolized in chapter 1 by the image of the Tower of Babel, suggest that persons who think about ethics in modern societies must come to grips with a distinction between *public morality* and *private morality*.

Let us say that your private morality is "what you think is the right way to live, for yourself or anyone." Public morality, by contrast, is "what you owe others *even if they do not agree with your private morality.*" Such a distinction seems to be required by the pluralism of modern societies, where individuals commonly disagree in their private moral views about issues ranging from pornography to abortion, capital punishment, homosexuality, euthanasia, gambling, economic justice, surrogate motherhood, and a growing list of other contentious social issues.[1] Persons' private morality may tell them that one or another way of acting or living is wrong, and yet, when there is no consensus, public morality counsels a measure of respect for the differing views of others.

Yet the distinction between public and private morality is controversial. Some think making such a distinction is a pernicious mistake. If you believe your private morality is the right way to live for yourself or anyone, they argue, how can you fail to try to make it *the* public morality? Is it not difficult, and perhaps immoral, to restrain yourself and be tolerant in the face of behavior you privately regard as wrong and deeply offensive, as many regard pornography or homosexual behavior or abortion?

But, as natural as this reaction may be, it leads to a central problem about *whose* private morality would become the public one and be imposed on everyone else. The fact is that societies in which the distinction between public and private morality entirely collapses are *totalitarian*—they are societies in which some person's or some group's morality is imposed on others and made the public morality. This, in fact, is the essence of totalitarianism, which seeks total control over the actions, minds, and consciences of citizens and amounts to collapsing public and private morality. In Nazi Germany Hitler made a law against having homosexual *thoughts*. That is the totalitarian mind at work. As Auden remarked, "being unacknowledged legislators of the world is not the dream of poets," as is often said, "but the dream of secret police."[2]

By considering the totalitarian alternative, we come to appreciate how the distinction between public and private morality is related to the existence of free and pluralistic societies, in which individual choice and dignity are valued. The distinction between public and private morality can be difficult to live with, to be sure, yet it is the price we pay for living in such societies. At a deeper level, it is the price we pay for the lost moral innocence described in the *Perelandra* story of chapter 1, which arises when one confronts views of right and wrong differing from one's own. The difficulty of living with a public/private morality distinction is a further consequence of having bitten into the fruit of the tree of knowledge of good and evil in this conspicuously modern manner.

PUBLIC MORALITY AND THE ENDS PRINCIPLE: INALIENABLE RIGHTS

The fact that the distinction between public and private morality is related to the unprecedented pluralism of modern societies and the resulting loss of moral innocence provides a clue about how to understand *public* morality. The suggested response of chapter 2 to pluralism and uncertainty was initially an openness or respect for the points of view of others, even if they do not agree with our point of view—letting them prove themselves objectively worthy or unworthy by their actions. Such a response eventually led to the Ends Principle with its attendant exceptions and levels of moral sphere breakdown. Since the Ends Principle counsels us to respect others, even if their values are different than ours (up to the limit of moral sphere breakdown), it coincides with what we are here calling public morality. For it expresses what we owe others even if they do not agree with our private morality.

In sum we can be guided by the suggestion that *public morality is embodied in the Ends Principle and related ideas about moral sphere breakdown*, and we can bring these ideas to bear on issues of public morality. Though private moralities may differ, public morality would be something we have in common. It would be a universal or absolute core, applicable to all persons, which they share as a consequence of respecting their differences.

This suggestion has significant consequences for social ethics and public philosophy. Consider, for example, the seminal principle stated by Thomas Jefferson in the Declaration of Independence: "All men are created equal and endowed by their Creator with certain inalienable rights," among which are "life, liberty, and the pursuit of happiness." To respect persons' rights to life, liberty, and the pursuit of their happiness is another way of describing what it means to treat them as ends according to the Ends Principle—to let them choose and pursue their own purposes and values, without interfering or imposing our conceptions on them against their wills (up to the point, of course, where they break the moral sphere). Interpreted in this way, the Jeffersonian principle—which Abraham Lincoln called "the father of all moral principle"—is an alternative way of expressing the Ends Principle and defining public morality. It is something we share despite differing private moralities.

Jefferson and Lincoln, like many others, regarded the principle of the Declaration ("all men are created equal . . .") as universal or absolute in its significance, true for all persons at all times. Lincoln said that all residents of the land, including immigrants who came after the American Revolution, recognize it as "the father of all moral principle in them" which "they have a right to claim . . . as though they were blood of the blood, flesh of the flesh, of the men who wrote the Declaration."[3] He thought that all persons of any land could rightly claim the principle of the Declaration and the rights it conferred as their own. It was not the property of any one people, but rather had absolute significance for all people at all times.

Many thinkers today would doubtless disagree. They no longer believe the basic rights of life, liberty, and the pursuit of happiness can be defended as universal or absolute rights because they no longer believe in universal or absolute values of any kind. We who live in this society and cherish our freedoms, they argue, may prefer the principles of the Declaration and free societies over political alternatives, but the justification is ultimately a matter of personal preference. This view has a powerful hold in the current intellectual climate and is clearly a correlate of the problems of pluralism and uncertainty, relativism and skepticism, discussed in chapter 1. But if the principle and rights of the

Declaration are indeed expressed by the Ends Principle, we can read the argument of chapters 2 through 4 as a way of supporting the older view of Jefferson and Lincoln that these rights have universal or absolute significance, that they apply to all persons at all times.

LAW AND PUBLIC MORALITY

Another consequence of viewing public morality in terms of the Ends Principle is that public morality will turn out to have more content than we might suppose. The tendency is to think that public morality in a free society counsels us merely to be tolerant and to respect other peoples' points of view and pursuits of happiness, whatever they may be. And this hardly affords much direction in moral matters. It would leave all the interesting disputes on the private moral side. But the argument of chapter 2 was designed to show that the Ends Principle covers considerably more moral ground than that. It does not lead to an openness of indifference or relativism, as one might think, or to the bland tolerance of an anything-goes attitude, but rather to the view that some ways of acting and living are less worthy of respect than others. It covers most of the traditional moral commandments and, in the form of the wide version of the Golden Rule, it is regarded in some religious traditions as the whole of "the Law and the Prophets" or "the Sum of Duty."

When translated into law, public morality as expressed by the Ends Principle would lie at the basis of much of our criminal and civil law. On the criminal side, it would cover laws against murder, theft, assault, rape, burglary, fraud, larceny, bribery, extortion, libel, and so on (which involve level 2 breakdowns of the moral sphere—discussed in chapter 2—where there is a guilty party). It would also deal with the criminal justice system, fair trials, punishment, and treatment of the guilty. The guilty are due some respect, though not the full measure of respect. Deterrence of criminal behavior is necessary to maintain and preserve the moral sphere. On the side of civil law, the Ends Principle would be the basis for fair contracts and the just resolution of civil disputes and conflicts of interest under imperfect conditions (that is, level 3 breakdowns of the moral sphere). On the political side, it would be the basis for ethics legislation governing the behavior of legislators, lobbyists, and others involved in the political process.

SOCIAL ETHICS AND THE HARM PRINCIPLE

In addition, public morality viewed in terms of the Ends Principle would support various principles of social ethics, which social philosopher Joel

Feinberg has called "liberty-limiting principles."[4] The most influential of these principles among political and legal theorists, first enunciated by John Stuart Mill in *On Liberty*,[5] is often called the "Harm Principle": *the liberty of individuals can be justifiably limited (by law or government or society) to prevent genuine harm to others.* This principle is clearly related to the Ends Principle, since moral-sphere breakdown is usually described as the point at which some person does "harm" to another.

But what exactly is harm and what is to count as "genuine" harm according to the principle? In social ethics, these questions pose problems that go well beyond the examples of moral sphere breakdown discussed in chapter 2. Consider that many people are offended by such things as obscenity, pornography, public nudity, or other forms of behavior they regard as indecent. Are these offended people being "harmed" by the presence of such things in their community even if they do not directly see them or partake in them? In his influential work on *The Moral Limits of the Criminal Law*, Feinberg defines harm as "the thwarting or violation of someone's interests."[6] People offended by nudity, obscenity, or pornography say their interests are being thwarted by the presence of these things in their community; so it would seem they are being harmed.

Can the liberty of others be limited in this manner because it is said to give offense to some members of the community (where "offense" means something like "shocked sensibilities at the violation by others of one's deeply held beliefs")? Most recent legal and ethical theorists have held that, in the absence of any further conditions, the answer must be No. To limit freedom on grounds of offense alone would mean the prohibition of many forms of behavior that cause no other harms beyond the fact that they are offensive to someone or other in the community whose views may be different from those of the offenders. Where disagreements in private morality are to be expected, and many forms of behavior are likely to offend someone or other, liberties would be unduly restricted. Consider the case of a nudist colony isolated from the rest of the community, access to which is restricted to those who wish to join. Can it be shut down merely because some other people in the community who never see it are shocked by its existence? Here is a clear example, say the legal theorists, where private moralities conflict and public morality in a free society must stand up for the rights of minorities.

INDECENCY, PORNOGRAPHY, AND OFFENSE

But that cannot be the whole story about offense in public morality, if the Ends Principle is a guide. Offended parties also deserve some respect for their points of view, even if they cannot be accorded the full measure of respect in every situation. Their moral and religious sensibilities do not override the rights of others in all circumstances, but neither can their moral and religious sensibilities be entirely ignored if we are to respect them "to the degree possible" under imperfect conditions. Thus, while a private nudist colony with consenting members is not prohibited by law even if its existence may offend people who never see it, nudity on main street or at the public park is another matter. Here the offensive behavior is thrown in the face of those offended. I recall a picnic in a large city in which families sitting on blankets were subjected to the scene of a man pulling down his pants and defecating on the grass while shouting "This is what I think of the Sheik of . . ." (I can't remember where). He claimed his act was an exercise of free speech, but the police were unimpressed and hauled him away for public indecency.

If there is a difference for social ethics between such cases of private nudity and public indecency, as most theorists suppose, then the difference has to do with what Feinberg calls the criterion of "reasonable avoidability."[7] If offended persons can reasonably avoid the behavior that offends them, then their feelings do not override the rights of others. This is the case of the nudist colony. If, by contrast, offended persons are confronted by the behavior while walking down the street or while innocently enjoying a picnic with their families, their offense can be grounds for limiting liberty because they cannot reasonably avoid what offends them.

For the same reason, sending unsolicited pornographic material through the mails is prohibited, since it is thrown in the face of people who might be offended. It is also the reason why an adult movie theater placed in a part of a city properly zoned for commercial use presents one kind of a problem, while placing it in a residential area or next to a church presents another. In the second case, mere offense becomes important because the offended parties cannot reasonably avoid what offends them.

These examples yield a second principle of public morality that is often discussed in connection with Mill's Harm Principle. Normally, mere offense is not grounds for limiting liberty in the public domain, but this second principle, usually called the "Offense Principle," tells us when it can become so: *the liberty of individuals can be justifiably limited to prevent offense to others, if the offending behavior is not reasonably avoidable by those offended.* This principle is subject to further qualification, but it is a good start in defining public morality for matters of offense. It explains, for example, why issues about stores selling pornographic material or adult movie houses can look different in small towns as opposed to large cities. In large cities the offending material is reasonably avoidable by those offended, if the city is properly zoned and other conditions are also met. But a small town is another matter. A single main street with a few stores, a gas station, a church, and a topless bar with gaudy signs provides too little reasonable avoidability for those offended.

It is a piece of folk wisdom that big cities are sinful and dangerous places compared to smaller towns ("How ya gonna keep 'em down on the farm after they've seen Paree?"). And there is some justification for this folk wisdom in public morality. The ambience of large cities allows more diversity of behavior and life-style, and hence more respect for those with different points of view, but less respect for those easily offended. Yet it is not the case that anything goes in cities either, according to the Offense Principle. Zoning in large cities is a moral issue, and not merely a political or legal one, since it can provide some measure of reasonable avoidability for those offended by various activities. Wherever issues of offense and reasonable avoidability are involved, it is a question of balancing the rights of all parties, including those who are offended, which fits the general pattern of fair resolution of level 3 breakdowns of the moral sphere discussed in chapter 2.

DISCRIMINATION AND PUBLIC ATTITUDES: DRAWING THE LINE

Viewing these liberty-limiting principles of social ethics in terms of the Ends Principle helps to resolve another troubling problem of social ethics concerning offense. Can reasonable avoidability be all that counts for restricting liberty on grounds of offense? Doesn't it also matter *why* persons are offended—what attitudes or beliefs cause the offense? Is the offense at public indecency in a park of the same order as the offense of white supremacists in the presence of black families in the park? Is the offense at the presence of an adult theater in one's residential neighborhood of the same order or nature as offense by some persons at the presence in their neighborhood of a Jewish synagogue, or at homosexual couples owning homes? Writers on social ethics have sometimes tried to distinguish morally acceptable cases of offense on the basis of how many people are offended or how deep the offense is. But this clearly will not do. Prejudicial attitudes may be widespread in a community and may run deep. The numbers of people offended and the intensity of their shocked sensibilities are not the relevant factors; the nature of their attitudes is the issue.

The Ends Principle can come to our aid in sorting out this issue of public morality. The offense of white supremacists, anti-Semites, and the like, is based on the attitude that some persons are *less worthy of respect than others* simply because of what they are, or because of the group to which they belong (racial, ethnic, religious, or otherwise). This is directly opposed to the attitude enjoined by the Ends Principle, and hence of public morality, to treat all persons with dignity—to respect them equally as ends, not means—the attitude required within the moral sphere. Of course, individuals can *make themselves* less worthy of respect by breaking the moral sphere, but in that case they prove themselves guilty by their actions. And this is altogether different than being assumed to be less worthy of respect from the start simply because of what they are. Indeed, this gives us a deeper insight into the attitude of openness that led to the Ends Principle described in chapter 2. By requiring that others must "prove themselves guilty" by what they do, or plan to do, one is also saying that they are not to be presumed guilty at the outset simply because of what they *are*—racially, ethnically, sexually, and so on.

So if the offense of white supremacists and their ilk is of a different order, it is not because of the number of people offended or the intensity of the offense. It is because the attitude that gives rise to the offense is somehow "out of bounds" to begin with—it is in violation of the Ends Principle and hence of public morality. The Offense Principle needs to be rewritten to include this qualification: the liberty of individuals can be justifiably limited to prevent offense to others, if the offending behavior is not reasonably avoidable by those offended, *and the offense is not based on attitudes of the offended parties that are themselves in violation of public morality as defined by the Ends Principle.* Public morality would then determine what attitudes get into the offense equation in the first place—what attitudes are worthy of respect in the delicate balancing of reasonable avoidability and liberty. Some attitudes are not worthy of respect in this balancing, and the conditions of public morality tell us what they are.

WHAT YOU ARE AND WHAT YOU DO: THE CASE OF HOMOSEXUALITY

Conflicting attitudes toward homosexuality may seem to present a problem for this aspect of the Offense Principle. Some people whose private morality is opposed to homosexual behavior say that they do not think homosexuals are less worthy of respect as persons simply because of their sexual predilections, which may have been determined by genes and/or early upbringing. What these people object to, they say, is not homosexuals as persons, but homosexual behavior, including sodomy, which they consider immoral. Such attitudes are often hypocritical or disingenuous, but if sincerely held they seem to present a problem for the last qualification to the Offense Principle, since the offense is claimed to be at what is done, not at what people are.

What such attitudes really show, however, is that the distinction between what people are and what they do is more complicated in public morality than we have implied. Consider the following example. Some people with strong negative feelings about homosexuality are offended by displays of affection in public (for example, kissing or hand-holding) by homosexual couples. In order to determine whether such offense is at what is being done rather than at what these couples are, one has to ask the following question: would these same people be offended by similar public displays of affection by heterosexual couples? If the answer is no, then the offense is taken not at what is done alone but at who is doing it. On the surface, the offense is at what the homosexual couple is doing (displaying public affection), but at the deeper level it is at what they are.

Similar reasoning applies to another much-discussed case in social ethics: offense taken by the people of a mostly white town at an interracial couple walking down the street holding hands and acting affectionately. Once again, if the townspeople are not offended by hand holding and minor public displays of affection generally, no matter who is doing it, then the offense is only superficially at what the interracial couple are doing. It is really at what they are (and in particular that one of them is black). (In a mostly black town it could be the other way around. Prejudice can go either way.) Offense at such behavior is thus of the same order as in the other cases just considered. The offending attitude is out of bounds as far as the Offense Principle is concerned because it is ultimately based not on what these people are doing but on who they are.

By contrast a different kind of problem for public morality is presented by prudish people who object to modest displays of affection in public by anyone. Their feelings really are about what is being done and not who is doing it and so they are not out of the public morality equation. The question in this case is not whether the feelings of the exceptionally prudish or squeamish count for something in public morality. They do. The question is whether they count for enough in the total equation. Their feelings must be balanced against the feelings of others in the community and against community standards about what is reasonable conduct in public. What may have seemed appropriate in eighteenth-century Puritan New England may not seem so in twentieth-century America. Public hand-holding or kissing is one thing, sexual intercourse in public quite another.

THE DEBATE ABOUT LEGISLATING MORALITY:
DEVLIN AND HIS CRITICS

The theme I am developing here, by way of examples, is that the "liberty-limiting principles" frequently discussed in social ethics can be fruitfully viewed as extensions of the Ends Principle and its attendant notions of moral-sphere breakdown. This provides an ethical foundation for these social principles as well as throwing light on their formulation and some of their applications. If the Ends Principle expresses public morality, it also places such principles squarely in the realm of public morality.

Such an approach throws light on other disputed issues of social ethics. One such issue concerns the extent to which morality can, or should be, enforced by law. The most widely discussed defense of the legal enforcement of morals is that of Sir Patrick Devlin, a respected British judge and legal theorist, who first presented his case while arguing against the liberalization of England's laws on homosexuality.[8] Devlin first noted that societies are based on a community of ideas, part of which must be a moral foundation, and that society has a right to protect this moral foundation for its own survival. "Society," he says, "is held together by the invisible bonds of common thought. If the bonds are too far relaxed, the members would drift apart." Devlin's second point concerns the standards by which societal morals should be judged. They should be the "community standards" as determined by the "reasonable person," or "man on the street," or the person "in the jury box." In matters of pornography, for example, questions about what is obscene or outside community standards are often put to grand juries that are supposed to be representative sampling of the community. Devlin insists that the community reaction through such representatives must be a strong one of disgust or indignation to justify legal sanctions, but when there is such a reaction, he believes, liberties can be restricted on moral grounds. (The liberty-limiting principle justifying restrictions of immoral behavior in such cases is sometimes called the Principle of Legal Moralism.)

This now-standard defense of Legal Moralism has been criticized on a number of grounds. Critics, like H.L.A. Hart, Ronald Dworkin, and Feinberg have argued that Devlin's appeal to the criterion of community standards is vague and potentially dangerous.[9] Community moral standards may be based on ignorance or prejudice. Should they be given the status of law simply because they are widespread? And how widespread must they be? Will a majority suffice, and if so, do we not have a potential for tyranny of the majority? As for consensus, or near-unanimity, it is not likely to be found in modern societies on the moral issues that concern Devlin, like homosexuality, pornography, or abortion. Dworkin nicely sums up these criticisms of Devlin when he says that the problem is not with Devlin's "idea that the community's morality counts, but his idea of what counts as the community's morality."[10] Restrictions on liberty to prevent "immoral behavior" (as Legal Moralism requires) fail to resolve the central question of pluralist societies in which private moralities differ: "Whose idea of immoral behavior will be enforced?"

COMMUNITY AND THE PUBLIC MORALITY PRINCIPLE: BEYOND NEUTRALITY

While suspicions of Devlin's strong Legal Moralism seem to be justified, there is nonetheless something to be said for his view that "society is held together by the invisible bonds of common thought," which must include some moral foundation or shared ethical beliefs, without which its people would "drift apart." Social philosophers— from Plato to de Tocqueville to modern communitarians—have supported such a claim. And many of Devlin's critics acknowledge it as well, when they say, as Dworkin does, that the problem with Devlin's position is not his idea that "the community's morality counts," but his idea of what counts as the community's morality.

A shared public morality does count for social life. Without it, social disorder and moral disintegration are ever-present possibilities; and they have become real dangers for modern societies, if the writings cited in chapter 1 are to be believed. But in modern societies, with differing private moralities, a shared public morality cannot simply be identified with the majority view, nor can one private morality be enforced on all by law. The proper alternative, I think, is to begin by taking seriously the conditions of pluralism and uncertainty, as we did in chapter 2, and to proceed by way of an attitude of openness to the Ends Principle with its attendant levels of moral sphere breakdown.

Public morality, arrived at by such a search, would not simply counsel tolerance or an openness of indifference, as we argued, but rather the view that many ways of living are less worthy of respect than others. Society must take that attitude too. It could not remain neutral to ways of life or plans of action that could break the moral sphere. In this respect, neutrality toward different ways of life, which is the same thing as openness of indifference, is a spurious ideal.[11] Neutrality, in the sense of unqualified openness to every point of view, is the first step in the search for universal truth, but it cannot be sustained and is not itself the universal truth.

What I now want to emphasize is that this nonneutrality must go well beyond its embodiment in criminal and civil law if it is to capture fully public morality as expressed by the Ends Principle. The reason is that commitment to the ideal of treating all persons as ends involves a commitment to *promoting and sustaining the moral sphere* (which is by definition the sphere in which the Ends Principle can be followed by everyone). This suggests a further principle of social ethics which might be called the "Public Morality Principle": *society has a legitimate interest in protecting and encouraging attitudes, practices, institutions, and social conditions that tend to sustain the moral sphere, and in discouraging attitudes, practices, institutions, and conditions that would lead to its breakdown.*

A Public Morality Principle of this kind has numerous implications for social policy and law that go beyond the Harm and Offense Principles.[12] Communitarian theorists have often criticized liberal individualist social theories for paying too little attention to social institutions, like the family, the extended family, the neighborhood, the church, and the school, which are involved in the moral education of the young. If such institutions are dysfunctional or ineffective, one can scarcely maintain a social order in which everyone is treated as an end and rights to liberty and the pursuit of happiness are universally respected. Instead, society is likely to degenerate into wars of all against all such as we already see in the gang warfare of our cities and the increasing amounts of random violence in society at large.

The Public Morality Principle would therefore guide all social policy and private initiatives having to do with the health of families, moral education in the schools, social programs, and community efforts, like Head Start, Big Brothers and Big Sisters, and others, which provide support in morally directing the young, programs to deal with problems of teenage pregnancy, drug abuse, drunk driving, disaster relief, job retraining, child abuse, gang violence, and society's other pressing social problems; in addition, it would encourage support groups for mental illness and alcoholism, rape crisis centers, suicide hotlines, centers for battered spouses, hospices for runaways, public service advertising to deglamorize cigarette smoking or alcohol abuse, campaigns against the use of drugs, and so on. Such efforts should not merely be viewed as "social" programs; and it is a further question whether and to what extent they should be done by government or by private organizations or initiatives. The point is that they have to be attended to in some way or another if the moral order of society is to be sustained. To the degree that such social programs contribute to the maintenance and preservation of the moral sphere, they are imperatives of *public morality.*

This is a way of acknowledging the truth in Devlin's observation that "society is held together by the invisible bonds of common thought," which must include a moral foundation, and society has a right to protect this moral foundation for its own survival. The inadequacies of the

Principle of Legal Moralism, which Devlin defends, do not require us to reject the idea of shared moral commitments. We can embody this idea in an alternative "Public Morality Principle" which requires that society must not only protect the rights to life, liberty, and the pursuit of happiness here and now, but foster those social conditions, institutions, and attitudes ("habits of the heart," as de Tocqueville called them) that are necessary to create a moral order in which rights can be protected.

CRIME AND PUNISHMENT: JUSTICE AND THE ETHICAL INFRASTRUCTURE

The Public Morality Principle also has a role to play in matters of criminal justice. No one knows better than those who work within the criminal justice system—police, prosecutors, judges, social workers—that the system cannot stem the tide of crime on its own if the support of the society at large through moral education and community efforts is wanting. One such prosecutor, Ronald Earle, district attorney of Travis County in Texas, puts the matter this way:

> Alexandr Solzhenitsyn said recently that when Western society was established, it was based on the idea that each individual limited his or her own behavior, because everybody knew what they were supposed to do. The law didn't control behavior. People controlled their own behavior. Behavior was controlled by ethics . . . each person's . . . sense of what was right. . . . We [are supposed to get this sense of right] from the value-teaching institutions of community—home, family, extended family, neighborhood, church, school—all those institutions of love that add up to community.[13]

Earle aptly refers to these value-teaching institutions as the "ethical infrastructure" of society, and he argues that if this infrastructure is not doing its job, the criminal justice system cannot protect the moral sphere on its own.

Such a view, which is gaining a wider hearing in an age of overcrowded prisons, implies that public morality, as regards criminal justice, cannot merely be a matter of making laws and prosecuting criminals; it must also involve creating and maintaining an ethical infrastructure in which laws can function. In other words, the goal is not merely to *restore* the moral sphere when it has broken down, but to *preserve* it over the long term. For several decades it has been fashionable to say that we can only deal with the effects of crime and cannot do much about the social conditions that breed it. But, as crime grows, and prisons in most states fill up beyond the willingness of citizens to pay for them, the pendulum may be swinging in the other direction. As Earle points out, criminologists are generally agreed about the major (though not the only) sources of crime, which are four in number: abusive families, problem neighborhoods, substance abuse (drugs), and poverty. And much can be done about these, he thinks, with more community involvement in the criminal justice system. Following the directive of a recently passed Texas state law, Travis County has created community action committees for each of these four problem areas, made up of volunteer citizens who work with the Department of Human Services and the police, overseeing community efforts to deal with child abuse, teen pregnancy, parent training, drug and alcohol abuse, and so on. This is a community approach to crime, in which an ethical infrastructure supports the criminal justice system, very much in the spirit of the Public Morality Principle.

MORAL ECOLOGY: VIRTUES AND RIGHTS

The concern for the moral sphere fostered by the Public Morality Principle is concern for what the authors of *Habits of the Heart* call the "moral ecology" of a society, for those attitudes and virtues, like honesty, generosity, loyalty, and integrity (de Tocqueville's "habits of the heart") that make it possible to maintain a moral order. As we saw in chapter 1, there is growing criticism of modern free societies for neglecting this moral ecology. For example, so-called virtue ethicists (who emphasize the cultivation of virtues and moral character for ethical theory) often ally themselves with communitarians in criticizing post-Enlightenment doctrines of liberal individualism, which stress individual rights to life, liberty, and happiness, while underestimating the cultivation of virtues and moral character that make the enjoyment of these rights possible.[14]

Our discussion of the Public Morality Principle supports this point. It is customary to think of public morality in free societies as merely a set of rules for adjudicating conflicts between individual rights and ways of life. What is missing in such an approach (as virtue ethicists and communitarians remind us) is a realization that the rights of life, liberty, and the pursuit of happiness are not self-sustaining. They require a moral sphere in which to exist; and that moral sphere is in turn a fragile thing that depends for its preservation on the virtues and character of those who are part of it. As James Madison put it, "If there be no virtue among us, no form of government can render us secure. To suppose that any form of government will secure liberty or happiness without any virtue in the people is a chimerical idea."[15] Public morality, then, requires far more than a set of rules for adjudicating disputes and resolving conflicts of rights. It requires the cultivation of institutions and social conditions that create a moral ecology, or ethical infrastructure, in which rights can survive and flourish. This is a shared social commitment that modern societies have too long neglected—and it must be seen as an essential part of public morality.

ABORTION: A TEST FOR THE PUBLIC-PRIVATE MORALITY DISTINCTION

In summary, this chapter has described some of the implications for social ethics of the ideas presented in chapter 1 through 4. These include a distinction between public and private morality and the suggestion that public morality can be expressed by the Ends Principle with its attendant ideas of moral sphere breakdown. I suggested that public morality so conceived has more content than we might suppose, providing a foundation not only for criminal and civil law, but also for ethics legislation in politics, for liberty-limiting principles discussed by social ethicists, like the Harm and Offense Principles, and for public policy relating to the moral ecology of society. We could also have discussed the relevance of public morality for other liberty-limiting principles[16] and other issues of applied social ethics (for example, in medicine, business, law, and so forth), but the examples given provide a good illustration of its scope.

As broad as the scope of public morality may be, however, some moral problems are beyond its reach at present and for the foreseeable future; and these turn out to be, not surprisingly, among the most contentious social issues of the day. I will conclude with a few words about perhaps the most contentious of all these issues—abortion—which is a good illustration of the limitations of public morality. Lying between the opposing prolife and prochoice positions on abortion lies the great mystery of fetal life, which deeply divides private moralities and which public morality cannot resolve. When does the fetus become a human person in the full sense of the term? Prolifers usually insist that it is at the moment of conception when the sperm joins with the ovum. If this is true, abortion would be murder from day one, except in special circumstances, like threats to the life of the mother. The Public Morality Principle, based on the Ends Principle, would rule it out like any other killing of an innocent victim.

But one can agree about the Ends Principle and still disagree about abortion, if one does not accept the view that the fetus has full human status at the moment of conception. Therein lies the special difficulty of the abortion issue. Prolifers argue that conception is the only clear line of demarcation between the distinctively human and the nonhuman, but most prochoicers disagree. Writings in journals of medical ethics in recent years have explored other possible lines of demarcation, like the advent of brain waves (whose cessation is the new medical criterion for death), and "brain birth," or various stages of development of the neocortical (higher, distinctively human) structures of the brain between the eighth and twenty-second weeks of gestation.[17] This continuing medical research does not settle the issue of the human status of the fetus, but it does show how complicated the issue is. Others debating this issue appeal to religion rather than medical science for an answer to the question of human status, but here again religious views on abortion differ. Prolifers insist that God creates and infuses a human soul at the moment of conception, whereas religious prochoicers ask why an almighty God could not do that at a later time, at eight weeks, say, or eighteen, when the brain has developed more.

The general problem is that, with abortion, we are dealing with something greater and deeper than an issue about rights and duties, even deeper than an issue about life and death. It is an issue about "being and not being," the most profound of all philosophical and religious questions. What *are* we human beings and when do we come to be what we are? Medical knowledge can help to answer the question, but it is not sufficient if we are more than merely physical beings; and questions about the soul are not ones on which we easily attain consensus.

For these reasons, the abortion issue is presently beyond the scope of public morality and will be the subject of continuing public debate. If the U.S. Supreme Court overturns the 1973 *Roe v. Wade* decision that legalized abortion, or continues to whittle away at it, as in recent years, abortion questions will increasingly be turned over to state legislatures. Some states will place numerous restrictions on the right to abortion, while other states will maintain freer access. These differences reflect an ambivalence in the general public. On the one hand, there is uneasiness about abortion on demand for any reason. But, on the other hand, most Americans incline to the view that, on profound questions of a religious or philosophical nature, where consensus cannot be reached, decisions should be left to individual conscience.

In summary, abortion is one of those issues through which humans continue to "forge in the smithies of their souls, the uncreated conscience of their race" (to paraphrase James Joyce's expressive language).[18] Such issues, as it turns out, lie beyond public morality, certainly at the present time, and are the ultimate test of our ability to live with the distinction between public and private morality.

6

Democracy, Politics, and Ethics

THE POLITICS OF A PLURALISTIC AGE

Democracy was a rare occurrence in the original Axial Period of human history. It appeared in only a few places (for example, in the city-state of Athens toward the end of the 5th century B.C.) and then only for a short time. Yet it seems to be the preferred political form of what may be a new Axial Period. With the demise of communism, nations throughout the world are lurching warily toward it from both left and right. In Eastern Europe, Russia, Latin America and other places, they are finding the transition is not easy. Democracy requires habits of heart and mind different from the totalitarian ones to which they are accustomed and there is a danger that some of them will change one authoritarian form of government for another. In Africa, Asia, and in scattered spots on other continents, there are added problems of tribalism and fundamentalism, both of which clash with the openness and pluralism of democratic ways of thinking.

These examples make clear that the ferment over democracy is not just about practical politics, but about "ways of thinking" as well. Democracy is intimately related to the story I have been telling since chapter 1. It is the politics of a pluralistic age, the political response to the Tower of Babel, and it is related to the contrasting ways of searching for absolute values described in chapters 2 through 4.

To see this, consider the following images. We can imagine values in a society seeping downward from the top—from the rulers to the people—or bubbling upward—from the people to the rulers. The former image is that of authoritarian and totalitarian governments. Some ruling groups or elites choose values for the rest of society and these are imposed from the top down. Often in the past, the access of rulers to the true values was legitimated by claiming the divine right of kings, or a right of succession through ancestors who came from the gods, or (in some ancient societies) by the rulers themselves claiming to be gods. The idea was that those at the top had special access to the God's-eye point of view—the absolute or true values for all—and therefore could impose them on others.

Democracy represents the opposite image. Values bubble up from the bottom to the top. They arise in the desires, feelings, and aspirations of the people and flow upward to the leaders who must be responsive to the "rule of the people." Democracy assumes no direct access to the God's-eye point of view by the leaders, whose power must be curbed by checks and balances and who can be thrown out of office when they fail. And even the people, though sovereign, are not infallible. Their search for the good is very much an experiment with values in a democracy—a search in the realm of aspiration—that does not rely on certainty. That is why even the sovereignty of the people (that is, the tyranny of the majority) must be curbed by constitutional checks and balances.

POLITICAL VALUES AND ETHICAL IDEALS

These two images—of values seeping downward from the top or upward from the bottom—correspond to the two ways of searching for absolute values described in chapter 2. The traditional way was to position yourself in one point of view (your own or that of your group or culture) and try to show that it was right and everyone else wrong. This corresponds to authoritarian and totalitarian ways of thinking about politics. If you think you are right and everyone else is wrong, you will not be uncomfortable about forcing your views on others. You will be doing it for their own good and may even claim a divine right for your point of view.

But we found there were problems with this traditional way of searching for absolutes—problems of pluralism and uncertainty. The alternative path suggested in chapter 2 was the path of openness, of not assuming yourself right and others wrong from the start, but of letting others prove themselves right or wrong. In politics, this is the path of democracy. Democratic governments do not claim to have the whole truth about how human beings should live, which can be authoritatively passed down from the rulers to the ruled. They require an *initial* attitude of openness to different points of view to allow individuals to prove themselves right or wrong by how they live. We also found that this initial attitude of openness, if consistently pursued, has ethical consequences. It leads to the idea embodied in the Ends Principle of respect for the values or points of view of others up to the point where they break the moral sphere, an ethical view that is grounded in turn in the idea that each person has objective worth.

If democracy is the political response to the same conditions of pluralism and uncertainty that led to these ethical conclusions, it could be given a similar ethical grounding. The image of values flowing upward from the desires and aspirations of the people to the rulers would be grounded ethically in the objective worth of each individual whose desires and aspirations are worthy of respect. But, as the argument of chapter 4 also showed, linking ethics and politics in this way would require that democracy not be conceived merely as a practical expedient of social life. Rather it would be viewed as ancient thinkers like Plato and Aristotle viewed politics in general, as part of an aspirational search for the objective Good.

PROBLEMS OF MODERN DEMOCRACIES

But if democracy is the political response to the age of pluralism and uncertainty, we should expect its problems as well as its virtues to be connected with the lost moral innocence that accompanies pluralism and uncertainty. This expectation is confirmed by the many problems facing modern democracies, according to their critics. On the moral side, the critics say, democracies encourage excessive pluralism, social division, permissiveness, relativism, skepticism, and other attitudes that tend to erode the spiritual center.[1] On the political side, there is a growing chorus of criticism about the way democratic politics is carried on in media-driven societies. Political systems in which lobbyists dominate the halls of legislatures, politicians spend more than half their time soliciting campaign financing, political campaigns are shallow and superficial, and discussion of issues often gives way to manipulation by public-relations experts—to name but a few problems—seem to have strayed far from the ethical ideals of democracy.

As a consequence of these and other problems, many observers of American politics, including a good many disenchanted politicians and ordinary citizens, believe that the U.S. political process is not working as it was supposed to and are wondering whether it needs an overhaul. Syndicated newspaper columns by David Broder, Michael Oreskes, and others have chronicled the growing disenchantment, as have recent books by Elizabeth Drew (*Politics and Money*), E. J. Dionne (*The War against Public Life: Why Americans Hate Politics*), and William Grieder

(Who Will Tell the People?).[2] Active and retiring legislators concede that the system is frustrating and increasingly ineffective,[3] and distinguished citizens call for radical changes, while many ordinary citizens express disenchantment with politics as usual.[4] Meanwhile, various institutes for public policy studies[5] and distinguished political scientists like Robert Dahl *(Democracy and Its Critics)*, Thomas Cronin *(Direct Democracy)*, and James Fishkin *(Democracy and Deliberation)* have made proposals or written books seriously considering alternatives to the present system;[6] and popular works, like John Naisbitt's *Megatrends* and Alvin Toffler's *The Third Wave*, argue that representative democracy as we have known it is becoming increasingly obsolete and will be unable to cope with the challenges of the twenty-first century.[7] The time has come, they believe, to "rethink the democratic architecture of tomorrow . . . from the ground up."[8]

Whether we are willing to go this far, it seems clear that democracy's current problems deserve a closer look. If democracy is indeed related to new ways of thinking about values and ethics, as I suggested above, then thinking about the future of democracy is very much a part of the ethical quest. We may agree with Churchill that democracy is the worst form of government, "except for all the others," and yet wonder how it might be better. For democracy is not one form of government, but many. There are many forms that rule of the people might take and some may be better—morally and politically—than others.

PLATO'S CRITICISMS:
IMAGE POLITICS AND FAILURES OF LEADERSHIP

Criticisms of democracy are not new and they have often had ethical as well as political overtones. In fact, most of the modern criticisms were anticipated centuries ago by one of the greatest thinkers of the original Axial Period. The writings of Plato, especially his *Republic*, contain some of the most penetrating criticisms of democracy ever written and they provide an excellent framework for understanding the current problems of democracy.[9] (Plato's own alternative ideal society has failings worse than democracy; but that is another story we will put aside for a moment.)

First, Plato argued that (1) *democracies encourage mediocre leadership* because leaders in a democracy must constantly court the favor of the people to stay in power.[10] In democratic systems the premium for successful leadership will be put on popularity with the masses rather than on wisdom and training, and the most popular leaders will be those most like ordinary citizens, that is, those who are not outstanding. Also, in a democracy, he argued that (2) *leaders must pander to the wishes of the electorate* rather than do what they think is right. If they do not satisfy the wishes of the people, they will not be returned to office.

As a consequence of these features, (3) *democratic leaders are tempted to focus on short-term goals at the expense of the long-term needs of society.* What happens ten or twenty years down the road will not effect the next election, which must be their primary concern. The difficulty of getting leaders to deal forthrightly with long-term policies is no accident of democratic politics, according to Plato; indeed, it is built into the system. They cannot afford to choose policies that have long-term benefits but cause short-term pain. For similar reasons, he argued, in democratic societies leaders would be more inclined to give things to the people than to ask something of them in the form of sacrifices, a consequence being that (4) *democracies have an inbuilt tendency to spend more than they take in,* by giving people what they want in the present and letting the costs be paid by future generations who have no present vote.

Plato also thought that democratic citizens would be more taken up by the "images" or "appearances" of things rather than their true substance, such that (5) *democratic political debate over time would become more superficial and focus less on substantive issues.* What we would call (6) *image politics would come to dominate the electoral process,* with more emphasis on how leaders looked and spoke rather than on what they said. Plato had no inkling, of course, about modern media and the extremes to which these predictions would be taken.[11] But he was well aware that (7) *a society which focused on images rather than issues was easy prey to manipulation by those more interested in winning arguments and manipulating beliefs than finding the truth*—a society in which the electoral process could be dominated by media consultants, advertising agents, and public relations experts.[12] (In Plato's day, they were called "Sophists.")

The excessive image-consciousness of democracies touches on deeper themes of Plato's work. The fundamental distinction of the *Republic* is the distinction between "appearance" and "reality" (how things seem to us versus how they really are). It is illustrated by what is perhaps the most famous image in all of Western philosophy, the Allegory of the Cave in book 7.[13] Ordinary experience, according to the allegory, is like living in a cave in which we only see the appearances of things, not the reality that lies outside. For Plato, all imperfect societies fail because they favor appearance over reality and so lose their way in the search for wisdom; and democracy is especially flawed in this regard. Because political debate in a democracy must aim at swaying the populace, which loves images and is impatient with reasoning about complex issues, political debates become superficial and focus less on real issues (5), elections emphasize how candidates look and speak

(6), clever people learn how to manipulate a public that lacks the wisdom to see through the images to the reality beneath (7), and long-term goals give way to short-term satisfactions (3). Such a society is slowly consumed by its own illusions and eventually begins to entertain the ultimate illusion, that one can have anything one wants without paying or sacrificing for it (4).

ILLUSIONS AND DESIRES:
SPECIAL INTERESTS AND THE COMMON GOOD

The image consciousness of democracies leads Plato to several other criticisms. He also thought that in democracies (8) *more emphasis would be placed upon emotion in public debate than upon reason.* Images and appearances appeal to the emotions; it takes a disciplined exercise of the mind to see behind the appearances to the reality. But democracy is not good at instilling discipline of any sort, he felt, especially intellectual discipline. It favors the emotional appeal of images and gut reactions over patient discussion of issues, just as it favors winning the argument over finding the truth.

The image consciousness of democratic societies spills over into other areas of life. In democracies, Plato held, (9) *people tend to eat poorly because a premium is put on the appearance (for example, the look and the taste of food) rather than on real (nutritive) value*—a criticism that has a contemporary ring.[14] While you can see that an orange on a grocery shelf is brightly colored and unspotted, you cannot see how rich in vitamins and minerals it may be. Nor can you see that the bright color is due in part to synthetic chemicals that colorize it and its lack of spots are due to pesticides and preservatives, some of which have been absorbed into the fruit. What it appears to be is not what it is; and in the marketplace, as in politics, those who live in a world of appearances are ripe for manipulation.

Illusions also eventually undermine habits of rationality. Consider that we put synthetic lemon juice in small, plastic, lemon-shaped containers to spray on foods, while putting real lemon juice in floor-wax. And we scarcely notice how bizarre this is. If one lives with appearances long enough, Plato suggests, they come to seem natural and ordinary—the reality itself. Something has to remind us that we are living in a cave. The final result of this process, as he portrays it, is that illusions come to affect our desires. Influenced by appearances and images, people begin to want more of everything, and the leaders, pandering to the public, tend to give them what they want. The result is that (10) *democracies are prone to unrestrained growth and a factionalism of competing special interests seeking to influence leaders in order to fulfill private desires at the expense of the public good.* In a contemporary context, the power of lobbyists, special interest groups, and money in politics would be the natural outcome of this criticism. Finally, the factionalism that Plato feared could lead to what the modern world has regarded as the most obvious problem of democracy, the danger of a (11) *tyranny of the majority.*

LOSS OF SHARED VALUES

Most of the above criticisms of democracy are "political" in nature. To them, Plato adds a few others of a "social" nature[15] that reflect concerns about the moral foundations of society discussed in chapter 5. One of the gravest dangers of democratic societies, he believed, was that (12) *people would gradually lose a sense of shared values—values that are held in common and upon which all agree.* Since democracies make the values and desires of individual citizens sovereign, and individual values and desires vary, each person will want to go his or her own way, do his or her own thing, and no longer would there be agreement about basic values. For similar reasons, democracies tend to be permissive and (13) *citizens put more emphasis on rights to do as they please while being less willing to accept responsibilities or make sacrifices for the common good.*

These trends in turn increase the possibility for (14) *social disorder,* (15) *rising rates of crime,* (16) *distrust of authority,* and (17) *a large generation gap* (because young people would not necessarily share the values of their parents and would want to do their own thing). Finally, in the absence of shared values, Plato held that (18) *there would be a value vacuum at the center of democratic societies that would be filled by a succession of intellectual and social fads and fashions* which would capture public attention for short periods of time before giving way to others. Citizens might wander from one thing to another, from Eastern religions to primal scream therapy, yuppie indulgence to the latest diet fads, in the attempt to fill this vacuum. In Plato's words, for the democratic personality, "one day it's wine, women and song, the next water to drink and a strict diet; one day it's hard physical training, the next indolence and careless ease. . . . Often [the democratic personality] takes to politics and keeps jumping to his feet saying or doing whatever comes into his head. . . . There's no order and restraint in his life [but] he reckons his way of living is pleasant, free and happy" (p. 381).

WHO GUARDS THE GUARDIANS?

There is much in this indictment of democratic character and politics worth pondering today, whether or not we agree with every point. It need not lead us to abandon democracy, but may help to explain why Churchill could say that democracy is the worst form of government, before adding "except for all the others." One of those other forms of government is Plato's own alternative, which has failings of an opposite kind. His ideal state lies on the authoritarian side of the political ledger, though it is meant to be a benign authoritarianism of the wise. He envisions a class of "guardians" to run the state, persons who are not elected by the populace, but who are selected by an elaborate educational program designed to train them in wisdom and virtue as well as technical competence.

In such a guardianship system (in direct opposition to the democratic pattern), values flow downward from the rulers who are supposed to be educated to a vision of the Good that is imposed on the rest of society. And therein lies the problem. Can one guarantee that the rulers so educated will be wise and good as well as competent? If not, one would hesitate to abandon the checks and balances of electoral government. Plato had enormous faith in higher education and founded the first university (his "Academy"), modeled on the *Republic* and dedicated to training leaders. But more than two thousand years of hindsight have taught us to be more cautious about what higher education can accomplish. It can produce competent and knowledgeable leaders; but wisdom, goodness, and virtue are more complicated matters, which it can teach, but not guarantee.

There is a good reason for this limitation, which is implicit in the arguments of chapter 4. Those arguments implied that the "Good"—in the objective and universal sense sought by Plato and required for wisdom and virtue (we called it objective worth)—cannot be an object of certain knowledge for human beings, but only an object of *aspiration;* and, because of that, the existence of an objective Good is consistent, for all we know, with there being more than one good way to live. This should make us suspicious of any political group that claims the right to impose its vision of the good on all, no matter how "expertly" trained. The proper question for any such group therefore would be the question posed for Plato's scheme by the Latin poet Juvenal: *Quis custodes ipsos custodiet?* (Who guards the guardians?). Thus we see that a central theme of chapter 4 has important political consequences: the idea that absolute value is a matter of aspiration and not of certain knowledge favors democracy—with all its flaws—over authoritarian alternatives.

THREE CENTRAL PROBLEMS

But if Plato does not convince us to abandon democracy, he does draw attention to its inherent flaws and challenges us to see what can be done about them. Earlier I mentioned distinguished political theorists and futurists, as well as ordinary citizens and politicians, who think these problems have reached critical dimensions in current democratic societies. Of these problems, three central ones tend to emerge in modern debates, which effectively sort Plato's criticisms into three groups.

1. *Direct (or Participatory) versus Indirect (or Representative) Democracy.* The influence of special interests, lobbyists, and money has seriously impaired traditional representative government, giving rise to the widespread feeling that elected representatives no longer effectively serve ordinary citizens or the general interest as they should. (Compare Plato's criticisms nos. 1, 2, 10, 11, and 13.) Critics who focus on this problem argue for more control of special interests, lobbyists, and money and for more direct citizen involvement in the political process.

2. *Informed Political Discourse and Debate versus Distorted and Manipulated Political Discourse.* In a recent *New York Times* report on American politics, Michael Oreskes reports that "politicians in both parties say government is being crippled by a new superstructure of politics that makes ideas harder to discuss and exalts public opinion over leadership. . . . Domestic politics has become so shallow . . . that ideas and leadership needed to guide [the country] in a rapidly changing world are not being produced."[16] Compare this to Plato's criticisms nos. 5, 6, 7, and 8—emphasis on the superficial in political debate, image politics, appeals to emotion rather than reason, and the manipulation of political discourse by consultants and experts.

3. *Long-Range Goals and the Common Good versus Short-Term Gains and Private Interests.* Since politicians cannot usually afford to choose policies that have long-term benefits but cause short-term pain, or policies that serve the common good while harming particular interest groups, or policies that take from the electorate rather than giving to it, gridlock exists when it comes to long-range planning for a host of pressing problems such as energy, environment, crime, health, welfare, and others. (Compare Plato's criticisms nos. 2, 3, 4, and 10.)

It is worth noting that these three problems are ethical and not merely political. If democracy gives political expression to the ideas of openness and respect for the values of every person, then it requires fair input of all into the political system and a concern for the common good. Since these three problems thwart both goals, addressing them is as much a part of the task of "public morality" as anything discussed in chapter 5.

ATTEMPTS AT REFORM:
MONEY IN POLITICS AND DIRECT DEMOCRACY

There have been many suggested solutions for the above three problems, but the most well-known ones are controversial or represent only partial solutions, or both. Some new thinking about the "democratic architecture of tomorrow" is definitely in order on this subject. To curb the influence of special interests, lobbyists, and money on representative government (problem 1), we have had proposals for (1) public financing of elections and for (2) controls on campaign contributions by individuals and groups (contributions by political action committees [or PACs]).[17] Both of these initiatives have cleared up some abuses and we especially need more of (2), but neither has been the panacea its proponents had promised.

The recent upswell of interest in (3) term limitations is another reaction to the unresponsiveness of representative government (problem 1). But term limitation is a two-edged sword. It might make elected officials more responsive to citizen input in the short term, but it is not likely to do much to curb the influence of lobbyists and money. In addition, it does not seriously address problem 2 (image politics and avoidance of difficult issues); and it could thwart a solution to problem 3 (long-range planning) by reducing the institutional memory and experience of elected officials, as many of its critics have noted. Whatever the actual merits of term limitations, however, the growing movement for them does send a powerful message to incumbent politicians to start paying more attention to the public interest—a message well worth communicating.

Another significant movement of recent American politics, sending a similar message, also addresses problem 1. This is the movement toward deciding more political issues by (4) Initiative and Referendum. Here is an exercise in direct (or participatory) democracy that allows citizens to put measures to the direct vote of the electorate after collecting a suitable number of signatures (Initiative) or vote to approve or repeal a law proposed or enacted by a legislature (Referendum).[18] The Initiative and Referendum movement has crept up on us in recent years, beginning in California in 1978 with tax-limiting Proposition 13 and now spreading to more than half the states. But we should not miss its significance. It is a symptom of voter dissatisfaction with normal representative government (problem 1) and an attempt to circumvent the legislatures—a movement toward direct, rather than indirect, democracy. The issues submitted are often ones that legislators themselves are too timid to address for fear of angering powerful constituents or contributors.

Yet Initiative and Referendum also have limitations as solutions to democracy's problems. In his recent book *Direct Democracy* political theorist Thomas E. Cronin offers a balanced assessment of the history and recent fortunes of Initiative and Referendum in U.S. politics, concluding that they can be useful tools in the democratic process, provided that the laws governing them are carefully crafted to avoid abuses.[19] But he also takes note of many problems that can be mitigated, but not eliminated. Ordinary voters are often ill-informed about the complex issues put to them, and usually decide on the basis of emotion and immediate reactions. Nor are the voters better informed by the campaigns for various propositions that are usually "explained" by means of thirty-second TV spots and on billboards. Proposals are often ill-drawn and appeal to public passions. Higher income voters and the more educated are often favored by the process; and special interests with a stake in the vote usually get into the fray with massive amounts of advertising, thereby obscuring the public interest.

In sum, Initiative and Referendum attack some problems of democracy while leaving others virtually untouched. They address problem 1 by providing a greater degree of direct democracy, but they do little to address concerns about superficial, emotional, and manipulated public debate (problem 2) and leave us wondering, as a consequence, whether the common good and long-term goals will be better served (problem 3). In addition, Initiative and Referendum do not really address the problems of special interests and money that are a part of problem 1. Special interest money is merely diverted in Initiative and Referendum from campaign contributions and lobbyists who patrol the halls of legislatures to media consultants who design advertising campaigns. In either case, it often turns out that the greater the amount of money invested, the greater the chances of victory.

TELEDEMOCRACY AND ITS LIMITATIONS

More-radical suggestions for direct or participatory democracy are contained in the recent interest in what has come to be called (5) "teledemocracy." Many see hope in modern communications technology for greater citizen involvement in the political process. Public debate and information about social issues is immediately available to virtually every citizen through TV and other media; and interactive systems make it possible for citizens to participate in public discussions with policymakers, experts, and other citizens. In his book *Video Democracy* broadcaster Richard Hollander foresees a future in which local governments have been replaced by direct democracy through cable television and computer hookups.[20] In his imaginary Mediaville, the city council is abolished and its chamber converted into a TV studio to which the whole town has been wired for two-way interaction. Hollander imagines citizens deciding on their own to make proposals and vote on them through the system. It would be participatory democracy in the true sense.

But critics of teledemocracy are not as optimistic as Hollander. In a book published by the Roosevelt Center for American Policy Studies, *Teledemocracy: Can Technology Protect Democracy?*, F. Christopher Arterton reports on a study of thirteen local experiments in the political use of communications technology, including examples described by Hollander.[21] Arterton concludes that while citizen awareness and access can be improved by electronic systems, the systems cannot bypass representative government to achieve direct democracy for two reasons. First, it takes a lot of work and expense to bring decision making into living rooms through cable TV and phone lines, and those who pay the costs or arrange for the systems want a say in setting the agenda. Influential groups often arrange to wield disproportionate amounts of power in the process. Second, most of the public lacked the time, energy, and interest to shoulder the daily burdens of making public policy decisions in their homes. Arterton concluded that too few citizens have the time or interest "to make plebiscites a feasible means of policy making" (p. 89).

In summary, teledemocracy, like other suggestions for direct democracy, fails to address problems of uninformed and distorted public debate (problem 2), and it points to an additional difficulty not previously mentioned. Ordinary citizens seldom have the time or interest to engage in the kind of lengthy deliberation necessary to decide complex social issues. To adapt an Oscar Wilde remark about socialism, a main problem with direct democracy is that it would take up too many Saturday evenings.

PUBLIC DEBATE: THE MINIPOPULUS AND DELIBERATIVE OPINION POLLS

To attack all three problems of democracy, one has to improve the quality of public debate. There have been a number of different suggestions for doing that. Improvements have been suggested in (6) televised debates between candidates, like televised presidential debates, which up to now have been little more than opportunities for short speeches by the candidates. Many observers feel they should be turned into real debates, with tough follow-up questions and candidates capable of questioning each other. More far-reaching is the suggestion of Max Kampelman, Elizabeth Drew, and others[22] that (7) radio and TV networks provide periods of free air time to candidates, as is done in many European countries and Japan, while limiting the amount of additional time they can buy on their own. Critics of free air time say it will be resisted by broadcasters, who are in business to sell commercial time, not to give it away. Yet in Europe and Japan the public sees nothing improper about free air time and broadcasters have accommodated themselves to it. The United States is behind the times on this matter and it is one thing that should be done, whatever else is done.

But many feel that even these proposals only scratch the surface of the problem of public debate. In *Democracy and Its Critics* distinguished political theorist Robert Dahl says that the central problem of modern democracies has never been solved and likely will not be solved without some radically new thinking.[23] The problem is how genuine rule of the people, with adequate citizen involvement, can be extended from small societies of the size, say, of the ancient Greek city-state, to large modern nation states. "If the democratic process is not firmly anchored in the judgments of the [people]," Dahl says, "then the system will drift toward quasi-guardianship," in Plato's sense of rule by knowledgeable elites. The key question thus becomes, "How can we get an *attentive* public that represents the *informed* judgment of the people themselves" in large modern democratic states? (p. 339). Teledemocracy and Initiative and Referendum provide neither an attentive public that can give the necessary time, nor an informed public that chooses wisely. In response, Dahl says:

> The idea seems self contradictory. Yet it need not be. Suppose an advanced democratic country were to create a "minipopulus" consisting of perhaps a thousand citizens randomly selected out of the entire [populace]. Its task would be to deliberate, for a year perhaps, on an issue and then to announce its choices. The members of a minipopulus could "meet" by telecommunications. One minipopulus could decide on the agenda of issues, while another might concern itself with a major issue. . . . A minipopulus could exist at any level of government—national, state or local. It could be attended—again by telecommunications—by an advisory committee of scholars and specialists and by an administrative staff. It could hold hearings, commission research, and engage in debate and discussion. (p. 340)

This quotation comes on the next-to-last page of a very long book, and Dahl says very little else about it, despite the fact that this suggestion seems to be his ultimate solution to the problems of representative versus direct democracy. The suggestion certainly raises many questions. Many of the problems of teledemocracy seem to arise once again for this proposal along with other problems; and it is also not clear how such a system would be related to the normal representative system of government.

Yet Dahl's suggestion is worth pondering, not only because it is the final suggested solution of a respected long-time student of democracy, but because similar ideas have been mentioned in recent years by other political theorists and constitutional scholars. Variations on Dahl's minipopulus idea are discussed by Toffler in *The Third Wave*. One variation, suggested by constitutional scholar Theodore Becker, would have citizen groups acting in something like the manner of juries to oversee legislatures or other branches of government.[24] Other variations would have them playing various advisory roles.

The latest variation on the minipopulus idea, suggested by James Fishkin in *Democracy and Deliberation*,[25] has received some popular attention. Fishkin suggests that we add to our primary election process what he calls a "deliberative opinion poll."

> Imagine a new beginning to the process of selecting a President . . . a national sample of the citizen voting-age population is transported to a single site for at least several days. . . . [where] they interact in person with the major candidates. . . . Democratic delegates go to the Democratic events, Republicans to the Republican events; independents are asked beforehand to choose one or the other. In some portions . . . the entire convention meets together. Some of the candidate appearances before these groups are individual and some are in debate formats. Many of the occasions for questioning and interaction are broadcast on national television. . . . [At the end] the delegates are polled on their preferences on both the candidates and the issues. (p. 2)

Fishkin envisages such a deliberative opinion poll being conducted before the first presidential primaries in Iowa and New Hampshire, providing a more-than-superficial reaction to the candidates by a representative sample of citizens, which would then inform the subsequent primary campaigns. A version of the idea was considered for the 1992 presidential campaign by PBS, though it was not carried through for lack of funding. The idea was to schedule a "National Issues Convention" organized on the deliberative opinion poll model, to be broadcast on national television, in which the candidates would interact with a national sample of six hundred delegates representing the entire electorate.

Fishkin's deliberative opinion polls are variations of the minipopulus idea, with some of the problems of the latter eliminated. They attempt to provide an "attentive" and "informed" body of citizens, who can give full time to the candidates and issues in a way that teledemocracy and Initiative and Referendum do not. Fishkin argues that many potential problems, like getting a genuinely representative sampling of citizens and getting people to participate, can be handled. It remains to be seen whether such an idea would work and how it might impact on electoral politics.

EXPANDING DEMOCRATIC POSSIBILITIES

But Fishkin also notes that, even if successful, deliberative opinion polls would be "only one step" toward curing the problems of deliberation in mass democracies. "In a time of experimentation with democracy around the world," he says, "we need a new research agenda for the general class of innovations that might bring 'power to the people' under conditions where [they] could exercise their power more thoughtfully. . . . Although we have experimented . . . with . . . democratic institutions, the experimentation has . . . been driven by an overly constrained vision of democratic possibilities" (p. 12).

I think he is right about this; and in the spirit of such a "new research agenda" for expanding democratic possibilities, I want to add some suggestions that go beyond the suggestions so far considered, yet also address the three problems of modern democracy we isolated. Deliberative opinion polls, and most other recently suggested reforms, apply to the process of electing candidates to political office, but they say little about what happens after the elections. Yet problems about special interests, lobbyists, money, legislating for the common good, pork-barrel spending, and a host of other ills are as much, if not more, a part of legislating and governing as of political campaigning. *Real reform that attacks the three problems of democracy will not succeed unless it addresses the way decisions are made in a democracy as well as how the decision makers are elected.*

We need some radical thinking about this truth if democratic institutions are to survive and flourish in the twenty-first century. The first of my own none-too-modest suggestions is this: at local, state, and even national levels, why not consider combining the minipopulus idea, or deliberative opinion poll, with Initiative and Referendum? Initiative and Referendum are already widely used in states to bypass legislatures that are too timid and afraid to deal with tough issues for fear that powerful interest groups will be angered and throw them out of office. People themselves are being asked to decide such issues. But Initiative and Referendum have problems because the populous in general has limited time and interest to follow patient debate on complex issues, which leaves room for manipulation of the process by special interests.

Suppose, however, that after the initial stages of Initiative and Referendum (the gathering of signatures to place an Initiative on the ballot or to hold a Referendum on a controversial law passed by a legislature), the issue was presented to a body of citizens chosen by lot according to the methods suggested by Dahl, Fishkin, and others to ensure a representative sampling of the citizenry.[26] Such citizens would function as a jury listening to the testimony from citizen groups and legislators on both sides of the issue and render the kind of informed verdict that is not possible for the populous at large. To provide the proper sampling, such citizen juries (let us call them "Citizen Commissions") might consist of twelve to twenty people at the local level, forty to fifty at the state level, and several hundred at the national level (the actual numbers are negotiable), and once in place they might deal with several issues at once. Service on them would be a civic duty, like jury duty in general, but income would be paid to the citizen jurors for the time lost on jobs. This system would cost money. But we will see in a moment how such Citizen Commissions (at local, state, and national levels) could actually save taxpayers more money than they would cost, by providing checks and balances on the spending of legislatures.

Unlike elected officials, these citizen jurors would not have to be looking over their shoulders at all times to ensure that they did not offend powerful interest groups. They would not have to worry about reelection, soliciting campaign contributions, or satisfying lobbyists or heavy campaign contributors because after their days or weeks of service are over they would return to their normal lives. Unlike ordinary citizens, they would have the time to be the "attentive" and "informed" voters that Dahl required to make democracy work. To limit outside influences on them, it would be made a serious crime, akin to jury tampering, to lobby or to even approach (much less offer money or inducements to) any citizen from the moment of their selection to the end of their service. Undoubtedly, jurors will have biases and interests of their own, but if there are sufficient numbers of them to balance each other, if they listen for hours to all sides of the issues, and if they understand that their job is to render a fair judgment for the common good, there is every chance they will come closer to doing this than our present legislatures. Juries, at present, usually rise to the occasion and we should expect the same from such Citizen Commissions.

CITIZEN COMMISSIONS AND
THE PROBLEMS OF PLATO AND DAHL

The above idea of citizen juries, or commissions, is one I concocted twenty years ago as a purely philosophical exercise while teaching Plato's *Republic*, in an attempt to answer his criticisms of democracy. How could we get genuine philosophical debate in a democracy, I asked, so that serious issues of the common good and long-term national needs could be fairly addressed without the distortions, manipulations, and sophistries of political debate that Plato had so presciently described? And how could we do this in large nation states with millions of busy citizens rather than in the small city-states familiar to Plato? This problem had troubled Rousseau and many other thinkers besides Plato; and we saw that Dahl calls it *the* central problem that must be addressed by democracies of the future.[27]

Reflecting on it, I came to the conclusion that the closest one could come to squaring this circle was through citizen juries of the above kind chosen by lot to be representative samples of the citizenry at large rather than being elected. These citizen bodies would not *replace* elected officials but would provide checks and balances on legislatures, presidents, governors, city councils, and so on, through Initiative and Referendum procedures or in other ways yet to be discussed. They would be empowered to play the role of Plato's "philosopher kings and queens" for a few days or weeks or months, whatever period deemed necessary, checking and balancing the actions of elected officials, and would then return to being ordinary citizens after their service.

At the time I first came to this conclusion, some twenty years ago, these ideas were a purely philosophical exercise, designed to get students thinking about Plato and the issues of "guardianship versus democracy." I thought the ideas too visionary to be taken seriously at the time—though perhaps in fifty to a hundred years or more they might have their day. But now it seems that with our democratic system unable to cope with its massive problems, and distinguished political theorists and constitutional scholars like Dahl, Fishkin, and Becker proposing similar ideas, the climate has changed.

In a recent article in the *Wall Street Journal* Stephen Adler, the *Journal's* editor for law, has gone so far as to suggest that Congress and state legislatures might be chosen by lot in the manner by which the ancient Athenians chose their governing assemblies. He thinks this would be an improvement over our present system of electing officials and he makes the same positive points about citizen jurors that I made in the previous section. Adler's idea of *replacing* Congress and state legislatures with citizens chosen by lot is certainly radical, and it is surely a sign of the times that it should be suggested by an editor of the *Wall Street Journal*. My own proposals are less radical even than the *Journal* editor's (which gives me hope), but they are in the same vein. My thought was to use citizen jurors chosen by lot to oversee and supplement legislatures rather than to replace them. The political system would stay more or less intact, but there would be greater accountability of elected officials to the people.

Another indication of movement in this direction is provided by the Jefferson Center for New Democratic Processes in Minnesota, which has experimented over the past few years with "policy juries" of twelve or more citizens that have grappled with specific issues such as agriculture, water policy, organ transplants, and so on.[28] The center suggests that such juries might function as advisory bodies at local, state, or national levels. Ned Crosby, president of the center, has also proposed electoral juries of citizens to monitor presidential elections around the country, weighing evidence and correcting distortions in the campaigns.

The convergence of such ideas is most likely not an accident. For I believe that anyone who seriously thinks through the standard criticisms of democracy from Plato to its modern critics, along with Dahl's problem of how to make democracy work in large nation states, will come to the conclusion that some variation of the Citizen Commission idea is the most promising way to go.

POWER TO THE PEOPLE

Here is another especially fruitful use of Citizen Commissions, which is actually the specific proposal I made twenty years ago. Its goal is to attack what Plato regarded as one of the most difficult of all the failings of democracies: the tendency of elected officials to pander to the desires of citizens, giving them what they want in the form of benefits while being reluctant to ask for sacrifices in taxes or other forms. The result of this tendency in our times is pork-barrel politics, overspending, massive deficits, and a host of related failings. Recent controversial suggestions for dealing with this endemic problem at the national level have included a balanced budget amendment and line-item veto power for the president, such as many state governors have. Both these proposals have their drawbacks, which surfaced in the public debates about them, though both are still alive as proposals. For example, most people believe that line-item veto power at the national level would tilt the delicate balance of power too much toward the executive. But rather than rehearse all the difficulties of these proposals, let us consider an alternative. Suppose we retain line-item veto power, but do not give it to the president. Suppose we give it to the *people* instead!

Imagine a body of 435 ordinary citizens chosen randomly, not elected, to be brought to Washington for a period of months to serve as a jury of citizens—a Citizen Commission—considering the national budget with line-item veto power over it. The selected citizens might be put up with their families at Camp David or some other suitable place in the manner of a partially sequestered jury for the months in question, with schools provided for their children. Their regular salaries would be paid by the government, with perhaps an additional bonus (you may have your own suggestions about this and other details) and their employers would be required by law to reinstate them in their original jobs without loss of status or seniority when their months of service were over. (A new group would be selected each year.) The idea would be to make it an honor and patriotic duty to serve in such a body, and for employers to go along—something similar to being called up to active duty from the military reserves (though these people would be going to war against government irresponsibility, not foreign invaders).

Citizens in special circumstances could be excused from serving (new mothers, the sick, persons starting up new business), but the exceptions would be far fewer than they currently are for jury duty because families could be brought along and salaries would be paid. The costs for such a commission could be several hundred million dollars a year, but the line-item savings are likely to be in the billions, when one considers the pork-barrel and special-interest legislation they would oversee—not counting the intangible benefits of greater citizen involvement and empowerment in the legislative process.

The number of citizens is negotiable, but the suggested number (435) has an obvious point. The idea is to account for regional variation by having the same number from each state as there are representatives in the House of Representatives from each state. Other requirements are also negotiable but should probably be kept to a minimum—say, a division of the populace into four income groups, from the most wealthy to the poorest, with proportional representation according to the numbers of citizens in each income group. With random selection, this should be enough to get proportional representation by gender, race, ethnicity, income, and the like, without requiring quotas. (Again, the details are negotiable.)

The selection process could be overseen by the federal judiciary, led by a federal judge with a staff appointed for one year by the Supreme Court, to make sure the selection process was fair and resulted in a representative group (there would be various other safeguards for this as well, such as Fishkin has outlined for his deliberative opinion polls).

Federal law would make it a serious offense, akin to jury tampering, to approach or lobby any member from the moment of selection, as indicated earlier. Keep in mind that we are talking about 435 citizen jurors. A lobbyist might get to a few of them, but that would be a small number in a group of 435, and it would be a dangerous game for any lobbyist to play. How long would he have before one honest citizen turned him in? If a lobbyist gets to very many without finding an honest juror to turn him in, then maybe we ought to give up on democracy after all! Note also that these citizens are not under the time-consuming constraints of elected officials, who often spend more than 50 percent of their time soliciting campaign contributions for their next election and engaging in public relations for the benefit of constituents and contributors. Their only job is to listen to the issues and decide as a jury would decide. Years later, they may tell their grandchildren about the all-too-brief time when they were in Washington at the center of power.

CITIZEN DELIBERATION: BEYOND IMAGE POLITICS

Of crucial importance is how such a Citizen Commission would actually function. It seemed evident to me from the start that citizen bodies overseeing legislatures should not function as legislative bodies themselves, but as *juries,* listening to evidence on all sides of each issue and rendering a verdict. The idea is to minimize grandstanding and emotional appeals, and to stick to the issues and facts. In addition, the group would, for the most part, not listen to *speeches* in support of one or another side, but to *witnesses* who would answer questions and be subject to cross examination. The citizens would then subsequently deliberate about each item among themselves. The entire proceedings could be televised (on C-Span, no doubt) and the text of its deliberations would be publicly available through the Library of Congress. The Congress would still make the laws and would submit a budget, and the president would continue to have veto power over the whole budget. But this citizens group would have an additional line-item veto power.

For each item on the agenda (or related set of items), sponsoring and supporting senators and representatives would agree on a few members of their staffs to represent that item before the Citizen Commission. Simultaneously, senators and representatives who had been opposed to that budget item would appoint staff to represent the opposition to it before the commission. These staff appointees would play roles analogous to lawyers for the prosecution and defense in a jury trial. They would call and question witnesses (who might be experts, government officials, representatives of citizen groups, and the like) in support or against the item in question, but *all witnesses would be subject to cross examination by the opposing staff* (and what they say, of course, would be on permanent record). Citizen jury members themselves could submit questions in writing for the witnesses. Supporting or opposing senators or representatives could also appear (as well as members of the president's staff or cabinet) but again as witnesses only, and their testimony would also be subject to cross examination. The idea is to make it as difficult as possible for anyone to play fast and loose with the facts, without perjuring or making a fool of themselves. Grandstanding testimony would also be discouraged by the rules and would prove counterproductive. Having to listen for hours, citizen jurors are not likely to suffer bloated or irrelevant testimony lightly. The testimony would become everything a campaign speech is not.

All of this would be presided over by the federal judge and his or her staff, the same ones who were appointed to select the Citizen Commission in the first place. The judge would set (lengthy, but finite) time limits on total testimony for each item (or set of items) so that the representing staffs would choose their witnesses carefully and avoid repetitious testimony, and the judge (with some associate judges taking turns) would preside over the day-to-day proceedings of the commission. The courtroom rules need not be exactly the same as for jury trials, but they would be similar.

Such details are matters for discussion, but the overall aim should be clear. The goal is to create, to the degree possible, conditions of fair debate and judgment on the *real* issues of the day, by an *impartially* selected group of ordinary citizens, who have the *time* to listen to the different sides of the issue, which time we ordinary citizens do not usually have ("philosopher kings and queens for a day"). How many pork-barrel projects designed by senators and House members for their states or districts would survive the line-item scrutiny of such a body of citizens, if citizen groups opposed to the projects exposed them in such a setting?

No human institution is perfect, but the question is whether a system of this kind would come closer to realizing the democratic ideal of rule by the people than others, including our current system. I recall de Tocqueville's statement in his classic *Democracy in America*, that the citizen jury, especially when it functions in civil (rather than criminal) cases, "is the most energetic means of making the people rule . . . [and] also the most efficacious means of teaching it to rule well."[29] I am extending this idea here, while trying to avoid one of the main problems of the jury system—bias in the selection of jurors.

Since the jurors are randomly selected, lawyers cannot play mind games in the selection process.

CAN THE PEOPLE RULE?

Do ordinary citizens know enough to decide national issues wisely? If the citizenry is as ignorant and as prey to images as it was made out to be by the earlier criticisms of democracy, why should we believe that it would function wisely in these Citizen Commissions? I have wondered about that question for years and now believe that most ordinary citizens are capable of deciding wisely about the vast majority of issues with which legislatures deal, *if they are given the time to be informed about them, and the leisure to deliberate in an impartial setting*. (For the small minority of issues where this is not true, other strategies can be devised.[30]) Citizens for the most part are not stupid, but they are often uninformed or misinformed about public affairs, and so they are easy prey to emotional appeals and manipulation. Make them sit down for hours, give them the background information, let them hear all sides of the issues, and they are capable of making wise decisions about most national and state issues.

If ordinary citizens could do this job, would they be willing to serve? I believe most of them would serve diligently. It could be made a high honor and patriotic duty to serve on such a national commission, as well as an interesting interlude from everyday life, without loss of income or status. (Those selected from among the poor would get a minimum stipend set above their ordinary income. And most selected citizens would make new friends for life.) The families might be feted at the White House when they first arrived and at the end of their tenure. Their swearing-in would be surrounded by ceremony and they would be told that their role was a sacred trust: no less than the public good and future of the country was in their hands.

People rise to such occasions. I recall an incident from the TV series "All In the Family" in which Edith Bunker is picked for jury duty. The jury has been sequestered for weeks because Edith will not agree to a guilty verdict. Edith's roommate and fellow juror is an influential businesswoman who wants to get back to her work. She pleads with Edith to give in, but Edith replies in something like the following fashion: "I don't know about you, Mrs. So and So, you're a very important lady. But in my whole lifetime, no one has ever cared to ask for my opinion on any important social issue. And now that they are asking me, *I'm going to do it right*." I think Fishkin is correct in saying that most citizens would approach the matter this way; and service on such citizen juries itself would promote greater faith in the system.

ETHICS AND POLITICS: FRIENDLY PERSUASION AND THE MORAL SPHERE

This is but one use of citizen juries to oversee government. There are indefinite numbers of other uses at local, state, and federal levels: as advisory bodies to officials at all three levels (as suggested by Dahl and the Jefferson Center), in the electoral process (as suggested by Fishkin), and functioning in conjunction with Initiative and Referendum (as I suggested earlier). At all these levels Citizen Commissions could be used to tackle the tough issues of long-term policy and the common good, which elected officials are often too timid to address for fear of being thrown out of office. In all cases, however, I think the ideal is for them to function in the manner described in the last few sections to get a genuinely fair hearing.

Though short of perfection, I think this ideal comes as close as any known alternative to addressing all three of the problems of democracy listed earlier. First, it provides checks and balances from ordinary citizens on the influences of special interests, lobbyists, and money. Second, it provides for lengthy, reasoned debate about substantive issues which Plato demanded as opposed to the superficial, image-dominated, and manipulated discourse that he criticized. And third, it provides a chance for citizens to decide issues about long-term goals in society and the common good without fear that they will be thrown out of office at the next election.[31]

Solving these problems at the present time, as I suggested, is not merely a political expedient, but an ethical imperative. Where special-interest lobbyists and distorted discourse reign, the moral sphere has broken down, and some people are being treated as means to the ends of others. What we called "friendly persuasion" in chapter 2 has given way to manipulative persuasion. To repair democracy in such circumstances is to repair the moral sphere.

7

Meaning and the
Mosaic of Life: Religion

SECULARIZATION AND
THE PLURALITY OF RELIGIONS

We could scarcely do justice to an account of the ethical quest without addressing the topic of religion, which for many people is inseparable from ethics. Ethics was traditionally grounded in religion and taught in childhood from a religious point of view, as indicated in chapter 3, and this traditional picture of the relation of religion to ethics continues to have a powerful hold on people's minds. Yet it has been challenged by two twentieth-century trends.

First, religion is also caught up in the modern Tower of Babel and faces problems of pluralism and uncertainty. In chapter 1, I noted the claims of Huston Smith and Hans Küng that one of the greatest challenges for religious believers in the twentieth century was coming to grips with the diversity of the world's religions, whose presence in the global community can no longer be ignored or lightly dismissed. Smith, Küng, and others also cite a second major modern challenge to religious belief, the growing "secularization" of life, an indifference to the sacred, brought on by the forces that characterize modern civilizations: science, technology, commercialization, modern media, mass society, and others.[1]

These two challenges to religious belief—secularization and the plurality of religions—are both challenges to the spiritual center. As I noted in chapter 4, people traditionally went in search of the spiritual center by trying to find out who was speaking from the divine, or God's-eye point of view—a sacred book, a prophet, a church, or an inspired person—whose claims about the good and the right would represent the

141

absolute point of view. (As a consequence, religion has been called, with some justification, the "temple of absolutes.") But in a world of conflicting religious voices and texts, each claiming to speak from the divine point of view, this path is clouded; and it is further clouded by the secularization of modern life which leads to suspicion of sacred books, prophets, and churches of all kinds. Thus, secularization and the plurality of religions conspire to erode the spiritual center in religion. When Archie Bunker was asked how he knew a certain message he had received had really come from God, he replied, "because God has one of those voices you never forget." The laughter of the audience made it unnecessary to express the response of a secular culture: "How did you know it was God the first time around?"

As in the case of ethics, pluralism and uncertainty in religion do not necessarily imply relativism. The mere existence of many religions does not exclude the possibility that one is right and others wrong. But the plurality of religions and the forces of secularization cannot help but make people wonder about the truth of their religious beliefs, as well as their ethical beliefs. Like the woman in *Perelandra*, we are led to question our own convictions in the presence of alternatives widely held by others. These similarities between the loss of spiritual center in religion and in ethics may provide clues about how to approach questions of religion in a new Axial Period. The aim of this chapter is to explore that possibility.

LOSING THE SPIRITUAL CENTER: MILOSZ AND SINGER

The concerns many people have about the effects of pluralism and secularization upon religious belief are vividly expressed by another author mentioned in chapter 1, Polish poet and Nobel laureate Czeslaw Milosz. He was mentioned along with Aleksandr Solzhenitsyn as an expatriate from the communist world who rejected communism, but who was also concerned about the loss of spiritual center in the Western world. Milosz's comments about this loss are worth hearing as we begin this discussion of religion. I should confess that I feel a special affinity for Milosz. As a young man in the 1950s I came upon a book of his in the library, translated into English from the Polish as *The Captive Mind*.[2] It is one of the most powerful indictments of communism and totalitarianism ever written—comparable to other great twentieth-century works in this vein, like Arthur Koestler's *Darkness at Noon* and George Orwell's *1984*[3]—and it had a profound influence on the youth that I was. The next time I heard Milosz's name was more than twenty years later, when he was awarded the Nobel Prize for Literature in 1980, and my thoughts reverted back to that book of my youth. Since then I have read some of his translated poetry and a recent work, *The Land of Ulro,*[4] partly biography and partly philosophical reflection, only to find that while the topics have changed, the spiritual affinity continues.

Milosz's actual words about the loss of spiritual center in the modern world are these:

> In the West, there has been a constant race between disintegration and creativity. . . . Freedom allows the new to be borne at the expense of tradition and history. Somehow it happened that the West has been racing for a long time in this way—it gets the prize for creativity. But if you look from a certain perspective, like my compatriot Isaac Bashevis Singer, in his last book, *The Penitent,* there is also an indifference to basic values. The narrator of that novel looks at life in America as sordid and becomes a convert to Orthodox Judaism in the Hasidic quarter of Jerusalem. He returns as it were to a search for the sacred.[5]

It is interesting that Milosz should refer to his compatriot Isaac Bashevis Singer in this connection, another great writer and Nobel prizewinner, originally from Poland. Milosz has more than a little sympathy for Singer's penitent, who is searching for the sacred. As Milosz says,

> I feel a great affinity with Singer because we both come from religious backgrounds, I from Roman Catholicism and he from Judaism. Constantly, we deal with similar metaphysical problems. . . . For me the religious dimension is extremely important. . . . Reverence toward being which can be formulated in strictly religious terms or more general terms, this is the basic value. . . . [Yet while] some people are optimistic about the state of religion today, . . . I am [not among them]. . . . I consider that both believers and nonbelievers are in the same boat as far as the difficulty of translating religion into tangible images. Or maybe we can say that the transformation that is going on in religion reflects something extremely profound in the sense of nihilism. . . . If nihilism, as Nietzsche says, consists in the loss of memory, recovery of memory is the weapon against nihilism.[6]

The recovery of memory that will support what Milosz calls a "reverence toward being" is one of the main tasks of religion, as he sees it, and one way it "protects us against nihilism." One is reminded of Mircea Eliade's statement that the sacred has not entirely been eliminated from modern life, but "survives buried in the subconscious."[7]

In the writing of Nobelists like Milosz and Singer we can discern one of the central features of religion and one of its connections to the spiritual center—its relation to the search for *roots,* for a historically defined sense of belonging in the cosmos (one of the three features of the spiritual center defined in chapter 1). The idea of roots is built into the very meaning of the term "religion" in English, which comes from the Latin *re-ligio* and literally means a "linking backward" to one's origins. There is a connection here to the fact that the religious quest is concerned with the "meaning of life." As linguists and etymologists remind us, the meaning of words and language (like the meaning of life itself) has a historical dimension; it cannot be understood apart from a known past and a projected future. When the penitent of Singer's novel returns to the Hasidic quarter of Jerusalem, he returns to his roots, which are related in his mind to finding meaning in his life. Such a relation is evident in Milosz's thinking about religion as well, though his roots are different from those of Singer's protagonist.

FUNDAMENTALIST RETRENCHMENT
AND HUMANIST SKEPTICISM

Yet the connection between religion and roots—this "linking" backward" to the past—is the source of a great problem about religious belief. The problem is connected to a paradox about the spiritual center, touched on in chapters 1 and 4. If finding the spiritual center means both finding one's roots and finding the absolute or God's-eye point of view, then there is a tension built into the very idea of a spiritual center that religion seeks. For our roots are always particular and local, since we are finite beings whose points of view are limited, whereas religion seeks what is true and right for all times and all points of view.

In the past this tension was eliminated in religion by claiming that one's own roots represented the absolute truth: "Our beliefs are the right ones, our gods the true gods." To find one's roots was therefore to find the absolute. But the situation is not so simple anymore in a world in which we are aware of the diversity of religious roots and the uncertainty of proof in religion. Singer's penitent returns to the Hasidic quarter of Jerusalem and to the ways of his ancestors in order to find the sacred. Milosz speaks nostalgically of his Polish Catholic roots that have played such an important role in freeing his homeland from communist domination. Each has distinctive rituals and beliefs in mind. And the diversity multiplies if we look at the Muslim in Baghdad or Islamabad laying a blanket on the ground and praying toward Mecca; the Buddhist monk sitting cross-legged in his temple; Hindus sacrificing to Shiva, creator and destroyer of universes; evangelical Christians singing hymns; and Sikhs worshiping in the temple of the Granth. Where is the spiritual center here? Members of these faiths are in conflict about the most fundamental beliefs. And if one is right and the others wrong, what avails the others to return to their roots?

The most common reaction of deeply religious people to this modern predicament is retrenchment to an older view. This is the orthodox or fundamentalist reaction, and we know how strong it is in many countries of the world today. "Stick fast to your own beliefs and your own sacred texts," it says, "Brook no deviation from them. Claim they are *the* truth and that you know they are the truth. Try to convince others of this, but do not expect they will agree. Their minds may be clouded by false doctrines and perverted by sinfulness. Their religious perspectives are wrong, after all, so we cannot expect them to be seeing things clearly." To such orthodox and fundamentalist minds (whether they appear in Christian, Jewish, Islamic, or other forms), this is the only way to reclaim the spiritual center. As Bruce Laurence describes their view in a book on fundamentalism throughout the world *(Defenders of God)*, we have to recapture and hold fast to the one Truth, the one set of beliefs, one prophet, one community, one reading of the one Book, or we are lost—indeed the world is lost.[8]

We may sympathize with the plight of some of those who hold such views. Many of them are deeply disturbed by the loss of a spiritual compass and moral decline in the modern world. And they rightly connect this predicament to the loss of a spiritual center. But fundamentalist reactions in religion have the same problems we found to be connected to older ways of searching for absolutes in ethics. In a pluralistic world some group's "Sole Truth" is not that of another, and if each holds to its own view as the absolute truth, viewing the minds of those who disagree as clouded by prejudice or perverted by sinfulness, the world is ripe for every kind of sectarian strife and fanaticism. Moreover, since those who accept such a solution cannot demonstrate the truth of their view and the falsity of all others in a non-question-begging way, their position does not escape the circularity associated with the traditional way of searching for absolutes discussed in chapter 2. Failing this, believers must fall back on a claimed authority of their point of view against all others, thus adding the dangers of authoritarianism to those of fanaticism and sectarian strife.

The opposite reaction to fundamentalist retrenchment in the face of pluralism and uncertainty is a humanist skepticism, or "secular humanism," that rejects religion altogether. Since the Age of Enlightenment humanist skeptics have argued (in the words of Kolakowski quoted in chapter 1) that we "have already suffered enough from struggles between various religions and doctrines whose adherents, on all sides, were deeply convinced of being the only privileged carriers of the absolute truth." The skeptical and secular answer to fanaticism, authoritarianism, and sectarian strife is to reject religion altogether.

UPROOTEDNESS AND UNCERTAINTY

For many people today the strife over religion remains a battle between these two opposing camps, religion's devoted followers, on the one hand, and its cultured despisers, on the other. Many of the rest of us who are sympathetic to religious aspirations, but questioning and often deeply troubled by the modern predicament, sit on the sidelines of this traditional battle between the true believers and the cultured despisers. For us the question is different. We would like to retain a religious faith in some form and pass it on to our children. It is a matter of retaining the spiritual center—of absolute values, human dignity, and rootedness—and hence of giving meaning to our lives. But we wonder how we can retain the intensity of genuine religious conviction held by believers in the past when we can no longer blithely hold the conviction that ours is the one true way, a conviction that enabled our ancestors to believe they had found the spiritual center. Failing to retain this intensity and commitment, we fear that we (and those we love) may escape fanaticism only to end up living in an ice palace made out of frozen sighs.[9] This problem lies at the source of the spiritual dilemmas of the time and it may require us, with fear and trembling, to rethink attitudes toward religion.

The first problem is secularization, the loss of a sense of the sacred and the inability, as Milosz puts it, to find "tangible images" that make religion relevant to modern life. A growing number of persons today are neither believers in nor despisers of religion: they are merely indifferent to it. Secularization has entirely taken hold of them and religion has become a dead issue. Some have never been inside a church or temple, and think of such buildings much as they think of museums or monuments to primitive cultures. Others may remember being taken to religious services when young, but their overwhelming impressions of this experience include a mixture of boredom and doubt about the simplicities they were hearing. Traditional religious beliefs do not measure up to the scientific and intellectual world into which they matured; moreover, the commercial culture has left no place in their lives for the sacred. Now and then they may end up in church for a wedding or a funeral of a family member, friend, or colleague, but on these occasions they have the same feelings as an anthropologist observing the rites and rituals of a primitive tribe. Or they may have thought of going back to religion to rear their children only to find such a thing impossible to accomplish when one lacks belief oneself.

For persons such as these and so many others deeply affected by the secularization of modern life, it might be better if the term "religion" were left out of the present discussion—tainted as it is for them by so many negative associations. But the problem we are discussing will not go away even if we drop the term "religion." It is the problem, identified by Milosz and Singer, of the loss of a spiritual center and the consequent desire to find ultimate meaning in life. If those who are indifferent to religion and its cultured despisers have not entirely given up *this* quest, then they are also part of the present conversation—describe it as they will.

A BROADER QUESTION:
MEANING AND WORTH OF LIFE

For there lies below the surface of what is normally called "religion" the real source of spiritual aspiration: the deeply ingrained human desire to find meaning in life in the sense of a broader purpose than a self-enclosed existence can afford. "Our concept of the absolute," in this sense, says Eliade, "can never be completely uprooted: it can only be debased."[10] Such aspiration manifests itself, among other ways, in the desire for recognition of the objective worth of our accomplishments, as Alan wished for his paintings, in the desire to be objectively worthy of another's love, as in the case of the *Solaris* story, or in the desire to be part of grander projects and quests for the good of humankind (to bring peace or relieve suffering or save the environment). Milosz speaks of such desires as manifesting a "reverence toward being which can be formulated in strictly religious terms or more general terms" and calls it "the basic value . . . [that] protects us against nihilism."

Thus, the first question to be asked about the reasonableness of religious belief is broader than religion. What, if anything, can justify this general attitude of "reverence for being," which inspires belief in and aspiration toward an objective meaning and worth to life that transcend our own personal existence? The drift of modern secular cultures seems to point to a clear answer to this question. The message of secularization is this: "There is no objective reality in which objective meaning and worth could be grounded, no God's-eye point of view because there is no God, no absolute point of view because no absolutes, no point of view of the universe because, as science tells us, the universe is nothing more than a vast physical mechanism with a beginning and perhaps an end."

It follows, according to this secular message, that the only points of view ultimately worth considering are your point of view and mine, and those of anyone else we may care about. The meaning and worth of life can only be found inside one's own life, in projects and undertakings that engage one's interest and bring one personal happiness. It may be true, the message continues, that we often aspire to some higher meaning in life, but this aspiration simply cannot be satisfied. Where such aspiration comes from we know not, but we can guess. It is most likely a by-product of evolution, stemming from our desire for love and the approval of others, coupled with the ability of our minds to imagine an objective point of view—perhaps a cruel joke played on us by evolution, but nothing more.

Max Weber aptly described the development of this secular worldview as the disenchantment of the world.[11] Some of the greatest modern writers, like William Shakespeare, were ahead of their time in recognizing its approach. "We are such stuff as dreams are made of," muses Macbeth, "and our little life is rounded with a sleep." We think of Hamlet as a sincere but melancholy young man, whose indecisiveness is his downfall. But he is one of the earliest figures of modern Western literature to be haunted by the ghosts of a secularized worldview. Hamlet was torn asunder by a burning aspiration for objective worth, on the one hand, and the belief, on the other, that there is no grounding for objective worth in the nature of things. His indecisiveness ("to be or not to be") stems from this deep conflict which now haunts all of civilization; and his melancholy may be called, in the apt expression of philosopher George Graham, a "metaphysical melancholy," the thwarted desire for genuine meaning in life.[12] T. E. Lawrence (known as "Lawrence of Arabia") expressed the point of Graham's metaphysical melancholy several centuries after Shakespeare, when he suggested that the paradox at the heart of modern culture is the longing for great acts combined with a sense of their irrelevance.[13]

SCIENCE AND THE SECULAR WORLDVIEW

Is reason on the side of this secularized worldview? Does secularization undermine the reasonableness of an attitude of "reverence for being," which inspires belief in, and aspiration toward, an objective meaning and worth that transcend our own personal existence? The honest answer, I believe, is that "reason" is not clearly on either side of this debate. It is often said that modern experimental science clearly comes down on the secular side—and science has become definitive in the modern period of what reason and experience allow us to believe.

Science, it is said, supports the secular view described in the previous section—a materialist universe without purpose or ultimate meaning or an Intelligent Designer, which are no longer needed to account for the origins and development of the universe, or of life, or human consciousness. Science has already explained much of what was once mysterious about the universe and ourselves and will inevitably explain more.

Such is the secularist message, we are told, from modern science. But we must distinguish in that message the specific and well-confirmed results of research from the meaning given to the whole. A decent respect for the canons of human reasoning, and an understanding of how science actually works, should convince us that the results of patient scientific experimentation cannot be ignored by those who want to know what is objectively real. But the specifics of the scientific message are one thing; the meaning of the whole is quite another. That meaning can be spelled out in a secular way, as in the above paragraphs, but it need not be, as many of the greatest scientists have realized. Albert Einstein eloquently expressed another view.

> The most beautiful thing that we can experience is the mysterious. It is the source of all true art and science. He to whom this emotion is a stranger, who can no longer pause to wonder and stand, wrapped in awe, is as good as dead; his mind and his eyes are closed. The insight into the mystery of life, coupled though it be with fear, has also given rise to religion. To know that what is impenetrable to us really exists, manifesting itself as the highest wisdom and the most radiant beauty which our dull faculties can comprehend . . . this knowledge, this feeling is at the center of true religiousness. In this sense I belong in the ranks of the devoutly religious men.[14]

This statement is surely on the side of Milosz's "reverence for being," and Einstein makes clear in other writings that he views such reverence as the source of the scientific drive to understand the objective nature of things, in much the same way that we earlier used the scientists' search for the final truth as an example of "searches in the realm of aspiration."

The point to be made is not that Einstein's view is unassailable, but that the specific results of scientific research are consistent with two general attitudes: you can interpret them in a secular way, which is reductive and deflationary, or you can view them in Einstein's way, as part of the quest for objective understanding of a reality that is worthy of reverence. Scientific research does not tell us which side of this divide to stand on; eminent scientists have stood on both sides. This is what is meant by saying that "reason" is not clearly on one side or another in this debate. It is more a question of aspiration than knowledge—a fundamental choice about how we want to view the world or ourselves. We should not be seduced by the thought that on the one side—the secular—lies "science," "reason," cold, clear "logic," and honest "realism" about the way things are, while on the other side—the aspirational—lies "speculation," "emotion," "wishful thinking," and woolly headed "idealism" about the way things ought to be. The fact is that, on a question of this depth, taking a position on either side is a mixture of science and speculation, reason and emotion, logic and desire, realism and idealism.

I once heard an eminent scientist talking about the question of whether intelligent beings lived on other planets scattered throughout the universe, or whether perhaps we humans on this earth were the only intelligent beings in the entire universe. His response was, "It's mind-boggling either way." Indeed, it is. The thought that there are other thinking beings out there in the universe (perhaps trillions of them) of unimaginably different species than our own fills us with wonder and awe. But it is no less difficult to believe that in this vast universe we are the only intelligent species, inhabiting one small planet orbiting an insignificant star in the spiral arm of an undistinguished galaxy in a universe of trillions of stars. It is mind-boggling either way.

WHAT WE CAN KNOW AND
WHAT WE SHOULD ASPIRE TO

So it is with the question of the ultimate meaning of life. Thanks to modern science and scholarship, we have lost our intellectual innocence (as well as our moral innocence) and it is difficult to believe that there is ultimate meaning in life, in religious or any other terms. And yet when we think for a moment about the alternative, we find it no less awesomely difficult to believe that this vast universe, with its many galaxies and stars, its long history and production of living things (at least on one part of it and maybe others) who suffer and die, and some of whom think about their existence, and about the incomprehensible injustices that surround them—it is also awesomely difficult to believe that this is all some bizarre accident with no ultimate meaning whatsoever. It is mind-boggling *either* way—a matter of wonder; and those who think otherwise have lost some of their capacity to wonder. Yet the choice is thrust upon us; we are forced to opt for such a reverence or against it. To avoid the issue is to choose in the negative. This is what William James called a "genuine option" in his famous essay "The Will to Believe."[15]

Recall Kant's claim that there are three great questions we can ask: What can we know?, How should we live?, and What should we aspire to? I argued in chapter 4 that the answer to the second question cannot be entirely based on an answer to the first. We do not know enough to base all the important answers about how to live on what we know. An adequate answer to the question about how to live also requires an answer to the third question about aspiration.

Now the secular response is that we cannot put much faith in aspirations for ultimate meaning and objective worth, because they can be explained away as products of an evolutionary process for survival. But the search for origins is only one way of understanding things. We can also look at our deepest aspirations as clues implanted in us about what we are and where we should be headed, as a signal about our destiny. Recall the root meaning of *aspiration*, mentioned in chapter 4, a "going outward," or "outflowing" of the spirit toward something greater than itself. The secular interpretation of aspiration looks backward to its origin in our evolutionary past. It may be a correct account of how such aspiration arose, so far as it goes, and yet not be the whole truth. We may also look upon the aspiration as telling us something about our future as well as our past, telling us something about the next stages of evolution yet to come. We might look upon it as a clue about (and a "calling" toward) a spiritual journey that lies ahead of us.

So the attitude we take toward our human aspirations falls across the same divide as our attitude toward scientific results in general: we can interpret the aspirations toward objective meaning and worth in a secular way, which is reductive and deflationary, or we can view them in the manner of Einstein and Milosz, as part of the quest for an understanding of a reality that is worthy of reverence. The mind-boggling choice confronts us once again: how we explain human aspirations for ultimate meaning and worth *is part of the choice to go with them or against them*. We have to read our inner selves and decide how important it is to believe in ultimate worth in order to give meaning to our lives. Kant said that the motto of the eighteenth-century Enlightenment was *"Sapere aude,"* "Dare to know."[16] Had we to choose a similar motto for a potential new Axial Period, it should be *"Aspirare aude,"* "Dare to aspire."

A WORLD OF MANY RELIGIONS

But even if we are prepared to cross this divide and go with Milosz's and Einstein's reverence for being, we are still some way from "religion," are we not, at least in the traditional sense of that term? An aspiration toward ultimate meaning isn't worth much unless we can put flesh on it in terms of what exactly to believe and how to live—which brings us to our second problem. There are many religions out there, making specific and controversial claims that go beyond the aspirations we have been talking about, contradicting each other and yet all claiming to have the truth. When we try to give content to our aspirations for ultimate meaning in terms of what to believe, do we not come face to face with the critiques of specific religious doctrines and the conflicts between religions?

This was the second challenge for religious believers in the twentieth century: the plurality of religions. It would appear that the two modern challenges, secularization and pluralism, cannot be separated. The question of *whether* to believe is related to the question of *what* to believe. For most people who have crossed the aspirational divide, the question is not simply whether they should be "religious" in some general or abstract sense, but whether they should be (or continue to be) a Christian of a specific kind, or an orthodox or reformed Jew, or Muslim, or Buddhist, or whatever. As Gandhi once remarked, it is hard to be religious without being so in some way or another, religion being more than merely a set of beliefs; it is a way of life, most often within some community of worshipers.

We are back to the connection between religion and *roots* and to the paradox of the spiritual center. All religions, including the ones into which we may have been born, are particular and local, with specific beliefs and practices based on scriptural writings and revelations; whereas religion, if it expresses our aspiration to objective meaning and worth, seeks the universal or absolute. The question is how, if at all, can we make sense of these conflicting aspirations in a world of many religions?

WAYS OF WORSHIP AND CLAIMS TO TRUTH

In the final chapter of his popular recent book on religion (*Who Needs God?*), Rabbi Harold Kushner directly addresses the question of different religions.[17] His answer provides a useful starting point on this issue, both for what it says and for what it leaves unsaid.

> Why *are* there so many separate religions, each claiming to be truer and more valid than the next? If religion were a provable matter, then we could assume that the multiplicity of religions was a temporary situation. . . . Religion would be like chemistry or astronomy. . . . But the problem is not only that religious statements are unprovable. . . . The problem is that religion is not first and foremost a series of teachings about God. Religion is first and foremost the *community* through which you learn to understand the world and grow to be human. (p. 194)

Rabbi Kushner elaborates on these claims a little later when describing a counseling session with two young people planning to marry. He explains to them that the issue is not so much what we believe about "God, sin, salvation," or even about "abortion or eating pork." The issue is rather about the language and community in which

> they express their religious impulses. . . . There are different religions because we come from different families, from different backgrounds, from different communities. I once heard a Buddhist theologian tell a Christian minister with whom he appeared on a panel, "To say that Christianity is the only way to God is like saying that your wife is the only woman in the world." For me to claim that my wife is the most wonderful woman in the world, or that my mother is the best cook, or that my local basketball team is the best in the country is a statement of loyalty, not of fact. Such statements do not conflict with what *you* may choose to say about your wife, mother or basketball team. It is at least in this sense that religious claims are statements of loyalty rather than historical fact, that two or more religions can be true even if they see the world differently. . . . If religious claims to truth were statements of fact, then when they differed at most only one of them could be true. (pp. 195–96)

These passages appear near the end of a book in which Rabbi Kushner dispenses a considerable amount of everyday wisdom about religious belief and practice. He comes across as a wise and humane shepherd of souls who has many true things to say about the role of religion in people's lives. But I think *these* particular passages should make religious believers as well as critics uneasy. To say there are different religions because we come from different families and communities is true enough, and worth saying. But the uneasiness arises when he adds that the issue is not what is "believed about God, sin, salvation, or even . . . of the morality" of this or that specific religion, but how we will "express our religious impulses." Religious claims are "statements of loyalty" rather than "statements of fact."

We can understand why spiritual counselors may want to say such things. They may want to assuage doubts caused by the existence of other religions or reduce intolerance to other faiths. But can we so easily separate religious *practice* from religious *belief*? Can religious impulses be disconnected from what is believed about God, sin, salvation, morality, and the like? To religious believers, it cannot be a matter of indifference whether God spoke to Moses on Sinai; whether Christ was the son of God; whether Mohammed was the seal of the prophets; whether there is an afterlife or resurrection, a heaven or hell; whether the object of religious worship is to be conceived as the one true God, or Brahman, or Nirvana, or the Tao; how salvation or enlightenment is to be attained; and so on. How we live cannot so easily be separated from what we believe.

Another way of putting this is to say that we cannot pretend to believe in religious doctrines just because it would make us feel good or live better. If we don't *really* believe, religious practice inevitably withers. Now and again, psychologists and sociologists tell us that religious belief can be beneficial for psychological health or the good of society, that it is helpful for raising children or teaching them morality. But, try as we will, we cannot believe what is otherwise unbelievable to us, just because it would make us feel good or because society would be better off if we did. Try as we will to be loyal to our inherited faiths and pass them on to our children, we cannot do so if we cannot believe what they teach. Religion, of all things, cannot be based on a lie.

The point is that there is an *objective* aspect to religion that cannot be ignored—a matter of the *truth* or *validity* of what is believed, which cannot be removed from religion without trivializing it. Rabbi Kushner emphasizes only one aspect of the spiritual center in the passages quoted, while downplaying another. He emphasizes the connection between religion and roots, but in doing so he downplays another aspect of the spiritual center, which has to do with the objectivity of what we believe. This is what makes us uneasy about the assertion that religious claims are merely statements of loyalty and not statements of fact.

But, of course, we know why he says this. For he adds, "if religious claims to truth were statements of fact, then when they differed at most only one of them could be true"; and he wants to say that "two or more religions can be true even if they see the world differently" (p. 196). Rabbi Kushner is a religious man fully committed to his Jewish traditions and faith. But he is also an educated man living "after the modern Fall" who is aware of the problems of pluralism and uncertainty. He cannot bring himself to take the fundamentalist line that his faith is the only right one and all others are wrong. So he downplays questions of truth and fact, viewing religion as a matter of loyalty to various traditions and communities of worship. This is a view that has become popular in recent years among some theologians, as well as among ordinary believers, troubled as they are by questions of objective truth in religion. But I think it is an unsatisfying view because it leaves too much out of account. The plurality of religions is acknowledged at the cost of abandoning claims to objective truth, without which religion becomes a hollow shell.

COMPARATIVE RELIGION

The problem, then, is how to make sense of the objectivity of religious claims and beliefs. You will note that "objectivity" in this sense is the same thing as what we have previously been calling "absoluteness" (or absolute truth), which was defined as truth from the point of view of the universe. The concern we have about the objectivity of religious beliefs is, therefore, connected to the search for absoluteness in religion, and hence to the search for the spiritual center—a fact that accounts for the reluctance of religious believers to abandon claims to objective truth in religion altogether.

But how is objectivity to be given its due? Are we to choose the fundamentalist view that if the claims of one religion are objectively or absolutely true, then the conflicting claims of other religions must be objectively or absolutely false? Or do we choose the relativist view that religions do not make truth claims from the point of view of the universe at all, but only from this or that limited point of view? Or perhaps the view that religious claims are merely mythical or symbolic, or statements of loyalty, galvanizing us to live better or binding us to communities of worship? For an older Axial Period, these may have appeared to be the only options. Must they be the only ones for a new Axial Period?

I don't think we can begin to answer these pivotal questions without returning to basic issues about the nature of religion. This is one of those places where answers seem to escape us because we have come to the end of one line of inquiry and must start another. To make headway with the issue of objective truth in religion, we have to return to square one as far as understanding what religion itself is; and I think we can get our first clues by turning to the very phenomenon that gives rise to the problem of objectivity in the first place: the plurality of the world's religions. One of the trends of the times is a growing interest in comparative religions and in the mythologies of East and West, which have much to teach us about the nature of religion and life in general. Recall Huston Smith's remark that in the present age we are "summoned to be Cosmic Dancers, who may have our own perspectives, but they can no longer be cast in the hard mold of oblivion to the rest."[18]

The first thing we learn from comparative studies of religion is that religions are not merely systems of belief or theories about the world. They are first and foremost *"Ways"* or *"Paths of Life,"* through which persons seek to overcome the evils of the world and attain some higher state. This accords with what Rabbi Kushner emphasizes about religion, but there is more to it. Buddhists, for example, hold that the religious goal is enlightenment (Nirvana) to be sought by way of what they call the "Noble Eightfold Path or Way" which consists of Right Belief, Right Desire, Right Speech, Right Behavior, Right Livelihood, Right Effort, Right Mindfulness, and Right Meditation. Buddhism, like other religions, is thus an entire way of life, including a good deal more than "Right Belief," which is only the first step. But notice also that "Right Belief" is an essential part of the Eightfold Way. Without the right beliefs, Buddhists hold, one could scarcely persist through the other steps of the Eightfold Way.[19]

The idea of religion as a Way or Path of Life, involving true belief, but more than merely belief, is common to the major world religions. In a well-known Gospel passage Christ says, "I am the Way, the Truth, and the Life,"[20] an interesting juxtaposition of terms. For it conjoins the elements I am emphasizing as characteristic of religion, the "Way" of "Life" with the "Truth," without which the Way of Life would not have the significance it is supposed to have. In a similar vein, the central notion of Chinese religious traditions, both Confucianism and Taoism, is the notion of the "Tao" (pronounced "Dow") which means literally the "Way." The Tao in Chinese thought is the Way of the universe, but also the Way for people to live if they are to be brought into harmony with the Way of the universe.[21] It is represented by a Chinese character composed of two other characters, one on top of the other, the bottom one signifying "walking" or "going" and the top one "thinking." The Way is a journey through life while thinking or reflecting about where one is going; it involves living and believing.

A second major feature of religion that emerges from comparative study is a further development of the first. Religion cannot be an ordinary way or path of living, because its goal is transcendent and therefore necessarily hidden from us in everyday life. We see it, if at all, only through a glass darkly. And this is suggestive in the light of previous chapters: if we think back for a moment, we will see that religions, conceived as Ways or Paths with transcendent goals, have all the earmarks of what we called in chapter 4 "quests," or searches in the "realm of aspiration." Their goals are more like finding the Holy Grail than finding a silver chalice in the forest, more like the scientists' quest for the final truth than for the best available theory. With quests, there are things we can do that are necessary to attain the goal, like the knight's search for the chalice or the scientists' search for the best available theory, but we cannot be sure in this life that these things will be sufficient. The goal of a quest is something we attain, if at all, with great effort and not *until the end of the journey.* So we find it often said that religion is concerned with "the last things" (what the theologians call "eschatology"). And it is also said that there is no "proof" in religion (at least so long as we are "on the way").

THEORIES OF VALUE AND THEORIES OF REALITY

The danger is that, in recognizing the absence of proof, we abandon the idea that there is objective truth to be sought in religion. It is a danger because, as we saw, religious belief and practice cannot so easily be severed. To avoid the danger, we need another clue.

As Ways of Life seeking to overcome the evils of the world, religions are not merely views about reality, they are also views about value. They seek to tell us not only what is ultimately *real*, but also what is ultimately *good*, or worth striving for. This combining of a theory of reality (what the philosophers call a "metaphysics") and a theory of value is, in fact, one of the distinctive features of religion. It accounts for one way in which religion differs from science and why evidence for the truth in religion cannot take quite the same form as in science. There is no proof, to be sure, in either domain (science or religion), if proof means certainty about the final truth. The scientists' quest for the final truth about the physical cosmos is also a quest in the realm of aspiration, as we saw. But even so, there are differences in the kind of evidence admissible in science and religion because religion is a theory of value as well as a theory of reality; it seeks to tell us what is ultimately good as well as what is ultimately real. Religion, therefore, should not contradict science, but must go beyond it.

The idea that religions combine a theory of reality and a theory of value has an important implication. At the summits of their theories of reality, religions usually identify a "supreme reality," variously called God, Allah, Brahman, Nirvana, Tao, and so on, which they understand in different ways. In their theories of value, they also characteristically identify a *summum bonum*, or highest good, also understood in different ways. For Christians, the highest good is Love; for Hindus, it is a combination of three values, "Sat" (infinite being), "Chit" (infinite consciousness), and "Ananda" (infinite bliss or joy); for Taoists, it is a disposition toward life variously described as actionless activity or creative quietude (*wu wei* in Chinese).[22]

But the remarkable thing is that, in the major religious traditions of the world, the supreme reality and the supreme value are usually viewed as convergent. In Hinduism, the highest values, Sat, Chit, and Ananda, are identified with the highest reality, Brahman. Brahman is said to be Sat-Chit-Ananda (infinite being, consciousness, and bliss) which Hindus often elide together as the name of the supreme reality. In Christianity, the supreme reality is God, the supreme value, love; and we are familiar with the assertion that God is Love. In Taoism, the highest value of creative quietude *(wu wei)* is exemplified most fully in the supreme reality, Tao, so that for a person to exemplify creative quietude is for that person to be brought into harmony with the Tao, or the ultimate Way of the universe.

The convergence of supreme reality and supreme value takes different forms in the different world religions, but some variation of it is always there working behind the scenes. For some religions supreme reality and supreme value are identical, for others the supreme reality exemplifies the supreme value in the highest degree. But the underlying theme is always the same. *You can find the one (supreme reality) by finding the other (supreme value).* And this theme in turn can be directly related to the two themes about religion previously mentioned, that religion is a Way or Path of Life, which includes belief but is more than merely belief, and that the goal of religion is transcendent and hidden from us.

Because the supreme reality is transcendent and hidden from us (the first theme), there is no direct intellectual path to it. The path must be indirect. But because the supreme reality and supreme value are somehow convergent (the second theme), there is an indirect path to the supreme reality: we can seek the supreme reality by way of the supreme value. To seek value of any kind, however, is to pursue a Way of Life whose object is the attainment of that value as its goal (the third theme). For this reason, religions insist that only those who live a certain kind of life find God (or the supreme reality)—"only the good find God"—and more to the point, that you *can* find the supreme reality if you live the right kind of life.

A CLUE: OBJECTIVE TRUTH AND OBJECTIVE WORTH

These three themes provide us with our first clue about how objectivity is to be sought in religion. Suppose that the supreme reality and the supreme value are convergent, as religions claim, so that we can seek the supreme reality by pursuing a Way of Life whose aim is to realize the supreme value. Then, if the supreme reality we seek is to be objectively real (real from all points of view), the supreme value through which we seek the supreme reality, and with which it converges, must be objectively valuable as well (valuable from all points of view). But objective value in this sense is what we earlier called *objective worth*. So one thing we look for in testing the objective truth of religions is whether the Ways of Life they require have objective worth. This will not be the only test, but it will be a necessary one if supreme reality and supreme value converge: objective worth will be something without which a religion cannot claim objective truth from all points of view.

Not only is this a clue about how objectivity is sought in religion; I think it also provides unique insight into some of the characteristics of religion identified by historians and anthropologists. Most importantly, it tells us why *ethics* is so closely associated with religion. We learned in chapter 4 that the two dimensions of objective worth were worthiness for love and worthiness for glory (clear recognition with praise) from all points of view. We also learned that a condition of the worthiness of love is that we ourselves love others for themselves and not merely for what they can do for us. It is precisely this claim, to love others for themselves alone, which is embodied in the ethical requirements of the Ends Principle and the wide version of the Golden Rule.

This accounts, I believe, for the widespread appearance of the Golden Rule in the major religious traditions of mankind, noted in chapter 2. It also accounts for the common requirement in religion that only those who have gone through various ethical steps (as in the "Right Speech" and the "Right Behavior" stages of the Eightfold Way), or have fulfilled various commandments (like those of the Mosaic Law), are worthy of salvation or enlightenment ("Only the good find God"). The Dalai Lama has recently said, "I maintain that every major religion of the world—Buddhism, Christianity, Confucianism, Hinduism, Islam, Jainism, Judaism, Sikhism, Taoism, Zoroastrianism—has similar ideals of love, the same goal of benefitting humanity through spiritual practice. . . . All religions teach moral precepts. . . . All teach us not to lie or steal or take others' lives, and so on."[23]

This is just what we would expect if religious lives were distinguished from secular undertakings by their quest for objectivity in the form of objective worth. *To seek objectivity for one's point of view, it is necessary to seek objective worth for one's way of life,* which means, among other things, to seek to be worthy of love by all. The ethical aspect of religion thus becomes an essential part of the religious quest for objectivity.

The point is not that all religions have sought objectivity in this way. They clearly have not. The normal way of seeking objectivity in religion, as we have seen, was to claim certainty and authority for one's own religion, rejecting all others who disagreed, and basing one's ethical views on that authority. This corresponds to the normal way of seeking absolutes in ethics which (as we saw in chapter 2) can lead to narrow versions of the Golden Rule ("Do unto others as you would have them do unto you, *if* they agree with you, or share your values").

One of the achievements of the great thinkers and religions of the original Axial Period was to begin (albeit tentatively) to move away from such ethnocentric views, to see religion in more universalistic terms (God is the God of all, not just of my people; Nirvana is available to all, not just the Brahmin caste), a tendency which is inevitable, I believe, insofar as religion seeks objectivity. Once this idea takes hold, traditional religion itself is inevitably put to an ethical test. "If the gods do evil," said the Greek tragedian Euripides in the original Axial Period, "then they are not gods"; and similar demands were made by other Axial figures, like Socrates and Plato: if gods do evil they are not the (objectively) true gods; if a religion preaches evil it is not the (objectively) true religion.[24]

THE IDEA OF THE SACRED

The ethical dimension of religion thus becomes an essential aspect of the religious quest for objectivity by way of objective worth. But it is only one aspect of the connection between objectivity in religion and objective worth. Two other features of religion, commonly mentioned by historians and anthropologists, point to the same connection.

One is the idea of the "sacred," which is regarded by many historians and anthropologists as the most significant and irreducible element in all religion.[25] The sacred is the realm set apart from the secular (which is the realm of everyday life) and the profane (the realm of evil or forbidden things). Sacredness in religious contexts may attach to many things: to places, to words (the Lord's Prayer or the Hindu word "Om"), to writings (the Bible or Quran), to objects (temples, icons, totems), to actions (prayer or sacrifice), to rites or rituals (baptism, ceremonial dance), to persons, times, events. But in each case the sacred has a special significance and special role in the economy of religious Ways of Life.

There is some truth in the influential view of sociologist Emile Durkheim that sacred places, objects, and rites play an essential role in the social life of religious communities, binding them together, rehearsing attitudes, and enforcing social obligations.[26] But there is also a dimension of the sacred in religion (not so often mentioned) that goes beyond the social and is related to my present theme, the religious quest for objectivity in the form of objective worth.

This is best illustrated by focusing on sacred rites or rituals. The tendency in religion is to mark the various stages of passage in human life (birth, coming of age, marriage, death) with rituals or ceremonies that set them apart from everyday life. Consider a description of the marriage ceremony of the Ngaju people of South Borneo by anthropologist Hans Schärer in his book *Ngaju Religion.*[27] Though very different from our modern religious ceremonies, there are many recognizable themes.

> The marriage ceremony, which, with all its rites, lasts a fairly long time, is conducted by the elders and they tell the couple from time to time what they have to do. The bride has to grasp the Tree of Life with her right hand and raised index finger. Then the bridegroom . . . encloses the finger of his bride and the tree of life with his right hand. . . .
> What does the wedding really signify. . . . It is clear that it has a deeper meaning and is somehow connected with the conception of God

and creation. It is not simply a social occasion . . . of pairing together, but one of the most important religious affairs. To be married means to enter a new stage of sacred life . . . it is death and life, passing away and coming into being. . . . The couple . . . return to the Tree of Life. . . . To clasp it means to be in the Tree of Life, to form a unity with it.[28]

The message is that the wedding is not merely a secular contract between two people. Turning it into a sacred bond means that the union of the man and woman has a significance that goes beyond themselves, linking them to the wider community and indeed the whole of creation (the "Tree of Life").

The role of the sacred, here as elsewhere, is what is sometimes called the "hallowing" of life, which means that everyday undertakings (in this case a marriage) are given a significance that goes beyond the parties immediately involved (which would only give them relative worth). Unlike merely secular undertakings, sacred undertakings must have worth from "the point of view of the whole of creation," that is, from "the absolute point of view"; they must have *objective worth*. And this means that they cannot be lived for personal happiness alone, but must serve the wider communities of which the persons are a part, and indeed all creation.

This role of the sacred in religion—of raising our lives above a finite, selfish point of view and giving them objective worth—pervades other important aspects of life from a religious point of view. Just as marriages are not to be perceived religiously merely as contracts between individuals for mutual satisfaction, so work and careers are not to be perceived simply as ways of earning a living, but as "vocations" or "callings" with a higher purpose. A woman may look upon a career in medicine as a means of making money or gaining fame, status, or prestige. So far these are secular goals. But if she sees it also and preeminently as a means of bringing some good into the world, of healing the sick and reducing needless suffering, she sees it as a calling or vocation. It becomes a *sacred* undertaking. *But note that this is just what is required to give her work objective worth, to make it worthy of recognition and praise from points of view other than her own and those close to her.* Hindus speak of social actions, like healing the sick, relieving suffering, and protecting the environment as "the maintenance of the world," and regard them as essentially sacred undertakings.[29] This wonderful phrase ("the maintenance of the world") is a way of saying that such actions have worth from the point of view of the universe—objective worth.

It should not surprise us, then, that persons who complain about the loss of spiritual center in modern societies also complain about the loss of a sense of "vocation" or "calling" in people's lives, and the tendency to see work as merely a means of attaining external goods like money or status. This is one of the themes of *Habits of the Heart,* the sociological study of modern American values mentioned in chapter 1. What I have added here is the connection of this theme to the search for objective worth by way of the sacred dimensions of life. By attacking the sacred, secularization undermines religion by undermining belief in objective worth itself.

SAINTS AND HEROES: CAMPBELL

A third way in which religion seeks objectivity by way of objective worth is through what we might call sainthood or heroism. Religions generally define certain ideal ways of life, or describe persons who play a special role in (or provide models for) the religious quest. In different traditions they are called saints or heroes, prophets or gurus, holy persons, monks, shamans, yogis, apostles, Buddhas, Bodhisattvas, sages, mystics, and so on.

The saintly or heroic aspect of the religious quest is a search for greatness of achievement in the religious life that may serve as an inspiration for others or have more specific benefits to the wider world. As such, it is a search for objective worth under its other aspect, as described in chapter 4, the worthiness for glory, or excellence of achievement deserving clear recognition with praise. But for the religious life, the search for objective worth through glory takes on a special cast. It is characterized by humility and associated with "sacrifice" of the self to some higher goal. The words of Christ express this nicely: "The greatest among you is the servant of all."[30] Excellence *is* sought in the religious life (who can doubt this if one thinks of the saints), but in order to serve some higher ideal, as in the case of the Confucian ideal of Chun-Tze, the ruler who strives to be great in order to serve the people rather than for self-gratification, or in the Buddhist ideal of the Bodhisattvas, beings who will not allow themselves to realize the fruits of enlightenment until every other creature and "every blade of grass" is enlightened.

In his classic study *The Hero with a Thousand Faces* Joseph Campbell has shown how pervasive is this saintly and heroic dimension in the myths of mankind.[31] The heroes of the world's myths wear many masks. They may be Indian maidens called to save their tribes or families, African shamans with special gifts, knights or warriors seeking some boon for mankind, or prophets or holy persons seeking and bringing spiritual renewal. But behind all the masks, Campbell finds a similar pattern. In the first stage, heroes are called to some higher adventure or quest. They must acknowledge their destiny and prepare to leave home, traditions, and everyday life in order to answer the call.

This symbolic death to former life is followed, in the second stage, by a series of trials and victories, won in great part through their own efforts, but with spiritual help. The heroes recognize at this stage that their outer victories must be matched by inner ones. To win out they must conquer the forces of evil and selfishness within themselves through self-knowledge and self-control. (In some of the myths the hero's journey is an entirely inner one—a removal from the world for a period of inner study, meditation, or mystical enlightenment.) Finally, having overcome all obstacles, and having died to their personal egos, the heroes in the third stage return home to reintegrate themselves with the society they had left. The object is to return to the world "transfigured, and teach the lesson [they have] learned of life renewed" (p. 91).

In this heroic pattern are contained most of the elements of the religious quest for objective worth. The leaving of home, traditions, and everyday life in the first stage is symbolic of the distinction between secular undertakings in which one seeks only personal happiness, on the one hand, and the religious quest in which one seeks objective worth, on the other. The return of the heroes with their boons for humankind makes clear that "the greatest among you is the servant of all." Excellence is sought, but only to serve some higher ideal. This is service, but not servility. The servant-of-*all* theme signifies that the worth which is gained is good from *all* points of view, that is, absolutely good.

TRUTH AND PRACTICE:
CAN THOSE OF OTHER FAITHS BE SAVED?

I have suggested that three central features of religion—the ethical, the sacred, and the heroic—are ways of seeking objective worth for religious lives. If the core of religious faith is belief in the ultimate convergence of objective reality and objective worth, then the ethical, the sacred, and the heroic become a part of the quest for objective validity in religion. They are ways of putting the believer in touch with the God's-eye point of view.

But we have still only scratched the surface of the problem of objective truth in religion. Perhaps we can rule out many religions as false in this way: if they do not require ways of life that have objective worth, then they are heading in the wrong direction. Such are religions that condone hate, selfishness, exploitation, and so on, as matters of principle. I feel confident that the view preached by Charles Manson to his followers would not qualify by this standard. (At one point, his followers were told to go out and kill innocent people to initiate a race war.) Nor would the religious cult of Jim Jones qualify (the fellow who took his followers down to Guyana where he forced them to commit mass suicide), nor would supremacist or Satanic cults, and many other religions, or so-called religions. The problem is more than one of having certain followers of a religion who fail to practice what it preaches, or live up to its standards, for this is an indictment of the followers, not the religion. The problem has to lie deeper, in what the religion actually teaches, or (as Nietzsche showed us) in the evil practices and attitudes a religion may systematically inspire, whatever it claims to teach.

But while considerations of objective worth may eliminate many religious views and cults, it need not narrow the options to one. Nor do considerations of objective worth answer all of our questions about objective truth in religion. Different religions have vastly different beliefs about the supreme reality and about the way to reach it. Where their doctrines disagree, it would seem that only one of them could be true—however ethical, sacred, or heroic the lives of their adherents might otherwise be.

This problem arises in a very practical way for religious believers. It takes the form of a familiar question. Can people in other religions be saved if they live good lives, though they do not have the right ("our"?) beliefs? In the West, Jews and Christians have wrestled with this question for centuries. The hardliners have always said "No." But the drift over the past few centuries has been toward saying "Yes," with varying qualifications. When the West discovered new peoples, Christians asked whether American Indians or Chinese or Hindus, who had never heard the message of Christ, could be saved; or if they had heard the message, could they be saved if they lacked the requisite background to truly understand it, or if it came to them distorted by poorly informed preachers (of which there were and are more than a few). To say such persons could not be saved, even if they lived sacred, heroic, and ethical lives in accordance with their consciences seemed inconsistent with the belief in a just, merciful, and loving God—that is, a God eminently worthy of love and praise.

Once this door was opened, such logic has gradually led many in mainline Protestant, Catholic, and Eastern Orthodox Christian churches to concede that persons may be saved in other faiths, even non-Christian ones (though fundamentalists have not gone along). The Second Vatican Council put it this way: "[M]en and women who through no fault of their own do not know the Gospel of Christ and of his Church, but who sincerely search for God and strive to do his will, as revealed by the dictates of conscience . . . can win eternal salvation."[32] In an important conciliatory gesture, considering Christian history, the council made a special point of saying that "God's saving will" can also extend to Jews and Muslims. Many mainline Protestant Christian denominations have made similar concessions.

In fairness, we have to add that such ecumenical statements, even when they are made by Christians (or followers of other religions), often are the reverse of earlier positions of these same churches and are surrounded with qualifications. (The "Way" of Christ is still held to be the true Way, and the others only second best, or sometimes the others are said to be really ways through Christ though they don't know it—their followers are said to be "anonymous Christians," to use the well-known expression of theologian Karl Rahner.) But even qualified and hesitant as they are, such ecumenical concessions, which are becoming more common in an age of increasing dialogue between the world's religions, show that the modern churches are wrestling with the issue of salvation in other faiths. And note how the ecumenical responses to this issue are connected to the search for objective worth in religion. People in other faiths can be saved, it is said, only on a condition—*if* they live lives that are sacred, heroic, and ethical, according to the lights of their own consciences, even if they do not have all the right beliefs.

THE VEDIC MANY-PATHS VIEW

The problem of other faiths becomes more complicated when we consider that in some of the world's religions, especially the Eastern ones, people are prepared to make even stronger ecumenical claims. The Hindu Vedas say "the truth is one, the sages call it by many names."[33] In the *Bhagavad-Gita* Krishna (an avatar, or incarnation, of the Divine) says that "howsoever men may approach me, even so do I accept them. Humans come to me in different ways, but whatever path they choose is mine."[34] Mahatma Gandhi, who was deeply influenced by these traditions and texts, insisted that in religion there are many paths to the one Truth—different paths, as he put it, up the mountain to the one summit.[35] He acknowledged that Christianity was a legitimate path to the divine (it was a version of what the Hindu traditions call "bhakti" yoga, the way to the divine through love), and Gandhi claimed to have learned much from the Christian Gospels as well as from other religions. Yet he insisted that his own religious consciousness—his own path up the mountain—was guided by the *Bhagavad-Gita* and other works of his own tradition.

To many Westerners, this Vedic "many-paths-up-the-mountain" image is appealing, but it also seems to come dangerously close to outright relativism in religion. Will any path do? No, not exactly, if objective worth is a precondition. In order to pass the tests of objective worth, a religion should not preach hate or oppression, or practice injustice as a matter of principle. So we can limit the "many paths" in terms of objective worth, as I think Gandhi would have had us do. But there are other problems.

Another typically modern reaction to the Vedic "many-paths" view might go like this: "If there are other ways up the mountain, why not look around for the easiest one?" We might call this the department store approach to religion: "When the going gets tough, the tough go shopping." It is easy to see why this reaction might occur naturally to those brought up in commercialized cultures. But to this reaction, Gandhi, and those who share the "many-paths" view, have a ready reply: "There *is* no easy way. The way to salvation is hard and steep, no matter which direction you are coming from. This is because the sacred life requires an emptying of the self and sacrifice, the heroic life is one of trials and dedication, and the ethical life is one of shared obligations and duties. No matter which religious path you choose, your worthiness for salvation will depend on *how* sacred, heroic, and ethical your life was, and the more of each it manifests, the harder it will be anyway. So forget this 'easy' stuff: the trek up the mountain is not easy, one way or the other." This may not be what a secular and commercialized culture wants to hear; but it would be the correct religious answer if objective worth is what is at issue.

ANOTHER CLUE: TWO VIEWS OF REVELATION

In such manner, some of the obvious objections to the Vedic "many-paths" view of religion may be answered. But other objections remain. We have not yet touched upon the problem of conflicting doctrines. If, for example, Christians are taught that Christ is the Son of God, and that redemption must go through Christ, how can they be comfortable with this "many-paths-up-the-mountain" view? Can they say that others who do not hold these Christian views and follow other paths can equally well be saved? Can they maintain their own beliefs with the same conviction and pursue the Christian life with the same intensity if they believed it might not be the one true way? And likewise for pious Muslims, Jews, and others.

We need at this point one further clue in our attempt to understand objectivity in religion, something that must be added to our earlier themes about religion as a Way or Path with transcendent goals. This clue has to do with yet another central feature of religion, namely, *revelation*, the disclosure of religious truths through scriptures, prophecies, and religious experiences. If the problem of objective truth in religion is to be adequately addressed, some further thinking about revelation is in order.

Revelation in religion can be looked at in two ways: as completed in the past and set down in some book or sacred document once and for all, or as a continuing process still going on, which may be completed only in a distant future. The first, or "past-directed," view was the dominant one of earlier ages, including the original Axial Period, but our arguments to this point suggest that the new Axial Period requires the second, or "future-directed," view. The past-directed view of revelation is associated with the traditional way of searching for absolutes and has all the problems associated with that way. You look to your own sacred texts handed down from the past, not only for revelation of the divine, but for the *whole and completed* revelation, and then try to convince others that your sacred text has the truth. In that direction lies uncritical authoritarianism, fanaticism, and sectarian strife.

The forward-directed view does not deny past revelations. Christians can and should believe that the Bible, and especially the New Testament, contains a large chunk of what is worth knowing about the supreme reality. (And believers in other religions should take similar attitudes toward their scriptures, if they really believe what they say.) Christians should believe this about their scriptures, and hope it is true, but they cannot know it is true. In view of the uncertainties of transmission, translation, and interpretation, well known to Biblical scholars; in view of what the Bible does not discuss or what it says conflicting things about; and in view also of the continuing revelations of Christian experience, believers in the Bible have no similar right to hold that it (on their interpretation or any other particular interpretation) is the whole and final truth. From the forward-directed view there may be as much or more revelation ahead of us as behind us. The spiritual quest of mankind is not over.

To be a Christian, for example, according to this future-directed view of revelation, would be to believe that fundamental Christian doctrines, like the Incarnation (that God has become man in Christ) and the Trinity (of three persons in one Godhead) *will turn out to express some profound truths in the final accounting of things, however inadequately those truths are now understood.* But it would also be to believe that these and other doctrines will be transfigured in the long process of future revelation so that our present understanding of them is akin to the way the cavemen understood the stars. In other words, we must take seriously the image of seeing "only through a glass darkly." The ancients were right to believe that the stars were sources of fire in the sky, though there is an immense difference between their understanding of fire and our understanding of nuclear fusion. A long history of continuing revelation stands between the two views, yet the ancients who believed that the stars were sources of fire were on the right track; what they believed turned out to be true by our present accounting, though inadequately understood.

CONFLICTING DOCTRINES

And so we should view our religious doctrines. It demeans the search for truth in religion to say that what we have in our scriptures and revelations are merely "myths," or "pretty stories," or "edifying symbols," with no foundation in reality—meant only to galvanize us to lead good lives. But it also insults the intelligence to say that our readings of these same scriptures and revelations are literally and completely true as they stand, knowing how deep are the mysteries they convey and the uncertainties of interpretation and transmission through generations of fallible humans. With regard to religious truths, we are as the medieval thinker Nicholas of Cusa put it, like owls squinting at the sun.

Of course, what is said here of Christian beliefs can be said also of those of Jews, Muslims, Buddhists, Taoists, and others. But what, then, is to be said about the contradictions in doctrines that so worried Rabbi Kushner? Jews and Muslims hold, contrary to Christians, that God could not become man, in Christ or anyone else. Muslims hold that Mohammed was the seal of the prophets, while many Jews and Christians hold that he was no true prophet at all. Buddhists believe that the supreme reality is an apparently impersonal state of Nirvana, quite different from the personal Deity worshipped by Jews, Christians, and Muslims. Could they all be true?

The answer, if we take seriously what has been said thus far, is surprisingly "Yes, much of what they say, which seems contradictory, could be true *in this future-directed view of revelation*—though not all—and surely not if they claim the *complete and whole* truth for what they affirm or deny." Consider that physicists once held that light was made up of particles of matter and then later that it was made up of waves. Today they believe that both views were right in a way, since light is both wave and particle, in a manner unimaginable to those who held the simpler views of the past. Each of the older views was right to a degree, but wrong insofar as it claimed the whole or complete truth, rather than just some aspect of the truth. So it may be with the conflict between the impersonal views of the supreme reality of some Eastern religions and the personal views of the Middle Eastern religions. Theologians have always held that the personhood of God is different from that of humans, though there is at least some faint resemblance. Perhaps there is some room in those differences for the "truth" of the Eastern impersonal views of the supreme reality to be consistent with the "truth" of Western beliefs that in some profound sense God is also a person. Any reconciliation would unquestionably transfigure our views of both alternatives, much as the modern physics of wave-particles transfigured traditional (and formerly contradictory) views of waves and particles.

In this view, religious believers can hold that the doctrines of their religion, which they believe and cherish, are not only valuable now, but will turn out to be *true* of an objective reality in the final accounting of things—the God's-eye point of view. But they must also hold that these doctrines are only inadequately understood at present, that revelation is not complete, that much of the spiritual journey of understanding is ahead of them, and that many (not necessarily all) of the cherished doctrines of other religions may also be true in the final accounting of things. *How* this may be so (given the apparent conflicts between religions) is one of those things that the spiritual journey can teach them, if they remain open to new revelation and do not assume they have the whole truth already.

Yet they may also hold that their own beliefs have something *unique* and *indispensable* to contribute to the final truth, something that is not now recognized by others who reject their religion, and something that needs to be learned by others if the whole truth is to be possessed. Thus, they can value what they have and preach it to others, so long as they recognize that being bearers of the truth does not mean being bearers of the whole truth.

SCRIPTURES AND PROPHETS:
A LIGHT UNTO THE NATIONS

Regarding the conflicting claims of religion about true scriptures and prophets, the situation is more difficult. But, again, we can see how apparently conflicting views may be right, so long as none claims the completed truth. A couple of examples will have to suffice to explain how we might learn to think in this way. It may be that God can become man in Christ, as Christians hold, and yet that God cannot become a man, as Jews and Muslims hold. This looks like a contradiction from our present vantage point. But the Incarnation is a mystery whose ultimate meaning is not fully known to Christians, by their own accounting. Christian theologians have labored for centuries over the question of how Christ could be an infinite God and a finite man at the same time, never quite resolving the contradictions. Is there not room here for Jewish and Muslim suspicions that the Incarnation cannot mean what Christians take it to mean when they use ordinary notions of identity? (Many Christian theologians would in fact grant this.) Yet even if Christians do grant it, if they are true to their beliefs, they must hold that there is some profound truth in the claim that God suffered in Christ out of compassion for the human race. They should insist that this message of divine compassion to the point of participation in human suffering will be part of the final accounting of things religious, and is an important message to all humans, not just to Christians, though it is not wholly understood at present. In other words, they need not say that the doctrine fails to be objectively true, only that it is not the whole truth and not now completely understood. This is what it means to call it a "mystery."

Or take another example. The sacred scriptures of Judaism, the Torah (or five books of Moses), along with the books of the Prophets, the Psalms, and other writings, tell the story of a special Covenant between God and the Jewish people made through Abraham. The Jews were to remain loyal to God, have no alien gods before them, follow the Law, and in turn God would be with them always and they would be a "light unto the nations." In the context of the future-directed account of revelation we are considering, to be a believing Jew would be to believe that this story will turn out to express some profound truths in the final accounting of things, however inadequately those truths are now understood. Nor would these truths be just for Jews; they would be "lights unto *all* the nations," if objectively true.

Imagine how this might be. One of the themes of the Hebrew scriptures is that worldly rulers are not gods, nor supreme authorities. Only God is the true King, and earthly sovereigns are not above the commands of God. Thus, the prophet Nathan chastises King David for sinning against God and Elijah rebukes King Ahab. This profound idea of subservience of human rulers to a higher law emerges for one of the first times in human history in these Scriptures. But it is an idea for all peoples, and may therefore be one of those things in the final accounting for which the House of Israel will have been a "light unto the nations." Yet another doctrine of Hebrew scriptures, which has been a scandal to many non-Jews, is a case in point. I refer to the doctrine of the "chosenness" of Israel, which is interpreted by most rabbis as imposing special responsibilities rather than as merely a form of favoritism. Moreover, it need not rule out the "chosenness" of other peoples. As Leo Trepp says, in a book on Judaism, "the chosenness of Israel, through the forces that have fashioned it, serves as an example of humanity to consider itself chosen for duty and held divinely responsible for its performance."[36]

In a similar manner, believers of other faiths can hold that their central doctrines will express profound truths in the final accounting—that they will be "lights unto the nations"—though inadequately understood and not the completed or whole truth. Not all cherished doctrines will survive these requirements of a future-directed view of revelation, to be sure. Any claim that our Way or religion is the *only* true Way, our prophet or scriptures (Moses or Mohammed, the Quran or Christian Gospels) the *only* true or fully right ones, will fail it. Literal interpretations of scriptural texts would also not survive such a view because they do not allow future reinterpretations and refigurations. We should not underestimate these changes; they are major and wrenching changes in the way religious revelation is viewed and they will not sit well with those who demand to see religion in the manner of the original Axial Period, in terms of past-directed revelations alone. But they can be reconciled with the idea that our particular religious beliefs, be they Christian, Jewish, Muslim, or something else, are objectively true—not just true for us, but lights unto all the nations.

A fitting motto for this view of revelation can be found in a theme often expressed by the great eighteenth-century dramatist and poet Gotthold Lessing, that no religion has the whole truth; only God alone has the whole truth.[37] The supreme reality is too great to be encompassed by any finite human tradition. If the goal of the religious quest is a transfiguration of human existence, should we fail to acknowledge that this might involve a transfiguration of our present limited beliefs and understandings as well?

THE MOSAIC OF LIFE

The final clue we need to make sense of this approach to religious truth is a theme introduced in chapter 4, the image of the great Mosaic of Life. The spiritual journey of humankind was represented as a mosaic composed of many different pieces of colored stones and glass that combined to create a larger pattern. The different pieces represent different Ways of Life through which humans have sought to connect themselves with the supreme reality, with the spiritual center—from Singer's penitent returning to the Hasidic quarter of Jerusalem to the Buddhist monk sitting cross-legged in his temple. They have different beliefs because they have an imperfect grasp of the reality and are seeing it through a glass darkly. But they are trying to see the whole more clearly by trying to reduce bias and narrow vision in their views.

Among the ways of reducing bias and narrow vision are the sacred, the heroic, and the ethical dimensions of their lives through which they seek objective worth, thereby viewing themselves, not selfishly, but from the point of view of the "whole of creation," the absolute point of view. Understood in terms of the mosaic image, the role of this search for objective worth in religion is to make one's point of view fit into the whole mosaic, so that it will represent part of the *objective* truth. With regard to factual beliefs and doctrines, the reduction of bias and narrow vision requires that religious believers be open to a continuing revelation and further understanding of what they believe (that they meditate on the mysteries of their faith, not assuming that those with differing views have nothing to teach them). Reduction of narrow vision also involves being open to secular learning, including science and philosophy. The idea that religion should not be reduced to science, yet should not contradict science, is of a piece with the goal of seeking objectivity by reducing bias and narrow vision. "Reason," as Arabic philosopher Al-Ghazzali once said, "is God's scale on earth."[38] In the mosaic image, the reduction of bias and narrow vision is signified by each piece attempting to reflect the whole while remaining unique. This is how a view becomes a "light unto the others" and obtains objective truth, or truth for all.

As we saw in chapter 4, the absolute point of view, which represents the objective in religion, is not a neutral point of view. It is the *summation* of all the partial points of view that have objective worth and truth, just as the complete description of New York City or the elephant of the Buddhist tale is a summation of all the partial descriptions from different points of view. The Mosaic was used as an image of this summative idea of truth. Removing any piece would make it less complete, just as removing one of the many possible descriptions will give us an incomplete picture of New York City or the elephant.

The problem about religion for many people is how to retain the intensity of conviction required to follow their particular religion—to follow the difficult, sacred, heroic, and ethical path it requires of them—while believing that it is particular and limited in its history and point of view, and without the assurance (which earlier believers may have possessed) of knowing that it is the sole right way and others wrong. It helps to be aware that there is no easy path, one way or the other, and that worth is measured by the difficulty of the struggle, no matter which path is taken. But it also helps to believe that your own religious tradition can be, as we said earlier, a unique and indispensable piece of a larger mosaic of spiritual truth so long as it manifests objective worth and remains open to further revelation and understanding of the supreme reality. For then your contribution and that of your religious tradition is required for the good of the whole, as is a piece of the mosaic. In Western religious terms, it contributes to the glory of God, though in its own distinctive way.

This frees us to return to our "roots," as Milosz and Singer would have us do, and yet find the "absolute." Rabbi Kushner approvingly quotes sociologist Robert Bellah's insightful comment that "the human race is just too vast to know who we are by belonging to it."[39] The image of the mosaic reflects this idea of different ways of being human. It speaks to the paradox of the spiritual center that requires people to reconcile *the particularity of their lives and traditions with the universality of their aspirations.*

Following this line of thought, the proper thing to say to those who belong to various religious traditions would be this: "If you are not disenchanted by your own religion and still believe you can find the sacred, heroic, and ethical dimensions through it, then it is the logical choice as a path up the mountain for you, because it represents your roots. But if you are concerned about its objective truth as well as its objective worth, knowing that it is only a finite way of life, then keep your mind and your heart open to the continuing revelation of your own and other points of view, for the objective truth and worth of your own Way require that it be true and good from all points of view, not merely from your own."

8

Environment, Gender, and Culture

THREE SOCIAL MOVEMENTS

I began this book by saying that we live in a world of too many voices and competing points of view about what is important in life—a Tower of Babel that is the source of moral confusion. The story which has been told since the first chapter would be incomplete if we did not give some attention at its end to three of these voices that have been heard in the last half of the twentieth century and are now challenging deeply held assumptions of an ethical kind.

These new voices appeared initially as social movements, often described as the environmental movement, the women's movement, and the movement toward multiculturalism. "Environmentalism," "feminism," and "multiculturalism" are fighting words in many quarters these days—an indication of the passions the corresponding movements arouse. Part of the reason is obvious: they represent power struggles between entrenched interests and forces of change. But we miss much of the importance of these movements if we see them only as power struggles. There is worldwide conflict over the environment, women's rights, and multiculturalism because these movements are also challenging deeply held assumptions about what is important in life. They are among the forces propelling us into a new Axial Period and have become a part of the current ethical quest.

FROM THE 1960s: DECADES OF CHANGE

In the United States all three social movements date back to the 1960s, that tumultuous period of change which is described by conservative critics, like Bloom, as the source of many of our current moral and social problems. The decade of the 1960s was certainly a period of many excesses. But, in retrospect, its excesses seem more like a premonition of impending moral and social turmoil than the cause of this turmoil. The real causes of social change since the 1960s lie far deeper than the disruptions of that decade can explain.

Many people identify the beginning of the environmental movement in the United States with the publication of Rachel Carson's popular book *Silent Spring* in 1962.[1] There had been warnings in the 1940s and 1950s about impending environmental problems by figures like Aldo Leopold (now regarded as one of the early prophets of the environmental movement).[2] But these warnings did not capture the popular imagination until *Silent Spring* appeared. Rachel Carson was dying of cancer when she wrote the book and her passionate campaign against the pesticide DDT contributed to its eventual banning.

It is interesting that *Silent Spring* appeared a year before the assassination of President Kennedy, which marks the real end of the comparative calm of the 1950s in American life and the beginning of the tumultuous 1960s. The assassination itself seemed to unleash new spirits of violent change. More assassinations of public figures followed, along with rioting in the streets of cities, the beginnings of the Vietnam War, plane hijackings and other unheard of acts of terrorism worldwide, campus revolts from Berkeley to Paris, and much more. It was as if the assassination had opened a door that could not be closed.

Of course, at this same time the civil rights movement was gaining momentum in the United States. The pivotal march on Washington at which Martin Luther King, Jr., gave his "I Have a Dream" speech occurred in 1964. The civil rights movement of that era is very much a part of our story, for it was the precursor of today's debates about "multiculturalism" in our schools and society at large. The struggle of black people since the 1960s to win a greater share of the power and fruits of American society has broadened in the 1990s into a debate about the degree to which American *culture* will or should change in order to accommodate its increasing minority population of African-Americans, Hispanics, Asians, and Native Americans. Many defenders of minority rights are now saying that social and economic progress for minorities cannot be entirely separated from cultural respect and acceptance.

It is an old story: human beings do not live by bread alone. But it has new overtones. According to the 1990 census, there are thirty million African-Americans in the United States, 12 percent of the population. Hispanics have increased to 9 percent of the U.S. population and Asians to 3 percent. The percentage of these three groups in the total population is now 24 percent and is expected to rise to nearly 40 percent over the next few decades.[3] (The United States is not alone on the multicultural front. While it leads the way in diversity, other industrialized nations are also facing divisive issues associated with immigration and minority populations.) We are becoming an increasingly multicultural society, many say, and this should be reflected in our general culture and our educational system. The current debates about multiculturalism in the U.S. universities is only the tip of the iceberg of this debate. Defenders of multiculturalism want to diversify the curriculum, with more emphasis on non-Western writers and culture, and less on the classic works and ideas of Western civilization. Critics of the multicultural movement, like Dinesh D'Souza in his recent book *Illiberal Education*, describe it as "a new cultural imperialism," and lament the politicizing of questions about what is to be taught and who is to be hired in our institutions of higher education.[4] This debate is only beginning.

The third movement I mentioned, the women's movement, also dates back to the 1960s in American society. Indeed, in its beginnings the women's movement took much of its inspiration from the civil rights struggle of the 1960s; and the connection between civil rights for minorities and for women continues to be a part of current political debates. Yet our understanding of the women's movement is also too narrow if we do not realize that it has likewise changed since the 1960s, or for that matter if we still associate it only with American women or with those who would call themselves "feminists." Women throughout the world, and not only those who accept the designation "feminist," are demanding more control over their lives and a greater share of power in the patriarchal societies to which they have been accustomed. In many places their struggle is only beginning, but the stirrings are noticeable, as in the example of the Saudi Arabian women protesting for the simple right to drive cars, or the poor women in Latin America, Africa, or Asia insisting on more control over the number of children they bear.

The women's movement in industrial nations also started as a struggle for power, but has become much more than that. In the 1970s and 1980s many women in the movement came to realize that what they were after was not merely an interchange of power—more women in what are now male-dominated positions—but fundamental changes in the cultural values of patriarchal societies.[5] Does equality of the sexes mean that women must fit into the existing social structures (which often means having a full-time job while still doing the bulk of the childrearing and homemaking) or does it mean gradual change of those structures into a new social order of some kind? Like the early movements for racial equality in the 1960s, the women's movement began as a struggle for power but has transformed itself into a broader debate about culture, values, and social change. This is the context in which we need to view all three of these movements.

ENVIRONMENTAL ETHICS

Until recently everyday ethical concerns, especially in the West, have focused almost exclusively on relations between human beings. In well-known injunctions like "Love thy neighbor as thyself," "Do unto others as you would have them do unto you," and "Thou shalt not kill," the references have been mainly to other human beings. *The significance of the environmental movement for the ethical quest is that it asks us to broaden our ethical horizons beyond the human species, to other living things and to the natural world.* It is difficult to overestimate how much of a change in human thinking this implies.

We may think of the growth of ethical consciousness as a series of ever-wider circles of concern, extending first from immediate family to clan or tribe, and beyond to village, nation, or ethnic group, or to those who share a language or culture, and eventually to the whole human race. At each stage there is a greater awareness of one's kinship with a larger circle of human beings. But the environmental movement asks for more—a drawing of the circle of ethical concern beyond the human race. It asks us to reconsider our kinship with the whole of creation—with what the Ngaju people call the Tree of Life—and to view ethics, in the apt Hindu phrase, as the maintenance of the world. This is the message of many of those who write in the new field of "environmental ethics."

Describing the birth of environmental ethics, J. Baird Callicott writes:

> During the mid-1960s an awakening occurred. People began to notice that many of the great rivers of the world had virtually become open sewers; that the atmosphere over many large cities was choked with noxious gases; that erstwhile open space and wildlife habitat had given way to highways, strip development, shopping malls and suburbs; that soil was eroding faster than it could be rebuilt; and that industrial and agricultural toxins were showing up everywhere, including of all places, in mother's milk and raptor's eggs.[6]

It began to dawn on many people, Callicott says, that this new kind of crisis would require not just technological fixes, but a change in the deep-seated cultural attitudes and beliefs of modern technological civilization, in sum, a new "environmental ethic." As Roderick Nash put it, "machines, after all, are only the agents of a set of ethical precepts. . . . The most serious sort of pollution is *mind* pollution. Environmental reform ultimately depends on changing values."[7]

One of the early debates in environmental ethics was over the relation of traditional ethical views to the environment—especially the views of the Judaeo-Christian tradition. Church historian Lynn White, Jr., and landscape architect Ian McHarg started a heated debate by suggesting that the human-centered ethics of the Judaeo-Christian tradition had permitted and encouraged environmental abuse in Western civilization.[8] They pointed to the declaration of Genesis 1:26–28, that humans are created "in the image of God" and given "dominion" over the earth and "every living thing that moveth upon the earth." Humans were commanded to "be fruitful and multiply, and replenish the earth and subdue it." To White and McHarg, this was an open invitation to human overpopulation and exploitation of other living things and of the earth and its natural resources. In any case, as they argued, Western civilization has read it that way ever since.

The White-McHarg thesis did not go uncriticized. Biblical scholars were quick to point out that there was an alternative "stewardship" interpretation of Genesis that points in another direction. In the words of biblical scholar James Barr, Genesis "contains no markedly exploitative aspect; it approximates to the well-known . . . idea of the Shepherd King."[9] According to this stewardship view, humanity's creation in the image of God confers not only rights and privileges on humans, but also responsibilities, including the responsibility to care for the earth. Defenders of such a view cite Genesis, chapter 2, where humanity, represented by Adam and Eve, is put into the Garden of Eden in order to dress and keep it, not to exploit it. Such examples suggest that the biblical texts allow for a less-exploitative, more environmentally enlightened attitude toward nature. But White and McHarg are surely right in saying that the Western tradition has often interpreted Genesis and other religious texts in an exploitative way. What was needed to finally shift the focus away from exploitation was a new understanding of the human relation to nature that has only arrived (for Western culture at least) in the twentieth century.

GOOD PLANETS ARE HARD TO FIND

This new understanding has several dimensions, but all have to do with broadening our ethical awareness beyond the human species. One dimension is signified by the word *ecology*, which, according to the dictionary, means both "the patterns of interrelationships between living things and their environments" and "the science which studies these patterns." The underlying story of this new science is one of interdependence. "The new hard problem," says Lewis Thomas in his popular work *The Lives of a Cell*, "will be to cope with the dawning, intensifying realization of just how interlocked we are."[10] Insecticides sprayed on fields turn up in the milk given to human babies. The lowly plankton of the oceans seems insignificant to humans, but it is the beginning of a food chain whose destruction would affect the quantity and quality of life throughout the planet. The same is true of the rain forests of Borneo and Brazil, though they seem so remote and insignificant to most of us.

Indeed, as Thomas and other biology watchers point out, we are learning that living things, ourselves included, normally live in interdependent, symbiotic relations with one another. This truth was obscured by the previous biological emphasis on the "survival of the fittest" and the struggle for existence, which did not always emphasize that the biological way to survival is to adapt to one's environment—an adaptation that requires cooperating and existing in symbiotic relations with other living things more often than competing with them.[11] Bacteria within the tissues of termites and other insects live in their hosts, but also perform special tasks without which the insects would die. Chloroplasts in plants are independent lodgers with their own genetic codes performing necessary functions for their cells. In humans, the mitochondria of our cells are independent organisms necessary for the production of cellular energy, bacteria in our intestines help us digest food, and benign microbes on our skin protect us from dangerous invaders. An interesting work by Theodor Rosebury about such microbes was appropriately titled *Life on Man*.[12] What we are learning is that "life on earth" too is a vast symbiotic system whose interconnections we are only now beginning to understand.

Such ecological awareness cannot fail to affect ethics. In fact, its ethical implications are among the reasons for the intense resistance to the environmental movement in many quarters. Put very bluntly, greater environmental awareness makes it more difficult not to be selfish—because we are forced to acknowledge that more of our private acts have harmful effects than we had previously believed. This is an inevitable result of the widening circle of ethical concern. As environmental ethicists like to say, we must now recognize that we are part of, and have obligations to, a "biotic community"—the ecosystem of the earth—as well as to the human community.

Lewis Thomas makes the striking suggestion that human beings at the present time could be considered something like the nervous system of the earth's biosphere.[13] We are passing information around the globe in staggering quantities, information that is capable of healing the ecosphere or of destroying it, and the future of the planet as a result depends in very large part on what we do. This is the old stewardship idea returned in a new form. We must care for the earth, but not by dominating or subduing it, but rather by understanding and respecting its rhythms and how we fit into them. The maintenance of the world is a heavy burden. But the time is long past when we can hide our heads in the sand and ignore it. "Good planets are hard to find," as Norbert Schedler has aptly said, and ours is a very good one.[14]

THE WOMEN'S MOVEMENT AND
THE DEBATE ABOUT PATRIARCHY

Like the environmental movement, the women's movement is not merely challenging existing power relations in societies, but also doing battle with deeply ingrained assumptions about values. I said earlier that women throughout the world—and not only those who accept the designation "feminist"—are demanding more control over their lives and a greater share of power in patriarchal societies.

The debate over "patriarchy" (the world literally means "rule by men") has been central to the women's movement from the beginning. Early feminists reluctantly acknowledged that almost all known human societies since the beginning of recorded history have been patriarchal or male-dominated; and they realized that the prevalence of patriarchy was something that needed to be explained as well as contested.[15] Anthropological evidence showed that only a few primitive societies (for example, several in central Africa) were less patriarchal and more egalitarian than the norm, but even these were not without traces of patriarchy. Some societies were also "matrilineal" (meaning that inheritance was through the female side), because of the ease of identifying the female parent, but the power within matrilineal societies generally was also in the hands of males. When we look at the major civilizations of the world, the patriarchal patterns of the past are especially clear. Consider the traditional positions of women in China, in Japan, in India, in the Arab and Islamic world, in Judaism, in Christian Europe, and in other parts of the globe, and it is evident that patriarchy has everywhere been the dominant pattern.

Early opponents of the women's movement argued that these historical facts showed patriarchy to be inevitable or natural for the human species. One sociologist pointed to the greater aggressiveness of males as a reason for the inevitability of patriarchy.[16] In a free and open society like ours, he argued, if there were true sexual equality of opportunity, more men than women would rise to positions of power anyway because of the greater aggressiveness of the male. The debate about "aggression" has consequently been a heated one within and around the women's movement.[17] Some feminists argued that women are not inherently less aggressive than males. The image of the compliant, nonassertive female is a product of nurture, they said, not nature— upbringing rather than genes. Opponents of this line countered with biological arguments that male hormones, given to those with diminished sexual drive or to transsexuals (who desire sex change operations), increase tendencies toward physical aggressiveness, while female hormones do the opposite; and sociobiologists weighed in with claims that comparative studies of primate species suggest greater male aggressiveness in humans.[18]

Such debates about aggression are ongoing. But it seems to me that they often miss an important point. People who relate aggression to issues of sexual equality usually fail to distinguish between physical *aggression*, on the one hand, and *competitiveness*, on the other. One may argue about the degree to which men are more physically aggressive and prone to violence than women, and about how much this may be due to nature or nurture. But competitiveness is not the same thing as physical aggressiveness. Any male who has competed with women— for example, in schoolrooms—knows from firsthand experience that women are not less competitive than men. So the argument that in free and open societies more men would rise to the top because of greater aggressiveness involves a confusion. In modern information-driven societies competitiveness of the kind that goes on in the schools is a much better indicator of who can get to the top than is physical aggression, which was better suited to the days when humans lived in caves. Too much physical aggressiveness can actually hinder advancement in modern societies.

The real problem for women (and for men) at present is not a lack of competitiveness, but something that results from too much competitiveness, namely, conflicts of interest between jobs and careers, on the one hand, and families, children, and personal relations, on the other. Feminists rightly insist that these conflicts are not just problems for women, but for men as well. Yet they weigh heavily on women, who continue to be regarded as the primary nurturers and homemakers. That is why there is much talk in the women's movement about changing cultural attitudes (toward the roles of men and women) and social structures (day care, for example, or parental leave) to deal with the conflicting demands of work and nurturing. There is no doubt that finding new ways to balance work, on the one hand, and the nurturing of the next generation, on the other, is one of central problems of our times, not just for women, but for human civilization. How it is solved will be one of the measures of a new Axial Period.

DOMINATOR VERSUS PARTNERSHIP SOCIETIES

This problem tells us why the women's movement, beginning as a struggle for power and liberation, has transformed itself into a broader debate about culture and values. As a consequence, the controversy over patriarchy has also taken a new turn in the past decade. We can best understand this by focusing on a distinction made by Riane Eisler in her much-discussed book *The Chalice and the Blade*.[19] Eisler speaks of two opposing models of human society:

> The first, [called] the *dominator* model, is what is popularly termed patriarchy or matriarchy—the *ranking* of one half of humanity over the other. The second, in which social relations are primarily based on the principle of *linking* rather than ranking, may best be described as the *partnership* model. In this model, beginning with the most fundamental difference in our species, between male and female—diversity is not equated with either inferiority or superiority. (p. xvii)

Eisler concedes that the dominator model—in the form of patriarchy— has been the prevalent one in human societies since the beginning of written history (from about 3000 years before the time of Christ, or 3000 B.C.E.). But she thinks the partnership model is superior and that we should be moving toward it in the future—a view that reflects much current thinking in the women's movement. The change from dominator to partnership societies is a useful way of explaining the cultural changes that women in the movement seem to be seeking.

But Eisler's most controversial claim is that dominator and patriarchal societies were not always the norm in human history, as commonly assumed. Drawing on the archaeological research of James Mellaert, Marija Gimbutas, and others, she claims that before the invention of writing and written history—that is, in the Neolithic period from about 8500 to 3000 B.C.E.—partnership societies prevailed.[20] In her accounting, these were agricultural societies that were less hierarchical and more egalitarian than the dominator societies that later replaced them, also less warlike, placing more emphasis on fertility and nurturing life than on promoting war and death. These Neolithic societies also worshiped female goddesses who represented life-giving and fertility, rather than the male gods of later patriarchal societies, who ruled over mankind by power and fiat; and the earlier societies were supposedly more environmentally conscious, living in harmony with nature, in contrast to later dominator societies, which tended to think in terms of dominance over nature as well as over other humans. Eisler's claim is not that these early societies were matriarchal (ruled by females), but rather that they were neither patriarchal nor matriarchal. They were not based on a model of domination by one group over another, but on partnership.

Her symbol for partnership societies is the "chalice," which provides sustenance and gives life, in contrast to dominator societies, whose symbol is the "blade," the instrument of domination. What happened in history, according to her view, is that the partnership societies of the Neolithic period in the Middle East, China, India, and Crete were overrun by a series of invasions by fierce, sword-wielding nomadic tribes from the north (approximately from 4000 to 2000 B.C.E.) and gave way to dominator societies from that point onward. Myths and legends persisted thereafter about an earlier "golden age" of human history in which humans had lived in a gardenlike setting in harmony with nature and each other, but dominator societies had become the prevalent pattern—until today, that is, when she thinks we can at least foresee the possibility of a return to the partnership societies of the distant past.

To assess this provocative view, I think we have to distinguish between Eisler's historical thesis (about how things were in the past) and her philosophical thesis (about how they ought to be in the future). The historical thesis about partnership societies in the Neolithic period is very controversial and is far from the majority view among archaeologists and prehistorians (though she is not the only one who holds it).[21] The more common historical view is that the agricultural civilizations of the Neolithic were not entirely peaceful or environmentally conscious; they fought over arable land and eventually expanded from the Fertile Crescent northward and eastward looking for new territories. In addition, critics of Eisler's view argue that the archaeological evidence from Neolithic villages in such places as Turkey is too thin to support everything she wants to say about the societies of this period. These villages do suggest agricultural civilizations that worshipped goddesses of fertility. Weapons are scarce in the archaeological sites and there is an absence of central temples or palaces that might suggest hierarchical or authoritarian social structures. But what the archaeological evidence ultimately means is a matter of speculation. Without written documents, we cannot be sure about the exact kinds of political system or social stratification in Neolithic villages; it may also be that their weapons were not of a kind to be preserved.

But if Eisler's historical thesis is open to question and will continue to be debated, it seems to me that her distinction between dominator and partnership societies is crucial for understanding the current intellectual scene. Whatever may have happened in the past, we must consider what ought to happen in the future; and if a new Axial Period is upon us, one of its defining issues is most likely to be whether traditional dominator and patriarchal models of society will continue to prevail or whether we will move toward some new kind of partnership society. Partnership societies would be more egalitarian (between the sexes, but also in general, between ethnic groups and races); less warlike and less prone to settle issues by violence or the sword; less interested in dominating nature than in living in harmony with it; and they would place a higher priority on the nurturing functions of society, which till now have been mainly the domain of women and were accorded less status than other kinds of work.

Such changes are far from inevitable; they would undercut powerful vested interests that are already lining up against them. But there is little doubt that the conflicts they represent will be among the pivotal issues of the future. The original Axial Period of human history (from 600 to 300 B.C.E.) consolidated the patriarchal structures of the past; the question for a new Axial Period is whether, and to what degree, these structures will be overturned.

MEN, WOMEN, AND MORAL DEVELOPMENT

The partnership model is also related to a final theme from the women's movement that is relevant to the ethical quest. I have in mind recent research by psychologists and philosophers on the differences between males and females in moral development and in ways of approaching ethics. Speaking of this, philosopher Virginia Held says:

> The work of psychologists such as Carol Gilligan and others has led to a clarification of what may be thought of as tendencies among women to approach moral issues differently. Rather than interpreting moral problems in terms of what could be handled by applying abstract rules of justice to particular cases, many of the women studied by Gilligan tended to be more concerned with preserving actual human relationships, and expressing care for those for whom they felt responsible. Their moral reasoning was typically more embedded in a context of particular others than was the reasoning of a comparable group of men. . . . [In the light of this research] many feminists see our own consciously considered experience as lending confirmation to the view that what has come to be called "an ethics of care" needs to be developed. Some think it should supercede "the ethic of justice" of traditional or standard moral theory.[22]

Gilligan's views on the moral development of women were developed in partial opposition to those of her mentor, Lawrence Kohlberg, whose pioneering work on moral psychology has influenced our present methods of teaching values in the schools.[23] Kohlberg's own views were built in turn on those of the great French developmental psychologist, Jean Piaget.[24]

Piaget's studies of children suggested to him that the moral or ethical awareness of young people develops in three stages. In the early years (up to about age six to eight), the orientation is self-centered and based on reward and punishment (Don't do that or you'll be punished. Be good and other people will like you). During a second stage, into the teen years, the orientation is social and conventional. One does the right thing for the good of the social group or the society to which one belongs and in order to be a valued member of that social group. Finally, at the third stage, which should come with the transition to adulthood, one acts upon abstract and universal principles of justice because it is the right thing to do, whatever society may think.

Kohlberg expanded Piaget's three stages of moral development into six (distinguishing two separate stages within each of Piaget's three) and did extensive cross-cultural research purporting to show that passage through the six stages was common to the moral development of children in different cultures. Kohlberg's work has influenced theorists and educators concerned with teaching values in the home and the school, but it has been criticized on a number of points. Not all children go through the six stages he describes, nor in exactly the order he describes. Among the critics were feminists, like Gilligan, who argued that Kohlberg's stage theory, like Piaget's, was biased toward the moral development of males. As Gilligan put it:

> Piaget, in his study of the rules of children's games, observed that, in the games they played girls were "less explicit about agreement [than boys] and less concerned with legal elaboration." In contrast to the boys' interest in codification of the rules, the girls adopted a more pragmatic attitude, regarding "a rule as good so long as the game repays it." . . .
> Kohlberg also identifies a strong interpersonal bias in the moral judgments of women, which leads them to be considered as typically at the third stage of his six-stage development sequence. At that stage, the good is identified with "what pleases or helps others and is approved of by them."[25]

The problem, as Gilligan sees it, is that stage three in Kohlberg's scheme is a deficient stage of moral development compared with stages five and six, which correspond to Piaget's third and highest stage, and involve doing the right thing *because it is right,* according to objective and impersonal principles. Gilligan continues in the same passage:

> Herein lies the paradox, for the very traits that have traditionally defined the "goodness" of women, their care for and sensitivity to the needs of

others, are those that mark them as deficient in moral development [according to Kohlberg's theory]. The infusion of feeling into their judgments keeps [women] from developing a more independent and abstract ethical conception in which the concern for others derives from principles of justice rather than from compassion and care.

To Gilligan, this is nothing more than bias toward a male point of view in ethics built into Kohlberg's stage theory. She thinks Freud had displayed similar bias when he said that the superego (the moral censor) was less developed in women than in men. A more reasonable approach, Gilligan suggests, would be to say that male and female perspectives emphasize different and legitimate aspects of ethical awareness. One perspective emphasizes objective and impersonal rules of justice which are needed to resolve disputes when there are conflicts of interest. The other perspective emphasizes caring interpersonal relations, rather than abstract rules; and it emphasizes compassion and nurturing of others, rather than merely the fulfillment of duties not to harm them.

AN ETHICS OF JUSTICE AND AN ETHICS OF CARE

These claims of Gilligan are the basis for the distinction between the "ethics of justice" and the "ethics of care" referred to in the passage by Virginia Held cited above. Philosophers like Held argue that the history of moral philosophy manifests the same male bias toward an ethics of justice and away from the ethics of care as does the history of psychology. While some feminists think this bias should be overturned— an ethics of care should supersede an ethics of justice—others argue, like Gilligan and Held, that we need an integration of both to have a complete ethics.

There is much to say in favor of this second view—that a fully developed ethical consciousness will integrate concern for objective principles of justice with concern for caring and compassionate interpersonal relations. One or the other of these concerns—for justice or care—is surely not the exclusive province of either sex. There is a danger in all psychological studies of moral development of stereotyping men and women. Not all men favor rules and abstract justice over care and compassion in their ethical thinking, and not all women do the opposite. If more women tend to be on the care side more often than men, we do not know how much this is a matter of nature or nurture, or how much of it could be changed if society itself were changed.

In any case, from the perspective of this book, we can say that what we have been calling "the ethical quest" involves a measure of both principles and caring—justice and love—which supports an integration of an ethics of justice and an ethics of care. The ethics of justice, according to chapter 2, is embodied in the Ends Principle or the wide version of the Golden Rule, which is an abstract principle to be sure, but one that allows exceptions in particular circumstances because it is rooted in the idea of respect for persons, rather than in the following of impersonal rules for their own sakes. And in chapter 4, we learned that the Ends Principle itself is rooted in the idea of love and worthiness for love from all points of view, which is why it favors persons over rules and allows for exceptions. (Love attaches, we said, to the inner self, or inscape, of other beings for which we should care and feel compassion.) In a certain way, then, the emphasis *is* on love and care—and justice is derivative. But this is not the whole story because there is also an emphasis on the abstract idea of worthiness for love from all points of view (objective worth), which is required for a sense of justice. Thus, a fully developed ethical consciousness would involve both a sense of compassion for the inscapes of others, and the ability to view things from an objective perspective—which is, I think, the basis for saying that it would involve both an ethics of care and an ethics of justice.

Finally, we should note a connection between this result and the earlier account of partnership societies. According to Eisler, people tend to think that if early human societies were not patriarchal, then they must have been matriarchal (if not one, then the other). But this is to assume a dominator model when in fact there is an alternative: partnership societies in which no group is thought to be superior or inferior to others. Similarly, those who argue that an ethics of justice is too narrow or one-sided might be inclined to replace it with an ethics of care—reasoning that if one does not predominate, the other must. But again there is an alternative: the ethical quest may require a partnership or integration of the two, an ethics of justice and an ethics of care. The ancient Chinese books of wisdom distinguished between Yang and Yin, the male and female principles of reality, respectively.[26] But they did not make the mistake of supposing that any being, including any human, was wholly one or the other. There is some of the Yin principle in every male and some of the Yang principle in every female; and attainment of the Good requires finding the right balance of the two within oneself.

THE DEBATE ABOUT MULTICULTURALISM

Defenders of what has come to be called "multiculturalism" in American universities want to diversify the curriculum, with more emphasis on non-Western writers and culture, and less on the classic works and ideas of Western civilization. They also want more diversity in faculties and student bodies, arguing for greater activism in the recruitment and hiring of minorities and women, and more power to promote diversification of the curriculum. According to critics of this movement, the struggle over these demands has politicized the universities in a manner unknown since the 1960s and poses a threat to the educational values of a free society and to our Western cultural heritage. One such critic, Dinesh D'Souza, whose *Illiberal Education: The Politics of Race and Sex on Campus* is a study of the multiculturalism debate on major U.S. campuses, says the following about it:

> There are [several] reasons why the changes inside American universities are worthy of close attention. The first is that the universities are facing the same questions as the rest of the country. The United States is rapidly becoming a multiracial, multicultural society. . . . . Immigration from Asia, Latin America, and the Caribbean has populated the landscape with an array of yellow, brown and black faces. Mine is one of them—I came to this country from India in 1978. When the United States starts to lose its predominantly white stamp, what impact will that have on its Western cultural traditions? On what terms will the evanescent majority and the emerging minorities relate to each other? . . . These challenges are currently being faced by the leadership of institutions of higher education. Universities are more than a reflection or mirror of society; they are a leading indicator and catalyst for change.[27]

Defenders of multiculturalism argue that our institutions of higher education have been remiss in not adequately teaching about non-Western cultures and that this will have to change in order to accommodate changes in American society, not to mention a shrinking world. On this elementary point, there is widespread agreement. But those who defend multiculturalism in the universities often have a broader agenda, which worries critics like D'Souza.

By his accounting, many of them argue that Western culture should no longer be given pride of place in the curriculum. It is not *our* culture, say these minority and women's voices, but the culture of white European males, who are the authors of almost all the great books of Western civilization that make up the traditional curriculum. The issue, for these voices, is not merely to broaden the curriculum but to weaken the commitment to the Western heritage which is identified by them with colonialism, sexism, and the oppression of minority groups. In support of such an agenda, many of them insist that the values of Western culture are not superior to those of other cultures; and some go further, asserting that no culture can be shown to be superior to others. There are no objective standards or truths that transcend cultures or support claims of superiority for the great works of Western culture.

Such views are lent support by some of the trendier academic theories of the day, which go by names like postmodernism and deconstructionism. Postmodernism is defined by French philosopher Jean-Francois Lyotard as "the rejection of all metanarratives."[28] For him, a "metanarrative" is any theory about the nature of reality that is true for all peoples and cultures at all times. In rejecting metanarratives, as Lyotard sees it, postmodernism is rejecting all objectivity or absoluteness of any kind—objective truth, goodness, beauty, and so on. People have their own personal narratives to give sense to their worlds, but no one narrative transcends different points of view and is valid for all. This postmodernist view is taken one step further by the deconstructionism of Jacques Derrida, which has influenced so much modern literary criticism.[29] According to many deconstructionists, there is no objective meaning to any literary or philosophical text, no one correct interpretation of it, and no correspondence between what any text says and an objective reality beyond it. One might say that, in this deconstructionist scenario, not only are there no metanarratives true for all, but our own local and personal narratives lack an inherent and final meaning, even for ourselves.

Such views are defended by numerous academics quoted by D'Souza, who play an important role in the multiculturalism debates at major universities. One such figure is Stanley Fish, chairman of the Department of English at Duke University, who argues that "objectivists" who believe in enduring intellectual and ethical standards fail to see that all "standards emerge and become sociologically and politically established" in particular historical circumstances. Since this is so, says Fish, "the best we can hope to do is convert someone from their set of beliefs to ours. This is persuasion. It has nothing to do with transcendent truth or knowledge."[30] To objectivists, such views lead to relativism and skepticism, but Fish believes that thinking in this way can be politically liberating: "Once you realize that standards emerge historically, then you can see through and discard all the norms to which you have been falsely enslaved." The changing of oppressive norms becomes, not a matter of objective rightness, but of political will and strength.

It is not difficult to see how such views could lend themselves to politicizing the universities in matters of hiring and curriculum and to questioning the status of Western culture. What is not so clear is how closely multiculturalism has to be aligned with such negative approaches to objective truth and value. D'Souza confuses issues by associating multiculturalism with its most radical postmodernist defenders, like Fish, which leads D'Souza to exaggerated conclusions. Expressing the worst fears of critics, he concludes by saying that the thirteen million students who go off to college each year "to shape themselves as whole human beings," are instead being taught that "standards and values are arbitrary, . . . justice is simply the will of the stronger, . . . the ideal of the educated person is largely a figment of bourgeois white male ideology; . . . all knowledge can be reduced to politics and should be pursued not for its own sake but for . . . political . . . power; . . . the university stands for nothing in particular and has no claim to be exempt from outside pressures." "In short," by D'Souza's grim accounting, "instead of liberal education, what many American students are getting is its diametrical opposite: an education in close-mindedness and intolerance—which is to say, illiberal education."[31]

POSTMODERNIST CHALLENGES: MULTICULTURALISM WITHOUT RELATIVISM?

These charges have much in common with what Allan Bloom says about American higher education in *The Closing of the American Mind*, referred to in chapter 1. And like Bloom's charges, these are exaggerated and one-sided. The vast majority of professors do not hold the views asserted by D'Souza in this last quote, much less do they teach them to their students, though they might support some of the aims of multiculturalism. The vocal minority that does hold such views is often influential, and influences many of those who want to change the power structure and priorities of the universities. But multiculturalism is a complex phenomenon that is ill-served by being defined only in the terms of its most radical defenders.

Multiculturalism starts with a simple idea that is widely shared: we live in an increasingly diverse society and a shrinking world, and American higher education must come to grips with this fact by broadening its curriculum to include such things as non-Western cultures, women's studies, and ethnic studies, and by diversifying its faculties to include more minorities and women. But exactly *how* all this is to be accomplished is a matter of dispute, as it ought to be, because coping with multiculturalism is one of the major challenges of a new Axial Period. Can it be done without forsaking fairness in hiring practices, without diluting academic performance, without losing roots in Western culture, without overturning belief in rational argument, or without throwing out standards of objective truth and excellence in arts and literature?

All these questions are before us and they are legitimate questions. But to assimilate multiculturalism to its postmodernist defenses is to give the impression that multiculturalism itself *implies negative answers to these questions* (for example, that ideals of objective truth or excellence or rightness must be given up). In fact, multiculturalism is more of a challenge than a position, and these negative answers are only one kind of response to it. Coming to grips with the diversity of cultures in the world, and within one's own society, without losing ideas of universal justice, objective truth, and excellence, and without losing one's roots, is one of the major challenges of the times—a challenge we have been discussing throughout this book.

My response to this challenge would differ from postmodernist and deconstructionist responses. In chapter 2, I argued that the correct *initial* attitude to the pluralism of cultures and the uncertainty of trying to prove the superiority of one's own should be an attitude of openness—keeping one's mind open in a search for truth to the possibility of learning from others. In the university setting, this surely means learning about diverse cultures. But openness does not imply relativism, or an openness of indifference. There are no initial grounds for saying, as some relativists do, that one culture is just as good as any other. In fact, the attitude of openness—if it is understood as the *search* (or quest) for truth rather than the final truth—leads not to relativism, as we saw, but to a belief in objective ethical standards embodied in the Ends Principle and the consequent belief that some ways of life (those that break the moral sphere) are inferior to others in an objective or absolute sense. (By contrast, a common charge against postmodernism and deconstructionism is that, as Charles Griswold, Jr., has put it, nothing in these doctrines provides objective grounds for rejecting even a position as heinous as Nazism.[32])

Thus, the university does "stand for something in particular" when it stands for academic freedom. It stands for openness in the search for truth, which implies an ethical point of view—respect for persons as ends and not means. Such openness is not indifference; it entails the idea that some views are inherently better or worse than others. But the position also holds that you can only find this out by initially opening your mind to other perspectives. Thus, in standing for academic freedom, the university carries a heavy ethical burden; yet it exercises that burden by letting all views be heard because its aim is to search for truth. The ethical burden and the openness are two sides of a single coin. Different views can be heard and debated because forceably imposing one view on others (including what is sometimes called the "politically correct" view in multiculturalism debates) would be to break the moral sphere. But views that advocate harming others cannot be acted upon, because that too would break the moral sphere. In sum, openness to other cultures and points of view does not entail abandoning objective standards of justice and rightness.

Nor does it entail abandoning ideals of objective truth and excellence, or worth. Modern trends like postmodernism and deconstructionism assert that we cannot have objective knowledge because we cannot transcend our own limited frameworks or points of view. But, as we argued in chapter 4, what follows from this is not that objective truth or worth do not exist, but that they are objects of aspiration, not knowledge. This means that we can never claim with certainty that we now possess them, but we can continually search for them by doing those things (like eliminating bias and error from our point of view) without which these ideals could not be possessed. Compare the scientists' search for the final truth of nature, an example used in chapter 4. If scientists assumed their present theories represented certain knowledge of that truth, they would not keep searching for new data, questioning prior assumptions, and proposing new experiments. But the absence of certainty need not, and does not, deter many of them from thinking that there is an objective truth about nature, which can be sought by engaging in just those experimental procedures that will produce the best available theory.

Thus, it is not surprising that the natural science departments in our universities (and related fields like engineering) are virtually untouched by trendy new philosophies denying the existence of objective truth, even though most scientists will grant that certainty is not to be found in science either. Humanists might say that scientists are stuck in their laboratories and are behind the times intellectually. But I think it is more likely that scientists have not lost the sense of what it means to patiently *aspire* to an objective truth in the face of uncertainty. As a result, though modern science was a product of Western civilization for its first three centuries, this has not prevented the non-Western world from embracing it in the twentieth century and producing scientists and engineers who have advanced it still further.

CULTURAL ROOTS, EXCELLENCE, AND OBJECTIVE WORTH

The situation of the humanities and the liberal and fine arts in the universities is more complicated, and this is where the real battle of multiculturalism is being waged. Objective excellence or worth in art, literature, music, and so on, is more controversial than in science. The problem in these areas, as argued in chapter 4, is that there are different ways to be excellent and different traditions from which excellence can be recognized and appreciated. Shakespeare's greatness will not be appreciated by those who have insufficient knowledge of the cultural traditions on which he draws, just as Bach's musical genius will not be appreciated by the tone-deaf or by those whose musical experience makes polyphonic music sound like noise. Yet, according to chapter 4, this does not preclude the achievements of a Shakespeare or Bach from being objectively excellent, or worthy of clear recognition with praise, from all points of view. Using the image of the mosaic, I argued that objective worth (in the sense of glory or clear recognition with praise) is the summation of different ways of being excellent from different points of view, just as the mosaic is the summation of its different pieces with their special shapes and colors contributing to the whole.

Another theme of chapter 4, however, was that excellence must be pursued within some context or other, in some tradition or culture that gives content and meaning to particular pursuits. Without that content and meaning there could be no standards by which to assess the worth of achievements. This theme explained the importance of *roots* to the pursuit of objective worth in chapter 4. You have to pursue excellence by being initiated into practices or ways of life (by studying music or literature, for example), and carrying them further. Cultures provide such roots; that is why it is important to be part of a culture, diverse as it may be, which provides some coherence to one's pursuits and a historically defined sense of belonging.

Of course, cultures too can change. As Alasdair MacIntyre says, a living culture or tradition is a continuing argument about what is *worth* pursuing or worth striving for in life.[33] Western culture today is engaged in such an argument. There is no question that our Western cultural heritage as transmitted in our universities will change, and is changing, to meet the demands of multiculturalism at home and in the world at large. Reassessment is going on in many academic departments about what to include in the curriculum and what to leave out. But to abandon Western academic traditions wholesale, rather than gradually transforming them to meet multicultural challenges, is an insanity that flies in the face of the need for cultural roots as a foundation for carrying on a meaningful debate about what is worth living for.

MINORITIES AND THE UNIVERSITIES

What, then, is to be said to African, Asian, and Native Americans who say that Western, European-based culture is not *their* culture? There is often a genuine sense of alienation expressed in such remarks that must be addressed. Many nonminority Americans are puzzled by this. Our ancestors came to this country, they say, and were alienated and discriminated against at first. But they learned to assimilate within a generation or two. Why can't current minorities do the same? An answer is suggested by Henry Louis Gates, Jr., a black scholar who has edited the *Norton Anthology of Afro-American Literature*.[34] "White ethnic groups came [to the United States] and they all became white. Previously, they didn't think of themselves that way—they were Latvians, Czechs or Germans [and so on]. . . . Of course, that option was never open to blacks and Hispanics and other Third World immigrants" because of the color of their skins; and as a consequence, people of color in this country, unable to melt into the general mix of peoples as easily as white ethnics, have sought an affirmation of difference. "That's why [many] black scholars study something black," says Gates, "we have to study ourselves, to find out what makes us different and what is most valuable about our experience."[35]

What is involved here is something else that cultures provide when they provide roots, namely, *identity*, and the dignity that goes along with having a valued identity. My experience with minority students at a major state university tells me that Gates has correctly identified what they desire. And if the fulfillment of this natural and significant desire requires offering courses or programs that discuss minority traditions, then such courses or programs should be made available. Academic purists sometimes say that courses in minority studies are often watered down and inferior, and keep minorities in intellectual ghettos. But I think Gates has the right response in this case as well. "I do believe," he says, "that some works are better than others. Some texts, black or white, use language that is more complex, more compelling, richer. . . . When I was in graduate school in the 1960s, everything black that could be found was reproduced. But some of it was terrible. We've got to make discriminations within the corpus of black literature, and keep what is worth keeping."[36]

Of course, that is also what scholars of Western European culture have been doing for centuries to find their Shakespeares, Bachs, and Michelangelos, which is why many are so reluctant to abandon their traditions wholesale or to concede that no works are objectively better than others. It is hard to concede this when you spend your life trying to discriminate between the better and the worse in your field of study. Our universities should therefore make a place for diverse cultures, letting them find and develop traditions of excellence. But rather than abandoning Western cultural traditions through which our universities have sought and found excellence for centuries, they should let Western culture change gradually by confronting alternatives. This is the beginning of wisdom in the multiculturalism debate. If a culture is a continuing argument about what has worth and is worth pursuing, this is how it should be.

Finally, the situation of women with respect to multicultural debates is different in certain ways from that of minorities. For one thing, those women who are not of minority groups also share a Western European background. The usual complaint is that women were systematically excluded from contributing fully to the Western cultural heritage, which is undeniable. Some did, of course, from Sappho, the ancient poet, to Hypatia, the ancient philosopher, to great modern novelists like Jane Austen and George Eliot. Women scholars are now busily ferreting out other women who have been overlooked; and women are now contributing to all areas of study in unprecedented numbers. While this is not exactly a case of Western culture changing by confronting foreign cultures, it is an example of how Western culture is changing by confronting ways of seeing the world that it had previously systematically devalued. So it is another case of a culture engaged in a continuing argument about what has worth and is worth pursuing.

CONCLUSION

In this chapter we have considered three social movements of the latter half of the twentieth century that are challenging deeply held assumptions of an ethical kind. Environmentalism, feminism, and multiculturalism had their origins in the 1960s as struggles for political power (the latter a struggle for civil rights of minorities), and have since become worldwide movements challenging traditional assumptions about values, ethics, and culture.

The environmental movement challenges us to widen our ethical horizons beyond the human race, to include other living things and the natural world—a monumental change in human thinking when put in historical perspective. The women's movement, no less revolutionary in its implications, challenges us to refashion long-standing patriarchal structures of society and to balance traditional ethical thinking about justice with an ethics of care. The multicultural movement forces us to come to grips with the emerging cultural diversity within nations and within the new global village as a whole; it challenges us to ask how we can maintain cultural roots and believe in the objective worth of our traditions while recognizing greater diversity.

All these problems we have been wrestling with throughout this book. Concern for the "maintenance of the world" (beyond private interests), the search for roots (amid cultural diversity), for the dignity of the person (regardless of race, sex, or ethnicity), and for the objective worth of our accomplishments and our ways of life (despite the limitations of cultures or points of view) are all searches for what we have been calling the "spiritual center." It is not surprising, therefore, that these movements should stir deep emotions or that they should be among the forces propelling us toward what is potentially a new Axial Period.

9

Moral Education

QUESTS AND INITIATIONS: PASSING ON MORAL VALUES

We come to our final subject, which has connections to nearly every other topic discussed in this book. It has been said that human history becomes more and more a race between education and catastrophe—a message that seems to apply with special urgency to moral education.[1] Throughout this book, ethics has been described not merely as a matter of following rules, or conforming to norms, but as a search in the realm of aspiration—a quest—to find meaning or significance in life. If there are norms to be followed (like the Ends Principle or the wide version of the Golden Rule), they are rooted in the aspiration for objective worth and meaning, which in turn is related to a search for the spiritual center. If we take the aspiration out of the ethical life, we are left with an aggregate of rules or inclinations, whose ultimate significance will elude us.

Now, as with any search in the realm of aspiration, the ethical quest requires some kind of initiation or education into it. When Joseph Campbell describes the varied quests undertaken in myth and legend, he notes that the first step is always one of initiation of the hero to prepare for the journey ahead; and the most difficult part of that initiation, Campbell says, is overcoming the hero's absorption in selfish interests that stand in the way of striving for a higher goal.[2] It would appear in this light that the ethical quest is part of every quest and every quest is part of it.

We are also learning that initiation into the ethical quest—what we call moral education—is not something that happens naturally. It is a difficult and precarious process that becomes more difficult as societies become more complex. In a publication of the Institute of American Values, Barbara Dafoe Whitehead reports the frustration expressed by many parents today who feel they are losing the struggle to pass on ethical values to their children.[3] When Whitehead asked about the basic responsibilities of parents, there was virtual unanimity of response: "putting a roof over their childrens' heads" and "teaching them right from wrong." But she also reported the feeling that these two responsibilities are on a collision course. Providing materially for children often requires that both parents work (when there are two parents in the home at all), leaving less time for moral education. At the same time, she continues, a culture increasingly focused by television and other media on material needs and goods, and absorbed with violence, is "increasingly hostile to families" and their role of morally educating the young. In the light of such dangers, moral education has become a primary concern.

STAGES OF MORAL DEVELOPMENT

In their book *Bringing Up the Moral Child* Michael Schulman and Eva Mehler sensibly remark that the main aim of early moral education is to teach children to be *kind* and *just*.[4] They argue that this generally takes place in three steps: first, an internalization on the part of the child of the parents' moral values; second, the development of empathy, or sympathetic concern for the feelings of others; and third, the development of personal moral standards of right and wrong that are held because they are right and not merely because they are socially acceptable.

These steps of moral development are reasonably close to those described by developmental psychologists, like Piaget.[5] In the earliest years the child accepts parental rules out of a desire to please the parents and avoid punishment. At the same time (from the age of two onward), a sense of empathy is developing, and later (from about ages four or five), a concern with fairness or equal treatment. Together these two senses— of empathy and fairness—provide the basis for a second, "socially" oriented, stage of moral development which lasts into the teen years. At this second stage, instead of thinking simply in terms of pleasing parents and avoiding punishment, children are learning the social dimension of morality: how it concerns the needs of others as well as of themselves. Finally, in the transition to adulthood, there should be the development of personal ethical standards that transcend social conventions, so that one acts on the basis of objective principles because they are right and not merely because they are socially acceptable.

Developmental psychologists sometimes talk as if the progression of children through these levels of moral development is inevitable and universal, when in fact there are numerous ways in which the process can go wrong, beginning in the earliest years if parents are abusive, neglectful, or absent. Later on, problem neighborhoods, conflicting messages from outside the home (for example, from television), or the wrong kinds of peer pressure can thwart or deflect the social stage of moral development. (It is interesting, in this connection, that three of the main causes of crime noted by criminologists and cited in chapter 5—child abuse, problem neighborhoods, and substance abuse—are connected to such failings.) Hence, the right way to look at these levels of moral development is the way that books on child raising, like Schulman and Mehler's, do—not as inevitable stages, but as normal and healthy steps that parents and others can bring about or thwart, depending on how they act.

It helps to know that children have natural tendencies toward moral behavior that will develop if not thwarted. Among the most interesting results of recent research by child psychologists is the recognition that children manifest capacities for moral behavior much earlier in life than was previously supposed. Distinguished child psychologist Jerome Kagan has gone so far as to suggest that nineteenth-century psychologists may have been partly right when they said that children have an innate moral sense.[6] "I did not begin my research with that idea in mind," Kagan says, "but it was imposed upon me after examining the data. We began by observing children in different cultures. My own research group worked in Cambridge, Massachusetts." Others worked with Vietnamese immigrant children in Southern California and with natives of the Fiji Islands in the Pacific. "In all three cultural settings," he says, "the same behavior appeared around the end of the second year. First, children became aware of actions that might displease an adult . . . [they] are bothered by many violations of adult standards after the middle of the second year." Second, when asked to do things by adults beyond their powers, they feel upset because they feel an obligation they cannot meet. "Finally, at about this time," he adds, "as every mother can tell you, children begin to show empathy with children who are hurt. And if they hurt another child, they become upset and often give their victims a gift."[7]

The first two of Kagan's points are important for the first level of moral development mentioned by Schulman and Mehler (an internalization of the parents' values by the child), while Kagan's third point (early tendencies to show empathy) is essential for the second, or social, level of moral development. Another implication of studies such as Kagan's is that the so-called levels or stages of moral development are not successive, but overlapping. Second-stage notions like empathy and fairness are beginning to develop during the first stage when parents' rules are being internalized, and third-stage notions of acting on principle begin to develop during the second, or social, stage.

Psychologists who accept Kagan's data may nonetheless be suspicious of his talk of an "innate moral sense" because it suggests to the unwary that children would grow to be moral naturally, if left alone. This is clearly not what Kagan and his psychological colleagues want to say. They concur with the claim made earlier that the propensity for moral behavior present in children must be cultivated and can easily be distorted. "I think the capacity for goodness is there from the start," says Thomas Lickona, author of *Raising Good Children,* but it must be nurtured, just as we help children to "become good readers or athletes or musicians."[8] As with language, the propensity to speak is there in every child, but it can be developed well or poorly, and in extreme cases not at all.

INTERNALIZING PARENTAL RULES

Thus, one way to bring into focus the problems of moral education in modern societies is to attend to these levels of moral development and ask *what can go wrong* at each level. This is not to suggest that the solutions will be obvious. Far from it: the social problems we now face in morally educating the young can seem overwhelming. But the first requirement is a compass to tell us where we ought to be headed.

In times past the first level of moral development mentioned by Schulman and Mehler was straightforward: the child internalized parental rules out of a desire to please the parents and avoid punishment. Nowadays, two factors complicate this process. From earlier ages than ever before children are influenced by social factors like television which present values that may conflict with those of the parents. (This is our familiar Tower of Babel once again, arising in the earliest stages of moral education.) Second, today's children demand explanations and justifications of parental rules and are less willing to accept them on authority. These two changes are obviously connected. The presence of values different from the parents, and of peers who live in homes with different points of view, requires that parents explain and justify *their* rules.

This is a source of immense frustration to parents, who often ask why kids don't just accept their authority in the manner that they themselves accepted *their* parents' authority when they were young—a wistful desire at best, because the social environment has dramatically and irreversibly changed. The Tower of Babel is upon us and will not go away. To meet the demands of childraising in this new environment one has to steer a middle course between the "authoritarian" upbringings of the past—in which rules were laid down without explanation—and the "permissive" homes of recent decades—in which there is little authority and no firm rules at all.

Lickona introduces the useful term "authoritative" (as opposed to "authoritarian") to describe this middle way.[9] He says that the adolescents who are most likely to follow their consciences in the face of peer pressure are those who grew up in authoritative homes, where rules are *firm but clearly explained or justified,* rather than either authoritarian homes, where rules are laid down without explanation, or permissive homes, where there are few firm rules. Lickona is, of course, aware of what every parent knows—that explanations often fail to convince and "the law" must eventually be laid down to children, whatever they think. But if parents develop habits of explaining and listening, he suggests, and are firm and consistent in their rules, then the occasions when explanations do not convince can be survived. There is now widespread agreement among experts that normal moral development in the early years requires firm parental authority of this sort, along with a stable environment, and clear, consistent direction.

EMPATHY AND FAIRNESS

By contrast, the second level of moral development (which overlaps the first in time, as we recall) requires entirely different strategies. To develop genuine senses of *empathy* and *fairness* in children requires more than laying down rules or even explaining or justifying rules. Sensitivity is more important at this stage than authority. We do know, as Kagan suggests, that feelings of empathy and justice begin very early. Babies imitate parents' facial expressions in an attempt to figure out what they are feeling and toddlers respond to the hurt of others from the second year onward. Somewhat later, but well before school age, children develop a sense of justice and will protest when they think a parental order or the distribution of a dessert is "unfair."

These feelings—of empathy and fairness—represent the beginning of what later will be a conscience, and they can be developed or stunted by what parents do in the early years. Psychologists Carolyn Zahn-Waxler and Marian Radke-Yarrow have shown that empathetic parents have empathetic children.[10] Youngsters whose mothers taught them altruism by example (helping a kitten tangled in a ball of yarn) helped others more often themselves. Parents who attempt to act fairly and to respond to their children's charges of unfairness with explanations produce children with a clearer sense of justice.[11]

One of the most exciting recent developments of moral education in the schools involves an application of these principles. In Chicago,

Denver, Atlanta, and other cities and their suburbs, children are taken on field trips to observe harsh realities like homelessness firsthand, and are encouraged to engage in such projects as collecting canned food for the local soup kitchens. A *Newsweek* article by Pat Wingert and Barbara Kantrowitz has this to say about such developments:

> Good works are part of the curriculum at more and more schools around the country, educators say. For the most part, these are grass-roots efforts, with projects ranging from field trips to fund drives, volunteer work to lessons on how to treat one's peers. In the past, the teaching of such values as caring and sharing fell squarely on family shoulders with church groups lending support. But nowadays with so many children in day care and church attendance not as popular, teachers are on the front line of moral education. Children in today's smaller families can be selfish and self-centered, says Deborah Battles, an Atlanta teacher who is developing a "values" curriculum for that city's schools. "And in urban areas," she says, "you're also talking about a large number of children who are children of children. You can't expect children to teach what they don't know."[12]

One can expect to see more of this in the future. It is a kind of moral education in the schools that ought to be less controversial than the "values-clarification" approach we discussed in chapters 1 and 2. Some might object that such projects could become ideological, pushing a narrow political point of view. If so, it is up to parents and school boards to see that this does not happen; and, as a matter of fact, few complaints of such kinds have arisen in the places where these projects have been tried. People recognize that the schools must begin to take up some of the slack where families fail and the churches do not reach. For one thing is clear from all psychological and other studies of childrearing: empathy and fairness can only be learned by experience, example, and practice. What these schools are doing is an extension of the mother helping the child to free the kitten entangled in a ball of yarn.

THE THIRD LEVEL AND
THE NEED FOR EXPLANATIONS

Practical writings on the moral education of children most often focus on the first two levels of moral development just discussed (internalizing parental rules and developing empathy and fairness) and are least helpful when it comes to the third level. One reason is that the third level is as much philosophical as it is psychological. Morality at the third level is no longer simply a matter of reward or punishment or of social acceptability, but of objective rightness or wrongness of actions based on universal principles which are supposed to hold for all persons, and not just for one's own social group.[13] This is a case of those widening circles of ethical concern we discussed in the previous chapter. The moral focus of children at the first level of moral development is on the family circle, on pleasing and not being punished by parents or other caregivers. At the second level the circle of moral awareness widens to the society beyond the home. But at the third level it must widen still further to all persons (and perhaps even beyond the human sphere), becoming universal and objective.

The question then naturally arises at the third level about the grounding or justification for universal principles of morality. We saw that children tend to seek reasons or explanations at earlier ages for the moral rules they are asked to obey, beginning at the first level. But the questioning is especially acute during the transition to the third level, which is supposed to take place in adolescence and represents a transition to adult ethical awareness. Here we find those philosophical questions that are so difficult for parents and teachers to answer: Why should I be moral at all? What is more important when the two conflict, personal success or absolute honesty and integrity? Why not favor my own needs (or those of my family or class) over the needs of others?

It is interesting that in nearly all households of the past and in many of the present, these questions were, and are, given religious answers. Moral behavior, honesty, integrity, and love of others are to be favored because God has commanded them and God will reward those who obey and punish those who do not. Thus, the traditional connection between ethics and religion begins with the first attempts to justify moral commandments. In fact, within religious households, the philosophical questions are given religious answers at the very first level of moral development when children ask why they should be kind or just toward others. In short, where religion is brought in at all in moral development, it pervades all three levels and children learn to think of morality as a set of absolute commandments from the very start.

Nonetheless, questions about the objective foundations of morality that are characteristic of the third level cannot be avoided. If morality is taught from a religious perspective, adolescent questioning about morality will take the form of questioning about religion. Is there a God to punish and reward us? Is the Bible to be believed? Which religion is to be believed when religions offer different accounts of what is ethical or moral? These are religious variants of the Why-be-moral? questions that arise in the transition to the third level. If such questions about the foundations of ethics do not get satisfactory answers (of a religious or any other kind), then adolescents or adults will not arrive at a third level and accept objective ethical standards, but are more likely to veer off into relativism, skepticism, or amoralism. This is a pattern that has become more and more prevalent.

Interesting evidence of this pattern of veering off into relativism or skepticism is seen in Kohlberg's research on moral development. In his later years Kohlberg was forced to concede that the transition from the second to the third level of moral development was not inevitable as he had earlier supposed. Evidence showed that many young people (especially in modern societies) never got to the third level because of doubts and philosophical questioning; or they reached the third level and then retreated from it. Unable to find a grounding for their moral commitments, they veered off into relativism or skepticism.[14] So prevalent was this pattern that Kohlberg actually introduced a new stage of his theory to account for it, which he called stage 4½. (Recall that Kohlberg adapted and refined Piaget's three-level theory by introducing two stages of moral development within each level. Stage 4 was the highest stage of Kohlberg's second level and stage 5 the lowest stage of his third level; so the stage between the second and third levels that represented a veering off into relativism became 4½.) Persons at stage 4½ could not convince themselves that morality was anything more than a set of conventional rules invented by societies to control behavior. This was the view of the Sophists of ancient Greece at the dawn of Western philosophy during the original Axial Period. And it led the Sophists to relativism, just as it leads many people today, at the dawn of their intellectual awakening, to relativism.

RESPONDING TO THIRD-LEVEL UNCERTAINTIES

It should now be clear why I said that the problems of moral development related to the third level are as much philosophical as they are psychological. Reaching and staying at the third level requires accepting universal standards of rightness. But for reflective persons, this has become no longer simply a matter of psychological training, but of philosophical justification, no longer an inevitable transition, but a choice to accept or reject an ethical point of view. This change in attitude about the third level of moral development is a major cause of the moral uncertainty and confusion of the times described in chapter 1, and one of the symptoms a new Axial Period.

It should also now be evident that many of the arguments of this book have attempted to address this problem—to suggest how the transition to the third level might be reconceived without veering off into relativism, skepticism, or amoralism. The modern Tower of Babel—with its twin symptoms of pluralism and uncertainty—tends to erode convictions that were formed in earlier stages of moral development and leads to doubts about whether any view can be shown to be objectively better or worse than any other. We confronted these problems in the first four chapters, showing how relativism might be avoided and objective ethical standards understood. The results have significant implications for moral education.

For example, in chapter 2, I criticized the standard method of values clarification used to teach values in the schools because it encourages relativism and skepticism, rather than answering them. The flaw in this method is that, while it begins with openness toward others as a response to pluralism and uncertainty, it fails to acknowledge that the attitude of openness breaks down where the moral sphere breaks down. Openness, in short, does not lead to relativism or indifference, but to the Ends Principle, which is judgmental, and tells us that some things are objectively right or wrong and that some ways of life are more worthy of respect than others. This suggested the following response, which teachers, parents, and others might make to ethical questioning that arises at the third level of moral development:

> Be open if you wish to other points of view. This may be a correct attitude *to start with* if you want to find the truth. But just remember that this attitude does not mean anything goes, ethically speaking. Quite the contrary, an attitude of openness leads to the conclusion that some things are really right and others wrong, and some ways of living are really better than others [as shown in chapter 2].
>
> And incidentally, some of those things that are really right or wrong are signified by those old commandments you have heard about. Don't kill or lie. Don't steal or cheat. Don't be unkind or inconsiderate or cause harm unnecessarily or be unfair. Don't treat others as means to your own ends, unless you are forced into it by their actions. And when you must, when the moral sphere breaks down, do what you can to restore and preserve conditions in this world where respect for others can flourish once again using minimum force and as fairly or justly as conditions allow. To love rightly is to recognize that you cannot love everything equally—except in a perfect world. But even where you cannot love equally in an imperfect world, you can love well by striving to make that world less imperfect.

This message can also be applied to higher education, as I suggested in the discussion of multiculturalism. The idea is that the cherished openness of mind of our universities, which goes by the name of academic freedom, is not an openness of indifference, but does in fact presuppose that some ways of life or points of view are absolutely better than others. Openness of mind in the search for truth, and an ethical attitude of respect for persons as ends and not means, are not antithetical, but two sides of a single coin. At the same time, there are limits to respect when the moral sphere breaks down. Not anything goes. In the universities, then, as in the schools, we can stand for something while openly searching for the truth.

IDEALISM AND ASPIRATION

There is one final problem to be addressed about the third level of moral development. Writers on moral education, like Schulman and Mehler, describe the third level as one of formulating "personal ethical standards," accepted because they are thought to be right, and not just because parents have taught them (first level) or society condones them (second level). At the third level, we reach the stage of ethical development where a sense of personal integrity enables people to resist the temptation to go along, or look the other way, even when grave injustices are at stake. But when books on moral education talk about what motivates people to adhere to such personal moral standards, it seems to me that the most important theme tends to be overlooked.

The ultimate motivator in ethics is a form of idealism, a striving to find meaning in life that transcends one's own narrow concerns. "The sense of greatness," Alfred North Whitehead once said, "is the groundwork of morals."[15] And in one of her novels Mary Renault has Plato say to his disciples, "Be what you wish to seem."[16] The latent idealism of the young is a crucial and too-often-neglected factor in moral education. Yes, the development of empathy, a sense of fairness, and compassion are essential. But if ethical consciousness is to get to the third level of moral development and stay there, one must tap the roots of idealism in people. That is why I have emphasized the notions of aspiration and objective worth in the ethical quest. Ethics has been described throughout this book not merely as a matter of following rules, but as a search in the realm of aspiration to find meaning and significance in life. The norms to be followed, such as the Ends Principle, do not exist in a vacuum, but are rooted in the aspiration for objective worth that provides such meaning.

Thus it is that fairy tales and myths, which aim to teach moral lessons to children, so often appeal to their love of heroism. If the young Indian maiden is to save her tribe from famine, she must suppress her selfish desires and continue searching for the hidden seeds of corn. Later in life, we can also be moved by inspiring stories of self-sacrifice in the face of great problems. David Putnam, director of *The Killing Fields* (the story of friendship between an American journalist and his Cambodian colleague during the dark days of Khmer Rouge rule in Cambodia) spoke at a news conference when the film appeared about showing motion pictures in all parts of the world. "No matter what the culture," Putnam said, "if it brings out the best ideals of humans, people will walk out moved by it, and having formed motives to do better things in the world." My own recent experience of this kind was seeing a PBS documentary on Le Chambon, the village in France whose populace hid and protected hundreds of Jews during the Nazi occupation, at great risk to themselves. The sheer courage and force of character of these simple villagers is the greatest moral teacher of all, and it would not be a bad idea if such films were shown in the schools as a part of moral education.

EARS TO HEAR

A final thought. Anyone who has tried to teach ethics in schools or universities knows what a precarious enterprise this is. It can be done, but there has to be a foundation to work upon. As I said in chapter 1, ideas can only work their way upon the evils of the world indirectly through people who care. And ethics can only be effectively taught to people who have already learned something about what it is to care and be cared for, to love and be loved, to respect others and be respected by them. We return, in other words, to the first two levels of moral development. At these levels, the family is the pivotal institution of moral education and we ought to be concerned about its current health. Attacking such social problems as dysfunctional families, child abuse, problem neighborhoods, and drugs is the ultimate frontier of moral education and must be done whatever else is done.

Of course, one needs good schools as well, but teaching values in the schools is not enough. Those who have suffered childhoods of deprivation of love cannot profit from such training. Their teachers are like Orpheus, in the poem cited in chapter 4, playing music to sway the beasts in Hades only to find that the beasts have no ears. Every teacher can tell you about such students. The ethical life is a harmony, as Plato called it, with its own subtle attractions.[17] But those who have been deprived of love when young cannot hear it. They have no ears.

Conversely, to teach a child in the early years what it is to love and be loved, to respect and be respected, is to give the child ears to hear whatever divine music the universe has to play. You cannot guarantee they will listen, but without those ears, life will be a terrible jumble of meaningless sounds, or worse, a dreadful silence. They will live in "an ice palace made out of frozen sighs." In this respect the family is the pivot of moral education. If it fails, teachers cannot succeed. Confucius put it this way: "When there is love in the home" he said, "there is peace in the kingdom."[18]

Appendix

Table of Contents with Section Headings

Notes

Chapter 1

1. See, for example, Stout 1988, introduction; Hauerwas 1983, chap. 1; Mitchell 1980, chap. 1.
2. For an overview of these trends, see Best and Kellner 1991.
3. MacIntyre 1981, pp. 1–4.
4. An excellent introduction to the problems of relativism, which is readable, yet demonstrates their depth, is Garrett 1990.
5. Solzhenitsyn 1978; Milosz 1985.
6. Bellah and coauthors Richard Madsen, William M. Sullivan, Ann Swidler, and Steven M. Tipton 1987; Bloom 1987. A more recent work in a similar vein by Bellah and the same coauthors is Bellah 1991. Sullivan 1986 is an insightful reconstruction of social and political philosophy that responds to some of the problems posed in *Habits of the Heart.*
7. Nussbaum 1987, pp. 20–26.
8. Eliade 1959, chap. 1.
9. Küng 1978, passim.
10. Smith 1958, p. 8. Smith's widely read *The Religions of Man,* from which this quote is taken, has been republished as *World Religions* (Smith 1991). The theme of the quote is further developed in Smith's recent *Essays on World Religions* (New York: Paragon House Publishers, 1992).
11. Lewis 1962.
12. Jaspers 1951, pp. 99–102. This period has sometimes also been called the "Great Awakening," after the image of the Buddha, one of its important figures. *Buddha* means "the enlightened one," or more literally, the one who "has awakened" (to a higher state of consciousness)—an appropriate image for the period.
13. The idea of a new era is suggested by a number of writers, most recently by Richard Tarnas in his interesting account of Western intellectual history (1991).
14. Toffler 1980, passim.

15. Reprinted in Kolakowski 1989, pp. 146–61. Originally a Jefferson Lecture in the Humanities, published in *New Republic*, 16 July 1986.
16. Rorty, "Solidarity and Objectivity," in J. Rajchman and C. West 1985, pp. 3–19; reprinted in Rorty 1989.
17. Williams 1972, pp. 22–26.
18. The sophisticated relativist views of contemporary philosophers like Gilbert Harman, David Wong, and Max Hocutt are more difficult to refute than "vulgar relativism," as is relativism in the broad sense of a denial of absolute values. For a critical review of recent relativist theories, see Stewart and Thomas 1991. For an insightful overview of recent debates about "relativism" and "rationality" see Bernstein 1983.
19. This image is suggested by Bernard Williams 1985, p. 28.
20. Yeats 1961, pp. 184–85.

Chapter 2

1. Nietzsche 1966, section nos. 5, 749, and 1011. I am indebted to Kathleen Higgins for references to passages in which Nietzsche expresses such thoughts.
2. I believe I am fairly crediting this marvelous quote to Brodsky since I recorded it from his writing some years ago; but I have not since been able to retrace its origin.
3. Philosophers will note that the argument will also have features of what Kant called "transcendental" arguments: that is, we will be looking for necessary presuppositions of consistently adhering to an attitude of openness. But, for all that, the argument is not really Kantian because the starting point (openness) is not assumed to be a *necessary* condition of rationality or purposive agency. In short, this is not a "rationalist" ethics in the Kantian sense (deriving ethical principles from necessary requirements of rationality) or in the similar sense of modern rationalists like Alan Gewirth (1978). I have doubts that these or any purely rationalist approaches to ethics can succeed (for reasons made clear in chapters 3 and 4). The argument of this chapter, as indicated, is better described as "dialectical" since the starting point is provisional, not necessary, and the question of why it should be taken must be further pursued. (For other interesting recent approaches to ethics inspired in part by Kant, but different from Gewirth's and from the approach of this chapter, see Donagan 1977 and Darwall 1985.)
4. Kant 1959, p. 47. See the preceding note for an account of the differences between the view put forward here and Kant's. Just as the argument of this chapter has Kantian features though it is not rationalist, so it arrives at a principle that is Kant-like, but differs from Kant's in essential ways, including the fact that it allows for exceptions to moral rules, a difference reflecting its dialectical origins.

5. Those interested in the fine points of the argument at this juncture should note that a deontic principle is at work: if you believe that a principle ought to be followed to the degree possible in all situations, then you ought to do what you can to eliminate situations in which it *cannot* be followed. This principle may be questioned, but I think it is an eminently reasonable and defensible extension of the familiar "ought" implies "can" principle (if you morally ought to do something, you must be able to do it). Assuming "ought" implies "can," if one believes that a principle of action ought to be followed *to the degree possible,* one should be concerned to reduce the occurrence of situations in which it cannot be followed, if one *can* do something about such situations.

6. In other words, it is not simply a matter of who acted first in time. A common plea in rape cases—that the victim provoked the situation by acting in a suggestive manner—is not a compelling defense for a good reason. Even if the women's walk did influence the rapist, precipitating the breakdown, it would not establish guilt on her part. For, as I argue in the rest of the paragraph, guilt and innocence are determined by the overall life-plans of the two parties and whether they are responsible for being the sorts of persons who have such life-plans that would break the moral sphere when provoked.

7. In his interesting work *The Moral Rules* (1973) Bernard Gert lists and discusses ten basic moral rules, which he takes to be fundamental to the ethical life, including such things as "Don't lie," "Don't steal," "Don't cheat," "Don't cause pain or suffering unnecessarily," and so on. I think it is the merit of the revised Ends Principle that it covers Gert's rules and accounts for reasonable exceptions to them in a systematic way, since the rules he discusses are commonly recognized consequences of many traditional ethical theories and religious traditions.

8. Walzer 1977; also see Axinn 1989 and Hartle 1989 for good accounts of the morality of, and in, warfare.

9. Selections from M. K. Gandhi, in Somerville and Santoni 1963, pp. 500–503.

10. I qualify here, saying that this has been "reputed" to have been said by Sitting Bull because I cannot track the reference of this quote which I jotted down years ago. If any readers know the reference, I would be pleased to get it (through Paragon House Publishers).

11. Berlin 1965, p. xl.

12. It seems to me that in level 3 situations, "utilitarian" considerations (about the "greatest happiness, or well-being, of the greatest number") come into their own in ethical theory. When the moral sphere has broken down and some innocent persons are going to be treated unfairly no matter what we do (as in the case of the raft or the airplane scenario), it may be necessary to weigh the numbers of people and the amount of suffering to determine the best course of action. This is sometimes also necessary in level 2 situations where stopping the guilty party is either not possible or requires harming many innocents. A classic case is the bombing of Hiroshima, where strategists had to weigh an estimated 200,000 victims of the bombing against an

estimated 2,000,000 Japanese and Allied dead if Japan had to be conquered by conventional means (assuming, of course, that these were the only options—a much-disputed issue). Ordinarily such calculations strike as as grotesque. But the moral sphere has badly broken down in this case (World War II) forcing difficult choices; since many innocents will suffer no matter what is done, numbers and amount of suffering matter. Utilitarianism is, of course, among the most widely discussed views in recent ethics. (See, for example, Sen and Williams 1982 and Hardin 1988.) I mention it infrequently in this book because I do not believe that *ultimate* ethical principles can rest on utilitarian grounds (mainly because utilitarianism has well-known problems about justice and lacks a notion of worth or desert, such as I develop in chapter 4). But I think that utilitarian considerations have a role to play in moral theory within a general framework constituted by the Ends Principle and moral sphere breakdown.

13. Bloom 1987, p. 61. For further information on the values clarification method, see Maury Smith 1977.

14. Mill 1956, pp. 21ff. The Milton lines are from *Areopagita.*

Chapter 3

1. From Dostoyevski, *The Brothers Karamazov* (1982).

2. Aristotle 1983, from the *Nichomachean Ethics,* book 1.

3. See George 1991; Finnis 1980; Grisez and Shaw 1974; and Veatch 1985. Budziszewski (1986) offers a qualified, but perceptive, defense of natural law; Hittenger (1987) is a challenging critique of new natural law theories.

4. Benedict 1946.

5. Sumner 1934, passim; Westermarck 1932, chap. 5; Herskovits 1947, chap. 5.

6. In partial defense of Benedict and other anthropological relativists, they would not have been happy with a defense of Nazism. Benedict and Herskovits argued that value relativism and the avoidance of ethnocentrism required that we be open or tolerant toward all other cultures. They may then have been sympathetic to the argument of chapter 2. But that argument shows, contrary to their conclusions, that we cannot be tolerant to *all* other cultures. It shows the limitations of relativism and provides an argument against Nazism, as their relativism did not.

7. Kluckholm 1955.

8. Sartre 1965.

9. Geertz 1965, pp. 93–118.

10. See Hofstadter 1955.

11. Wilson 1975, 1979; Alexander 1987; Dawkins 1976; Ruse 1986.

12. Kluckholm 1955.

13. Lorenz 1975, chap. 3.

14. Spinoza 1948, pp. 195–96.

15. Schiller 1945, pp. 90–91.
16. Pugh 1977.
17. Lovejoy 1961.
18. Darwin 1955, pp. 395ff.
19. Turnbull 1972.
20. Lorenz 1975.
21. Harré 1980, passim.
22. MacIntyre 1981; Sandel 1983; Hauerwas 1983; Hauerwas and MacIntyre 1983; Rasmussen 1990.
23. Haynes 1984, p. 433.
24. Nielsen 1984, pp. 88ff.
25. Wilson 1975, p. 1.
26. Reciprocal altruism is also frequently associated with what is known as a "prisoner's dilemma," a situation in which rational agents are better off in the long run if they cooperate rather than acting on their own self-interest (called a "prisoner's dilemma" because the original example involved two prisoners being questioned separately and given a choice of whether or not to confess and implicate each other). Successions of prisoners' dilemmas have been used by biologists and social scientists to explain the evolution of cooperation in humans. See Axelrod 1984.
27. The notions of reciprocal altruism and prisoner's dilemma (see the previous note) also play a role in some presently popular "contractarian" ethical theories which trace their origins to Thomas Hobbes; see Baier 1958, Gauthier 1986, Kavka 1986. Hobbes (1958) argued that a state of nature in which individuals pursued their own self-interests would be one of perpetual strife and misery. It would therefore be in the long-term interests of individuals to enter a social contract promising to curb self-interest when it came in conflict with the interests of others. Hobbes believed such a contract would have to be enforced by an all-powerful sovereign, but modern contractarians, like Baier and Gauthier, dispense with this part of Hobbes's theory, arguing that rational persons will voluntarily submit to such a contract when they see it is in their long-term interests. It is evident that theories of this kind have much in common with the "reciprocal altruism" of the sociobiologists, and similar limitations as *ethical* theories. Just as sensible knaves and free riders can be reciprocal altruists, so they can enter into a Hobbesian social contract, if it suits their interests, but violate the contract when they can get away with it. As Gauthier concedes, on the Hobbesian view, it seems that "we care about morality, not for its own sake, but because we lack the [wherewithal] to dominate our fellows or . . . avoid interaction with them" (p. 307). Gauthier therefore argues that if there is to be sufficient motivation to abide by a Hobbesian contract, other human motives must be brought in; and he specifically appeals to several of the Social Values of my category 3: desires for affection and social acceptance and to engage in cooperative tasks with others. But this brings us back to the general problem

of appealing to the Social Values discussed in the previous section. Sensible knaves and so forth, may well satisfy the Social Values within a restricted circle while otherwise living selfish lives.

28. There is a similar limitation to many modern value and normative theories, which argue that the so-called fact/value gap can be overcome. It *can* to a degree, as is amply demonstrated by some excellent recent works on values and norms—for example, works by E. J. Bond (1983), Panayot Butcharov (1989), Robert Audi (1988), and Allan Gibbard (1990). But one arrives at objective-yet-relative values in this way, not absolute ethical ones.

Chapter 4

1. Putnam 1987.
2. This is the theme of Plato's dialogue, *Euthyphro*, (Plato 1937, pp. 383–400).
3. Popper 1965a, passim, and 1965b, chap. 1.
4. Kirk and Raven 1960, fragments 189 and 191. I have used Popper's translation in Popper 1965b, p. 18.
5. I am not claiming that science must be viewed in this way. Some scientists and philosophers of science deny that there is any real or final truth out there to be found. But I am claiming that *if* science is viewed in this way as a search for the truth of nature, as it is by many scientists, then it is an example of a quest in the realm of aspiration which can teach us much.
6. See *Cassell's Latin-English Dictionary* (New York: Funk and Wagnall's, 1955), p. 533.
7. Descartes 1979, Meditation I.
8. Wittgenstein 1980, p. 75. I am indebted to Hilary Putnam for drawing my attention to this wonderful quote.
9. Chuang-Tzu, in Eliade 1977, p. 102; Maya referred to in the *Bhagavad-Gita* (Prabhavananda and Isherwood 1956, p. 50); trickster gods in Larson 1985, p. 102.
10. Philosophers will recognize a connection between this example and Robert Nozick's well-known example of the "experience machine" in his *Anarchy, State and Utopia* (1974), p. 18. This is not accidental because Nozick's experience machine is another way of getting to the idea of objective worth. But I am going to use different examples—several different ones—to bring out features of this complex notion which Nozick does not discuss.
11. Nagel 1986. The theme of Nagel's intriguing work is that many of the deepest philosophical problems arise because we are capable of having two different, often conflicting, ways of looking at the world: the objective and the subjective view.
12. Rilke 1963, "Ninth Elegy," p. 73.
13. Lem 1971.

14. Kierkegaard 1954, p. 196ff.
15. *Basic Writings of St. Augustine.* Edited by A. Pegis (New York: Random House, 1948) 2 vols; especially vol. 1 "Confessions" (pp. 3–258) and "On Nature and Grace" (pp. 521–82).
16. Hopkins 1953.
17. Gilbert 1962.
18. A study of the nature of desert or worth that is somewhat different than the one put forth in this chapter, but containing many valuable insights is Sher 1989.
19. Aquinas 1950, *Prima Secundae,* Question 2, article 3, p. 11. *"Gloria nihil aliquid est quam clara notitia cum laude ut Ambrosius dicit."*
20. Kant 1959, p. 53.
21. MacIntyre 1981.
22. Putnam 1987; Post 1987, 1991.
23. Williams 1985; Slote 1983.
24. Nozick 1981, chap. 5.
25. Goethe 1960.
26. From a lecture delivered at Yale University in the spring of 1963.
27. Nietzsche is the most conspicuous case of a philosopher who would deny this connection between love and glory. Nietzsche's celebrated "nihilism" does not mean he is a philosopher without ideals, as many commentators have reminded us, but his basic ideals lie on the glory side, not on the side of love as agape.
28. Kant 1958, p. 165 (A805; B833). Kant's second and third questions are more accurately translated as "What should I do?" and "What can I hope for?" I have adjusted their wording (but not, I think, their spirit) to my purposes. I am indebted to Thomas Seung for bringing to my attention the importance of these Kantian questions.
29. Melville 1982, p. 15 (end of chapter 2).
30. From a letter of Yeats to Lady Elizabeth Pelham written four weeks before Yeats's death; quoted in Unterecker 1959, p. 6.

Chapter 5

1. For an interesting account of the public debate over these and other divisive social issues, see Hunter 1992.
2. From a lecture delivered at Yale University in the spring of 1963.
3. Lincoln 1953, vol. 2, pp. 499–500. I am indebted to historian George Forgie for this reference.
4. Feinberg 1973, pp. 33–35.

5. Mill 1956, p. 13.

6. Feinberg 1982–88, vol. 1, p. 3.

7. Feinberg 1982–88, vol. 2, p. 26.

8. See Devlin 1965.

9. Hart 1965, passim; Dworkin 1978, chap. 10, pp. 240–59; Feinberg, 1982–88, vol. 4.

10. Dworkin 1978, p. 242.

11. The extent to which "neutrality" toward different ways of life is an essential feature of liberal societies is a much-discussed issue of recent political theory and social ethics. See, for example, Berlin 1956, Dworkin 1978, Sandel 1983, Rawls 1971, Ackerman 1982, and Scanlon 1982. In addition to defending a qualified neutrality toward ways of life, Rawls's now-classic *A Theory of Justice* (1971) also introduced into moral and political philosophy a different kind of "contractarian" ethical theory than the Hobbesian kind discussed in the footnotes to chapter 3. Rawlsian contract theory does not have the same problems as the Hobbesian theories, but it has other problems. Rawls initially seems to have wanted to ground a basic ethical commitment of equal respect for persons (and ways of life) in his hypothetical social contract. But critics argued (and Rawls later conceded [in Rawls 1985, pp. 223–51]) that such an ethical principle of equal respect for persons must be presupposed if the contract is to be adequately motivated; it cannot be generated by the contract itself. Thus, in his later work, Rawls concedes that his contract theory will only hold for those who already accept certain ethical ideals of respect for persons, such as most persons in modern Western societies do. I think he is right about this. The ground for ethical ideals of equal respect presupposed by social contract theories, like Rawls's, lie, as I see it, in the Ends Principle (and in considerations of Objective Worth) and not the other way around. (Of course, whether the Ends Principle would lead to a social contract theory like Rawls's or some other kind is an interesting further question not decided here.)

12. In addition to examples given in the text, the Public Morality Principle can support laws prohibiting behavior when other means are lacking. What it then adds to the Harm and Offense Principles is that harm cannot be narrowly limited to particular harms to specified individuals. There are also *harms to society,* for example, contempt of court, tax evasion, minor traffic violations, or air pollution, which may not injure specific individuals on each occurrence but which endanger practices or weaken public institutions (for example, respect for courts of law), and these are also covered by the Public Morality Principle.

13. From "On Ethics" and "The Structure of the Community Justice Process." Unpublished lectures.

14. See, for example, MacIntyre 1981, Hauerwas and MacIntyre 1983, Pincoffs 1985, Foot 1981, Wallace 1978, and Kekes 1989. The recent revival of interest

in "virtue ethics" has introduced a useful corrective into moral philosophy for the reasons cited. As I see it, a virtue ethics must be an essential part of any adequate moral theory, but cannot be the whole of such a theory. Note, for example, how MacIntyre's ideas about virtues, excellences, and traditions were incorporated into the theory of chapter 4 and how virtue ethics enters into the account of public morality in this chapter. But if a virtue ethics is not supplemented by some universal principles, like the Ends Principle, it is threatened by relativism or ethnocentrism, since tables of virtues may differ from society to society and era to era, as MacIntyre's own works show. Note also that if we *do* supplement a virtue ethics with the Ends Principle along with its grounding in Objective Worth, some virtues of a distinctly moral kind turn out to be universal—for example, justice, kindness, fairness, empathy, honesty, trustworthiness (not being prone to cheat), along with the master virtue, wisdom, defined in chapter 4 as knowing what is worth loving and worth praising in life. (It also follows that possessing such virtues [such as justice] would not mean adhering to simple exceptionless rules, since the moral sphere may break down.) In addition, given the two sides of Objective Worth (worthiness for love and glory), some virtues, like the moral virtues just named (justice, kindness, and so on) would be on the love side of the ledger, while other virtues, like self-discipline, educability, courage, and "excellences" of specific kinds, like artistic skills, leadership abilities, and the like, would be on the glory side. (Some virtues, like self-discipline, tact, and integrity, would lie on both sides.) The Greek term for virtue, *arete*, has the broader meaning of "excellence" (as is well known) and Greek thinkers, like Aristotle, tended to include in their accounts of the virtues both what we would count as moral virtues (for example, justice) and nonmoral excellences (for example, intellectual virtues). This puzzles many modern readers, but sense can be made of it if excellences or virtues in general are related to Objective Worth with its two aspects of love (moral virtues) and glory (nonmoral excellences).

15. Quoted in Draper 1982, p. 47.

16. That is, the so-called Harm to Self or Paternalism Principle, which is invoked, for example, to limit drinking ages or for regulations of prescription drugs, food, consumer safety, among other uses.

17. Flower 1985, pp. 231–51; Jones 1989, pp. 173–78.

18. I have adapted this from the closing paragraphs of Joyce 1960. I go forth "to forge in the smithy of my soul the uncreated conscience of my race."

Chapter 6

1. A theme of many of the works cited in chap. 1: Bellah et al., Solzhenitzyn, Bloom.

2. Oreskes 1990; Drew 1983; Dionne 1991; Grieder 1992; Broder has written numerous articles on the topic, some of which will be referred to later in the chapter.

3. Most recently, Senators Warren Rudman (R-N.H.) and David Prior (D-Ark.) and Congressmen Donald Pease (D-Ohio), Mickey Edwards (R-Ok.), and David Obey (D-Wis.). See Oreskes 1990.

4. No less an avuncular and respected figure than Walter Cronkite has said that the system is not working and we may have to "think the unthinkable," the possibility of consitutional changes by way of a constitutional convention. In a speech at MIT Dartmouth president John Kemeny expressed similar sentiments. Disenchantment with the system among ordinary citizens was tapped by the Perot candidacy of 1992.

5. For example, the Charles F. Kettering Foundation of Dayton, Ohio, and the Jefferson Center for New Democratic Processes in Minnesota (to be referred to later in the chapter).

6. Dahl 1989; Cronin 1989; Fishkin 1991.

7. Naisbitt 1983; Toffler 1980.

8. Toffler 1980, p. 433.

9. Plato 1987.

10. Most of the following criticisms appear in the sections on democratic character and democratic societies in book 9 of *The Republic* (1987, pp. 373–82); some occur by implication in other parts of that work (pp. 122–25). In my statements of the criticisms, I develop Plato's themes in ways that make them relevant to modern democratic societies.

11. A powerful illustration of these Platonic themes was Bill Moyers's celebrated PBS series "The Public Image," which discusses the roles of media, advertising, and public relations in modern politics.

12. Relevant here is another recent work by Mitroff and Bennis (1988).

13. Plato 1987, pp. 316–26.

14. Plato 1987, p. 328.

15. Many of these "moral" criticisms are reflected in current communitarian critiques of "liberal individualism." See chap. 3, note 22.

16. Oreskes 1990.

17. Drew 1983.

18. Some states also allow Recall, citizen initiatives for removing elected officials from office.

19. Cronin 1989.

20. Hollander 1985.

21. Arterton 1988.

22. Drew 1983; Kampelman 1989, p. 27.

23. Dahl 1989, p. 339.

24. Toffler 1980, p. 425.

25. Fishkin 1991. The book develops themes of Fishkin 1988.

26. Fishkin 1991, chaps. 1 and 8.
27. Rousseau 1978, pp. 72–78.
28. Discussed in Fishkin 1991, pp. 96–98.
29. De Tocqueville 1974, vol. I, p. 340.
30. For issues demanding expertise beyond that of ordinary citizens, similar juries could be formed of experts to function in the same way. The crucial addition would be that legal representatives on different sides of the issue would have veto power over prospective expert jurors until a reasonably unbiased panel on the issue in question is agreed upon. Beyond that, the expert juries would hear and discuss evidence in a similar manner. Some people claim you could not get impartial experts on many topics because the experts would inevitably have some ties to the relevant industries (for example, nuclear engineers to the nuclear industry). But experts do not have to be exactly in the field in question (for example, many trained physicists would have enough background knowledge to understand and assess testimony on nuclear power even if they were not nuclear engineers). A recently successful commission of experts was the one that looked into the *Challenger* disaster in which seven astronauts were killed. This might be a model for other expert juries.
31. For the process of hammering out long-term policies, other variations of Citizen Commissions might be considered. Some might function as representative citizens required to agree on trade-offs, such as the one described in a column by David Broder some years ago. Broder, whose ear is usually attuned to innovative democratic proposals, described a conference on energy policy arranged by two western-state governors, which brought together more than a hundred citizens with divergent views on the environment and energy (from oil executives to Sierra Club officers). Their experimental task was to hammer out a compromise before the weekend was over. At first, there was general hostility, but eventually, aware of the deadline, sensible compromises were suggested and agreed upon. (That a similar compromise could ever have been reached in our legislatures is hard to imagine.) This was only an experiment, of course, but it suggests a useful role for another kind of "Citizens Commission."

Chapter 7

1. Smith 1992; also see Smith 1982; Küng 1978, 1981.
2. Milosz 1953.
3. Koestler 1941; Orwell 1961.
4. Cited in chapter 1, note 5.
5. From Milosz 1986, p. 35.
6. Milosz 1986, p. 35.
7. Eliade 1959, chap. 1.

8. Laurence 1989.

9. Melville 1987, p. 15.

10. Eliade, "Patterns of Comparative Religion," in D. Eisenberg et al. 1990, p. 26.

11. Weber 1958, p. 182.

12. See Graham 1990 for an insightful discussion of this state and its philosophical implications.

13. A theme of many of Lawrence's writings; see Lawrence 1976.

14. From Untermeyer 1955, p. 54.

15. James 1959, p. 3.

16. Kant 1959, p. 85.

17. Kushner 1989.

18. H. Smith 1958, p. 7.

19. See H. Smith 1991, and Robinson and Johnson 1982.

20. John 14:6.

21. H. Smith 1958, chap. 5.

22. H. Smith, pp. 19–22 (for the Hindu values), 207–11 (for the Taoist ideal).

23. Dalai Lama 1984, p. 13.

24. Plato, *Euthyphro*; Plato 1937; for the Euripides quote, see Grube 1941, p. 62. I am indebted to Barbara Goff for the latter reference.

25. For example, Eliade 1954, chap. 1.

26. Durkheim 1964.

27. Schärer 1963; Selections are reprinted in Eliade 1977.

28. Eliade 1977, pp. 165–66.

29. H. Smith 1991, chap. 2.

30. Matthew 23:11.

31. Campbell 1956.

32. Second Vatican Council Constitution of the Church, Article 16. Referred to in Küng 1978, p. 97.

33. Prabhavananda and Manchester 1957, pp. 125–26.

34. Prabhavananda and Isherwood 1955, p. 51.

35. The relevant passages are quoted in Radhakrishnan 1939, pp. 25ff.

36. Trepp 1982, p. 9.

37. See, for example, Lessing's play *Nathan the Wise*, in Lessing 1906, pp. 227ff.

38. Quoted by Berger 1979, p. 163.

39. Kushner 1989, p. 195.

Chapter 8

1. Carson 1962.
2. Leopold 1966.
3. These figures are reported by Parsons 1991.
4. D'Souza 1991a.
5. For an overview of these changes as they relate to ethics, see Held 1990, pp. 321–44; Jaggar 1983; Calhoun 1988, pp. 451–63. All three works contain further references.
6. J. B. Callicott "The Search for an Environmental Ethic," in Regan 1980, p. 381.
7. Nash 1983; Quoted by Callicott in Regan 1980, p. 382.
8. White 1967, pp. 1203–7; McHarg 1969.
9. Barr 1974, p. 64.
10. Thomas 1974, pp. 1–2.
11. Thomas 1974, pp. 11–17, 81–88.
12. Rosebury 1969.
13. Thomas 1974, pp. 107–13.
14. Schedler 1989.
15. See, for example, Rosaldo and Lamphere 1974.
16. Goldberg 1973.
17. See Jaggar 1983 for one side of the debate; Goldberg 1973 and E. O. Wilson 1979 for the opposing view.
18. Wilson 1979, chap. 3.
19. Eisler 1987.
20. Eisler 1987, chap. 1.
21. Marija Gimbutas, whose works are cited in Eisler, is one of the most well-known defenders of this view.
22. Held 1990, p. 323.
23. Gilligan 1988; Kohlberg 1981.
24. Piaget 1932.
25. Gilligan 1988, pp. 76–77.
26. H. Smith 1991, pp. 214–15.
27. D'Souza 1991b, p. 58. (This is an article excerpted from D'Souza 1991a.)
28. Lyotard 1987, Introduction. On postmodernism and deconstructionism generally, see Best and Kellner 1991.
29. Derrida 1978.
30. D'Souza 1991b, p. 72.
31. D'Souza 1991b, p. 79.

32. D'Souza 1991b, p. 79.

33. MacIntyre 1981, p. 222.

34. Gates 1990.

35. Quoted in D'Souza 1991b, p. 71.

36. Quoted in D'Souza 1991b, p. 71.

Chapter 9

1. H. G. Wells is supposed to have first made the claim about education and catastrophe, though I am uncertain whether he is the source.

2. Campbell 1956, chap. 1.

3. B. D. Whitehead 1990.

4. Schulman and Mehler 1985.

5. Piaget 1932.

6. Kagan 1982.

7. Kagan 1982, pp. 55–56.

8. Lickona 1985.

9. Lickona 1985, passim.

10. Their views are described in Begley and Carey 1984.

11. An interesting recent philosophical work on justice by Robert C. Solomon (1991) shows how important the emotions are in the cultivation of a sense of justice throughout life. Justice, Solomon argues, is not simply a matter of following abstract rules, but a virtue intricately tied to varied aspects of our emotional life.

12. Wingert and Kantrowitz 1990, p. 41.

13. Jurgen Habermas 1990, pp. 32–37, makes this point about Kohlberg's stages 5 and 6.

14. Kohlberg 1981.

15. Quoted in Silber 1989, chap. 2.

16. Renault 1978.

17. Plato, *The Republic* 1987, book 5.

18. Quoted in Smith 1958, p. 196.

Bibliography

Ackerman, Bruce. *Social Justice and the Liberal State*. New Haven: Yale University Press, 1982.

Alexander, Richard. *The Biology of Moral Systems*. New York: De Gruyter, 1987.

Aquinas, Saint Thomas. *Summa Theologiae*. 3 vols. Rome: Marietti, 1950.

Aristotle. *The Ethics of Aristotle: Nichomachean Ethics*. Translated by J.A.K. Thomson. Hammondsworth, England: Penguin Books, 1983.

Arterton, Christopher. *Teledemocracy*. New York: Sage Library of Social Research, 1988.

Audi, Robert. "The Architecture of Reason." *American Philosophical Association Proceedings* 62; no. 1 (1988): 227–56.

Augustine, Saint. *Basic Writings of St. Augustine*. Edited by A. Pegis. New York: Random House, 1948.

Axelrod, Robert. *The Evolution of Cooperation*. New York: Basic Books, 1984.

Axinn, Sidney. *A Moral Military*. Philadelphia: Temple University Press, 1989.

Baier, Kurt. *The Moral Point of View*. Ithaca: Cornell University Press, 1958.

Barr, James. *Man and Nature: The Ecological Controversy and the Old Testament*. New York: Harper and Row, 1974.

Begley, Sharon, and John Carey. "Raising Children Who Care." *Newsweek*, 12 March 1984.

Bellah, Robert, Richard Madsen, William M. Sullivan, Ann Swidler, and Steven M. Tipton. *Habits of the Heart*. New York: Harper and Row, 1985.

———. *The Good Society*. New York: Knopf, 1991.

Benedict, Ruth. *Patterns of Culture*. New York: Pelican Books, 1946.

Berger, Peter. *The Heretical Imperative*. Garden City, N.Y.: Anchor Books, 1979.

Berlin, Isaiah. *Four Essays on Liberty*. London: Oxford University Press, 1965.

Bernstein, Richard. *Beyond Objectivism and Relativism*. Philadelphia: University of Pennsylvania Press, 1983.

Best, Steven, and Douglas Kellner. *Postmodern Theory*. London: Macmillan, 1991.

Bloom, Allan. *The Closing of the American Mind*. New York: Simon and Schuster, 1987.

Bond, E. J. *Reason and Value*. Cambridge: Cambridge University Press, 1983.

Budziszewski, Jay. *The Resurrection of Nature*. Ithaca: Cornell University Press, 1986.

Butcharov, Panayot. *Scepticism in Ethics*. Bloomington: Indiana University Press, 1989.

Calhoun, Cheshire. "Justice, Care, Gender Bias," *Journal of Philosophy* 85 (1988): 451–63.

Campbell, Joseph. *The Hero with a Thousand Faces*. Garden City, N.Y.: Anchor Books, 1956.

Carson, Rachel. *Silent Spring*. Boston: Houghton-Mifflin, 1962.

Cronin, Thomas. *Direct Democracy*. Cambridge: Harvard University Press, 1989.

Dahl, Robert. *Democracy and Its Critics*. New Haven: Yale University Press, 1989.

Dalai Lama. *A Human Approach to World Peace*. San Francisco: Wisdom Publications, 1984.

Darwall, Stephen. *Impartial Reason*. Ithaca: Cornell University Press, 1985.

Darwin, Charles. *The Origin of Species and the Descent of Man*. New York: Modern Library, 1955.

Dawkins, Richard. *The Selfish Gene*. Oxford: Oxford University Press, 1976.

Derrida, Jacques. *Writing and Difference*. Translated by A. Bass. Chicago: University of Chicago Press, 1978.

Descartes, Rene. *Meditations on First Philosophy*. Translated by D. A. Cress. Indianapolis, Ind.: Hackett, 1979.

De Tocqueville, Alexis. *Democracy in America*. 2 vols. New York: Schocken Books, 1974.

Devlin, Patrick. *The Enforcement of Morals*. London: Oxford University Press, 1965.

Dionne. E. J. *The War against Public Life*. New York: Simon and Schuster, 1991.

Donagan, Alan. *A Theory of Morality*. Chicago: University of Chicago Press, 1977.

Dostoyevski, Fyodor. *The Brothers Karamazov*. Hammondsworth, England: Penguin Books, 1982.

Draper, Theodore. "Hume and Madison: The Secrets of Federalist Paper No. 10" *Encounter* 58 (February 1982): 434–48.

Drew, Elizabeth. *Politics and Money*. New York: Macmillan, 1983.

D'Souza, Dinesh. *Illiberal Education*. New York: Free Press, 1991a.

———. "Illiberal Education" *The Atlantic Monthly*, March 1991b, pp. 51–79.

Durkheim, Emile. *The Elementary Forms of the Religious Life*. Translated by J. W. Swain. London: George Allen and Unwin, 1964.

Dworkin, Ronald. *Taking Rights Seriously*. Cambridge: Harvard University Press, 1978.

Eisler, Riane. *The Chalice and the Blade*. New York: Harper and Row, 1987.

Eisenberg, D., George deForest Lord, Peter Markman, Robert Merrill, Megan Scribner, and Charles S. J. White. *Transformations of Myth through Time*. New York: Harcourt Brace Jovanovich, 1990.

Eliade, Mircea. *The Sacred and the Profane*. Translated by W. R. Trask. New York: Harcourt, Brace, 1959.

————, ed. *From Primitives to Zen*. New York: Harper and Row, 1977.

Feinberg, Joel. *Social Ethics*. Englewood Cliffs, N.J.: Prentice Hall, 1973.

————. *The Moral Limits of the Criminal Law*. 4 vols. Oxford: Oxford University Press, 1982–88.

Fishkin, James. *Democracy and Deliberation*. New Haven: Yale University Press, 1991.

————. "The Case for a National Caucus" *Atlantic Monthly*, August 1988; pp. 16–18.

Flower, Michael J. "Neuromaturation of the Human Fetus" *Journal of Medicine and Philosophy* 10 (August 1985): 231–51.

Foot, Phillippa. *Virtues and Vices*. Berkeley and Los Angeles: University of California Press, 1981.

Gamwell, Franklin. *The Divine Good: Modern Moral Theory and the Necessity of God*. San Francisco: Harper San Francisco, 1991.

Garrett, Richard. *Dialogues Concerning the Foundations of Ethics*. Savage, Md.: Rowman and Littlefield, 1990.

Gates, Henry Louis, Jr. *Norton Anthology of Afro-American Literature*. New York: W. W. Norton, 1990.

Gauthier, David. *Morals by Agreement*. Oxford: Oxford University Press, 1986.

Geertz, Clifford. "The Impact of the Concept of Culture on the Concept of Man." In *New Views of Human Nature*, ed. J. Platt, 93–118. Chicago: University of Chicago Press, 1965.

George, Robert P. *Natural Law Theory: Contemporary Essays*. Oxford: Oxford University Press, 1991.

Gert, Bernard. *The Moral Rules*. New York: Harper and Row, 1973.

Gewirth, Alan. *Reason and Morality*. Chicago: University of Chicago Press, 1977.

Gibbard, Allan. *Wise Choices, Apt Feelings*. Cambridge: Harvard University Press, 1990.

Gilbert, Jack. *Views of Jeopardy*. New Haven: Yale University Press, 1962.

Gilligan, Carol. *In a Different Voice*. Cambridge: Harvard University Press, 1988.

Goethe, J. W. *Faust*. Translated by P. Wayne. Hammondsworth, England: Penguin Books, 1960.

Goldberg, Steven. *The Inevitability of Patriarchy*. New York: William Morrow, 1973.

Graham, George. "Melancholic Epistemology." *Synthese* 82 (1990): 399–422.

Grieder, William. *Who Will Tell the People?* New York: Simon and Schuster, 1992.

Grisez, Germain, and Russell Shaw. *Beyond the New Morality.* Notre Dame, Ind.: University of Notre Dame Press, 1974.

Grube, G. M. A. *The Drama of Euripides.* London: Methuen, 1941.

Habermas, Jurgen. "Justice and Solidarity." In *Hermeneutics and Critical Theory in Ethics and Politics,* ed. Michael Kelly, 32–52. Cambridge: MIT Press, 1990.

Hardin, Russell. *Morality within the Limits of Reason.* Chicago: University of Chicago Press, 1988.

Harré, Rom. *Social Being.* New York: Littlefield, 1980.

Hart, H. L. A. *Law, Liberty and Morals.* Stanford, Calif.: Stanford University Press, 1965.

Hartle, Anthony. *Moral Issues in Military Decision.* Lawrence: University of Kansas Press, 1989.

Hauerwas, Stanley. *The Peaceable Kingdom.* Notre Dame, Ind.: University of Notre Dame Press, 1983.

Hauerwas, Stanley, and Alasdair MacIntyre, eds. *Revisions: Changing Perspectives in Moral Philosophy.* Notre Dame, Ind.: University of Notre Dame Press, 1983.

Haynes, Ruth. "Indian Immigrants of the Fijian Islands." (British) *Journal of Psychiatry* 145 (1984): 433.

Held, Virginia. "Feminist Transformations of Moral Theory." *Philosophy and Phenomenological Research* (Fall 1990): 321–44.

Herskovits, Melville. *Man and His Works.* New York: Knopf, 1947.

Hittenger, Russell. *A Critique of the New Natural Law Theory.* Notre Dame, Ind.: University of Notre Dame Press, 1987.

Hobbes, Thomas. *Leviathan.* Indianapolis, Ind.: Bobbs-Merrill, 1958.

Hofstadter, Richard. *Social Darwinism in American Thought.* Boston: Beacon Press, 1955.

Hollander, Richard. *Video Democracy.* New York: Lamond Publications, 1985.

Hopkins, Gerard Manley. *Poems and Prose of Gerard Manley Hopkins.* Edited by W. H. Gardner. New York: Viking Penguin, 1953.

Hunter, John Davison. *Culture Wars: The Struggle to Define America.* New York: Basic Books, 1992.

Jaggar, Alison M. *Feminist Politics and Human Nature.* Totowa, N. J.: Rowman and Allanhead, 1983.

James, William. *The Will to Believe and Other Essays.* New York: Dover, 1955.

Jaspers, Karl. *Way to Wisdom.* New Haven: Yale University Press, 1951.

Jones, D. Gareth. "Brain Birth and Personal Identity." *Journal of Medical Ethics* 15 (1989): 173–78.

Joyce, James. *Portrait of an Artist as a Young Man.* New York: Noonday Press, 1960.

Kagan, Jerome. "Interview with Jerome Kagan" by C. Hall. *Psychology Today,* July 1982, pp. 51–57.

Kampelman, Max. "Cut Campaign Costs, Not Spending." *New York Times,* 20 December 1989.

Kant, Immanuel. *The Critique of Pure Reason.* Translated by N. K. Smith. London: Macmillan, 1958.

———. *"Foundations of the Metaphysics of Morals" and "What Is Enlightenment?"* Translated by L. W. Beck. Indianapolis, Ind.: Bobbs-Merrill, 1959.

Kavka, Gregory. *Hobbesian Moral and Political Theory.* Princeton: Princeton University Press, 1986.

Kekes, John. *Moral Traditions and Individuals.* Princeton: Princeton University Press, 1989.

Kierkegaard, Soren. *Fear and Trembling and the Sickness unto Death.* Translated by W. Lowrie. New York: Anchor Books, 1954.

Kirk, G. S., and J. E. Raven, eds. *The Presocratic Philosophers.* Cambridge: Cambridge University Press, 1960.

Kluckholm, Clyde. "Ethical Relativity" *Journal of Philosophy* 52 (1955): 663–77.

Koestler, Arthur. *Darkness at Noon.* London: Macmillan, 1941.

Kohlberg, Laurence. *The Philosophy of Moral Development.* San Francisco: Harper and Row, 1981.

Kolakowski, Leszek. *Modernity on Endless Trial.* Chicago: University of Chicago Press, 1989.

Küng, Hans. *On Being a Christian.* New York: Pocket Books, 1978.

———. *Does God Exist?* New York: Vintage Books, 1981.

Kushner, Harold. *Who Needs God?* New York: Pocket Books, 1989.

Larson, E. Thomas. *Religions of Africa.* San Francisco: Harper San Francisco, 1985.

Laurence, Bruce. *Defenders of God.* San Francisco: Harper San Francisco, 1989.

Lawrence, T. E. *Seven Pillars of Wisdom.* Hammondsworth, England: Penguin Books, 1976.

Lem, Stanislaw. *Solaris.* Translated by J. Kilmartin and S. Cox. New York: Berkeley Medallion Books, 1971.

Leopold, Aldo. *A Sand County Almanac.* New York: Ballantine Books, 1966.

Lessing, Gotthold. *Dramatic Works of Lessing.* Translated by P. Bell. London: George Bell and Sons, 1906.

Lewis, C. S. *Perelandra.* New York: Collier Books, 1962.

Lickona, Thomas. *Raising Good Children.* New York: Bantam Books, 1985.

Lincoln, Abraham. *The Collected Works of Abraham Lincoln.* Edited by Roy P. Basler. New Brunswick, N.J.: Rutgers University Press, 1953.

Lorenz, Konrad. *On Aggression.* Translated by Marjorie Wilson. New York: Harcourt Brace, 1975.

Lovejoy, A. O. *Reflections on Human Nature.* Baltimore: Johns Hopkins University Press, 1961.

Lyotard, Jean-François. *The Postmodern Condition*. Minneapolis: University of Minnesota Press, 1987.

McHarg, Ian. *Design with Nature*. Philadelphia: Falcon Books, 1969.

MacIntyre, Alasdair. *After Virtue*. Notre Dame, Ind.: University of Notre Dame Press, 1981.

Melville, Herman. *Moby Dick*. New York: Modern Library, 1987.

Mill, John Stuart. *On Liberty*. Edited by C. Shields. Indianapolis, Ind.: Bobbs-Merrill, 1956.

Milosz, Czeslaw. *The Captive Mind*. Translated by Jane Zielenko. New York: Knopf, 1953.

———. *The Land of Ulro*. New York: Farrar, Strauss and Giroux, 1985.

———. "An Interview with Czeslaw Milosz" by Nathan Gardels. *New York Review of Books*, 27 February 1986, pp. 34–35.

Mitroff, Ian, and Warren Bennis. *The Unreality Industry: The Manufacturing of Falsehood and What It Is Doing to Our Lives*. Berkeley, Calif.: Birch Lane Press, 1988.

Nagel, Thomas. *The View from Nowhere*. Oxford: Oxford University Press, 1986.

Naisbitt, John. *Megatrends*. New York: Warner Books, 1983.

Nash, Roderick. *The Environmental Student Program, 1983–4*. Santa Barbara: University of California, 1983.

Nielsen, Kai. "Why Should I Be Moral Revisited?" *American Philosophical Quarterly* 21 (1984): 81–91.

Nietzsche, Friedrich. *The Will to Power*. Translated by W. Kaufman and R. G. Hollingdale. New York: Random House, 1966.

Nozick, Robert. *Anarchy, State and Utopia*. New York: Basic Books, 1974.

———. *Philosophical Explanations*. Cambridge: Harvard University Press, 1981.

Nussbaum, Martha. Review of *The Closing of the American Mind*, by Allan Bloom. *New York Review of Books*, 5 November 1987, pp. 20–26

Oreskes, Michael. "Politics' Shallowness Blinds Its Vision." *New York Times News Service*, 25 March 1990.

Orwell, George. *1984*. New York: New American Library, 1961.

Parsons, Arch. "Predominant Groups Grapple with U.S. Diversity." *Baltimore Sun*, 14 May 1991.

Piaget, Jean. *The Moral Development of the Child*. New York: Harcourt, Brace, 1932.

Pincoffs, Edmund. *Quandaries and Virtues*. Lawrence: University of Kansas Press, 1985.

Plato. *The Dialogues of Plato*. 2 vols. Translated by B. Jowett. New York: Random House, 1937.

———. *The Republic*. Translated by Desmond Lee. Hammondsworth, England: Penguin Books, 1987.

Popper, Karl. *The Logic of Scientific Discovery*. New York: Harper Torchbooks, 1965a.

———. *Conjectures and Refutations*. New York: Harper Torchbooks, 1965b.

Post, John. *The Faces of Existence*. Ithaca: Cornell University Press, 1987.

———. *Metaphysics: A Contemporary Introduction*. New York: Paragon House Publishers, 1991.

Prabhavananda, S., and C. Isherwood, trans. *The Song of God: Bhagavad-Gita*. New York: Mentor Books, 1956.

Prabhavananda, S., and F. Manchester, trans. *Upanishads*. New York: Mentor Books, 1957.

Pugh, George. *The Biological Origins of Human Values*. New York: Basic Books, 1977.

Putnam, Hilary. *The Many Faces of Realism*. Lasalle, Ill: Open Court Publishing, 1987.

Radhakrishnan, S. *Eastern Religions and Western Thought*. London: Oxford University Press, 1939.

Rajchman, J., and C. West. *Post-Analytic Philosophy*. New York: Columbia University Press, 1985.

Rasmussen, David, ed. *Universalism versus Communitarianism*. Cambridge: MIT Press, 1990.

Rawls, John. *A Theory of Justice*. Cambridge: Harvard University Press, 1971.

———. "Justice as Fairness: Political Not Metaphysical." *Philosophy and Public Affairs* 14 (1985): 223–51.

Regan, Tom, ed. *Matters of Life and Death*. New York: Random House, 1980.

Renault, Mary. *The Mask of Apollo*. New York: Bantam Books, 1978.

Rilke, Rainer Maria. *Duino Elegies*. Translated by J. B. Leishman and S. Spender. New York: W. W. Norton, 1963.

Robinson, Richard H., and Willard Johnson. *The Buddhist Religion*. Belmont, Calif.: Wadsworth Publishing, 1982.

Rorty, Richard. *Contingency, Irony and Solidarity*. Cambridge: Cambridge University Press, 1989.

Rosaldo, Michelle, and Louise Lamphere, eds. *Women, Culture and Society*. Stanford, Calif.: Stanford University Press, 1974.

Rosebury, Theodor. *Life on Man*. New York: Viking Press, 1969.

Rousseau, Jean Jacques. *The Social Contract*. Hammondsworth, England: Penguin Books, 1978.

Ruse, Michael. *Taking Darwin Seriously*. Oxford: Basil Blackwell, 1986.

Sandel, Michael. *Liberalism and the Limits of Justice*. Cambridge: Cambridge University Press, 1983.

Sartre, Jean-Paul. "Existentialism Is a Humanism," In *Existentialism from Dostoyevski to Sartre,* ed. W. Kaufman, 345–68. New York: New American Library, 1965.

Scanlon, T. M. "Contractarianism and Utilitarianism." In *Utilitarianism and Beyond,* ed. Amartya Sen and Bernard Williams, New York: Cambridge University Press, 1982.

Schedler, Norbert O. "Don't Treat Me like Dirt: A Philosophical Reflection on the Ecology Crisis." Unpublished lecture delivered at Central Oklahoma State University, Edmond, Oklahoma, 9 November 1989.

Schärer, Hans. *Ngaju Religion.* Translated by R. Needham. The Hague: Reidel, 1963.

Schiller, Friedrich. "An der Freude." In *Deutsche Lyrik,* ed. von W. Urbanek. Frankfurt, Germany: Ulstein Bucher, 1945.

Schulman, Michael, and Eva Mehler. *Bringing Up the Moral Child.* Boston: Addison-Wesley, 1985.

Sen, Amartya, and Bernard Williams. *Utilitarianism and Beyond.* New York: Cambridge University Press, 1982.

Sher, George. *Desert.* Princeton: Princeton University Press, 1989.

Silber, John. *Shooting Straight.* New York: Harper and Row, 1989.

Slote, Michael. *Goods and Virtues.* Oxford: Oxford University Press, 1983.

Smith, Huston. *The Religions of Man.* New York: Harper and Row, 1958.

———. *Beyond the Postmodern Mind.* Wheaton, Ill.: Quest, 1982.

———. *World Religions.* San Francisco: Harper San Francisco, 1991. (New edition of Smith 1958.)

———. *Essays on World Religions.* New York: Paragon House Publishers, 1992.

Smith, Maury. *A Practical Guide to Values Clarification.* La Jolla: University of California Associates, 1977.

Solomon, Robert C. *A Passion for Justice.* Boston: Addison-Wesley, 1991.

Solzhenitsyn, Aleksandr. *The Moral Order.* New York: Erdmann's, 1978.

Somerville, John, and Ronald Santoni, eds. *Social and Political Philosophy.* Garden City, N.Y.: Anchor Books, 1963.

Spinoza, Baruch. *Ethics.* Edited by J. Guttmann. New York: Hafner Publishing, 1948.

Stewart, Robert M., and Lynn L. Thomas. "Recent Work on Ethical Relativism." *American Philosophical Quarterly* (April 1991): 85–100.

Sullivan, William M. *Reconstructing Public Philosophy.* Berkeley and Los Angeles: University of California Press, 1986.

Sumner, G. M. *Folkways.* Boston: Ginn and Co., 1934.

Tarnas, Richard. *The Passion of the Western Mind.* New York: Harmony Books, 1991.

Taylor, Charles. *Sources of the Self.* Cambridge: Harvard University Press, 1989.

Thomas, Lewis. *The Lives of a Cell.* New York: Bantam Books, 1974.

Tinder, Glenn. "Can We Be Good without God?" *Atlantic Monthly,* December 1988, pp. 69–85.

Toffler, Alvin. *The Third Wave.* New York: Bantam Books, 1980.

Trepp, Leo. *Judaism: Development and Life.* Belmont, Calif.: Wadsworth Publishing, 1982.

Turnbull, Colin. *The Mountain People.* New York: Simon and Schuster, 1972.

Unterecker, John. *A Reader's Guide to W. B. Yeats.* New York: Noonday Press, 1959.

Untermeyer, Louis. *Makers of the Modern World.* New York: Simon and Schuster, 1955.

Veatch, Henry. *Human Rights.* Baton Rouge: Lousiana State University Press, 1985.

Wallace, John. *Virtues and Vices.* Ithaca: Cornell University Press, 1978.

Walzer, Michael. *Just and Unjust Wars.* New York: Basic Books, 1977.

Weber, Max. *The Protestant Ethic and the Spirit of Capitalism.* New York: Charles Scribner's Sons, 1958.

Westermarck, Edward. *Ethical Relativity.* New York: Littlefield, Adams, and Co. 1932.

White, Lynn. "The Historical Roots of Our Ecological Crisis." *Science* 155 (1967): 1203–7.

Whitehead, Barbara Dafoe. "Parents Struggle to Raise Children Amid Shifting Values." Cox News Service Report, 7 October 1990. Excerpted from *Family Affairs,* a publication of the Institute of American Values, New York, 1990.

Williams, Bernard. *Morality: An Introduction to Ethics.* New York: Harper and Row, 1972.

———. *Ethics and the Limits of Philosophy.* Cambridge: Harvard University Press, 1985.

Wilson, E. O. *Sociobiology: The New Synthesis.* Cambridge: Harvard University Press, 1975.

———. *On Human Nature.* New York: Bantam Books, 1979.

Wingert, Pat, and Barbara Kantrowitz. "Teaching Children Who Care." *Newsweek.* 1 January 1990, p. 41.

Wittgenstein, Ludwig. *Culture and Values.* Translated by P. Winch. Oxford: Basil Blackwell, 1980.

Yeats, William Butler. *The Collected Poetry of William Butler Yeats.* New York: Macmillan, 1961.

Name Index

MacIntyre, Alasdair, 2, 7, 86–87, 88, 194, 219(22), 222(14), 23
Madison, James, 114
McHarg, Ian, 179, 234
Mehler, Eva, 200, 202, 208, 236
Mellaert, James, 183
Melville, Herman, 98, 234
Michelangelo, 94
Mill, John Stuart, 44, 105, 234
Milosz, Czeslaw, 2, 3, 142–144, 147, 151, 234
Milton, John, 44
Mitroff, Ian, 234
Moyers, Bill, 224(11)

Nagel, Thomas, 75, 220(11), 234
Naisbitt, John, 120, 234
Nash, Roderick, 178, 234
Nicholas of Cusa, 168
Nielsen, Kai, 61, 219(24), 234
Nietzsche, F., 5, 13, 164, 216(1), 221(27), 234
Nozick, Robert, 94, 220(10), 234
Nussbaum, Martha, 3, 234

Oreskes, Michael, 119, 125, 234
Orwell, George, 96, 142, 234

Parsons, Arch, 234
Piaget, Jean, 186, 200, 234
Pincoffs, Edmund, 222(14), 234
Plato, 7, 46, 68, 119, 120–125, 133, 134, 139, 209, 230
Popper, Sir Karl, 70, 220(3), 235
Post, John, 90, 235
Prabhavananda, S., 235
Pugh, George, 53, 54, 55, 56, 235
Putnam, David, 209
Putnam, Hilary, 67, 90, 220, 235

Radhakrishnan, S., 235
Radke-Yarrow, Marian, 203
Rahner, Karl, 165
Rajchman, J., 235
Rasmussen, David, 235
Rawls, John, 222(11), 235
Regan, Tom, 235
Renault, Mary, 208, 235
Rilke, Rainer Maria, 75, 220(12), 235
Robinson, Richard H., 235
Rorty, Richard, 8, 235
Rosaldo, Michelle, 235
Rosebury, Theodor, 180, 235

Rousseau, J.J., 133, 235
Ruse, Michael, 235

Sandel, Michael, 222(11), 235
Sappho, 196
Sartre, Jean-Paul, 48, 236
Scanlon, T.M., 222(11), 236
Schärer, Hans, 160, 226(27), 236
Schedler, Norbert, 181, 236
Schiller, Friedrich, 52, 236
Schulman, Michael, 200, 202, 208, 236
Sen, Amartya, 218(12), 236
Sher, George, 221(18), 236
Silber, John, 236
Singer, Isaac Bashevis, 142–144, 171
Sitting Bull, 36, 217(10)
Slote, Michael, 236
Smith, Huston, 5, 7, 141, 155, 215(10), 236
Smith, Maury, 218(13), 236
Socrates, 19
Solomon, King, 40
Solomon, Robert C., 228(11), 236
Solzhenitsyn, Alexander, 2, 113, 142, 236
Somerville, John, 236
Spinoza, Baruch, 52, 236
Stewart, Robert M., 216, 236
Sullivan, William M., 236
Sumner, G.M., 236
Sumner, W.E., 47

Tarnas, Richard, 215(13), 236
Taylor, Charles, 236
Thomas Aquinas, Saint, 80, 221(19), 229
Thomas, Lewis, 180, 237
Thurber, James, 51
Tinder, Glenn, 237
Toffler, Alvin, 7, 120, 130, 237
Trepp, Leo, 170, 237
Turnbull, Colin, 54, 237

Unterecker, John, 237
Untermeyer, Louis, 237

Veatch, Henry, 218(3), 237
Voltaire, 9

Wallace, John, 222(14), 237
Walzer, Michael, 30, 237
Weber, Max, 148, 237
West, Mae, 22, 55
Westermarck, Edward, 47, 237

Subject Index